ALL ABOUT
BIRDS
NORTHWEST

PRINCETON

press.princeton.edu

The**Cornell**Lab
of Ornithology

White-breasted Nuthatch ©Evan Lipton/Macaulay Library

ALL ABOUT BIRDS
BIRDS
NORTHWEST

Published in 2022 by Princeton University Press
41 William Street, Princeton, New Jersey 08540
6 Oxford Street, Woodstock, Oxfordshire OX20 1TR

press.princeton.edu

Requests for permission to reproduce material from this work should be sent to
permissions@press.princeton.edu

Library of Congress Control Number: 2021940655
ISBN: 978-0-691-99003-3
Ebook ISBN: 978-0-691-23009-2

Front cover photo: Rufous Hummingbird ©Fred Forssell/Macaulay Library

Back cover photos (left to right): Sandhill Crane ©Ad Konings/Macaulay Library; Varied
Thrush ©Brian L. Sullivan/Macaulay Library; Rufous Hummingbird ©Matthew Pendleton/
Macaulay Library; House Wren ©Matt Brady/Macaulay Library

Cover-flap illustrations: ©2022 Pedro Fernandes; Cover-flap extracted photos: Common
Murre, Common Loon ©Brian L. Sullivan/Macaulay Library; Northern Shrike ©David Mitchell
https://flic.kr/p/9y6tA8; American Dipper ©Russ Morgan/Macaulay Library

Editor: Jill Leichter

Assistant Editors: Michael L. P. Retter, Caroline Watkins

Photo Editors: Michael L. P. Retter, Jill Leichter

Design concept and layout: Patricia Mitter, Jill Leichter, Diane Tessaglia-Hymes,
Brian L. Sockin, Regina Miles

Printed in Malaysia
10 9 8 7 6 5 4 3 2 1

TABLE OF CONTENTS

WELCOME TO YOUR
ALL ABOUT BIRDS, NORTHWEST GUIDE

Wherever you live, we hope you'll enjoy the amazing diversity and beauty of the birds around you. Birds stir our imaginations with their songs, dazzling colors, and flight. Whether in the wilderness, on farms, or in the heart of cities, birds open up a door into endless discoveries and fascination with the natural world.

Mallard

So how exactly do you go about identifying an unfamiliar wild bird likely to fly away before you can figure out what it is? This guide will help you with a treasure trove of information, best practices, and advice about bird identification. By starting with the birds in your backyard, neighborhood, and region, you'll get to know more about the diversity, behaviors, and seasonal changes in birds—a foundation for endless explorations.

In these pages, you'll find information about the most common bird species in your region, drawn from the Cornell Lab of Ornithology's comprehensive website, *AllAboutBirds.org*, used by more than 22 million people each year. Each species profile includes a map and four photographs that will help you recognize and appreciate the diversity of birds' plumages within and between species. You will also discover information about the Cornell Lab's vast online resources and learn about the Lab's free **Merlin® Bird ID** app to help you identify the birds around you based on your observations, photographs, and sound recordings.

We've also included a special section about the Cornell Lab's "citizen science" projects—scientific studies driven by contributions from bird watchers just like you—including the Cornell Lab's Project FeederWatch, NestWatch, and Great Backyard Bird Count. Our largest citizen-science initiative, eBird, provides a free portal for you to create and keep your own bird lists while sharing them for use in science, conservation, and outreach. Each year, participants record more than 100 million bird sightings! These projects empower you to participate and contribute to important science, while enjoying the outdoors or the view from your window. So, let's get started and have fun!

Miyoko Chu
Senior Director of Communications
Cornell Lab of Ornithology

Brian Scott Sockin
CEO/Publisher
Cornell Lab Publishing Group

GETTING STARTED

All About Birds is a field guide for new and developing birders, based on *AllAboutBirds.org*, your online guide to birds and birding from the Cornell Lab of Ornithology. The content you will find in this book was curated by some of the world's leading bird experts and is presented in a friendly, easy-to-understand manner, just like the *All About Birds* website.

The first section of this book is presented as **Birding 101**, a primer for beginning and novice birders, but also a refresher for more advanced birders. You will learn how to identify birds with best practices, how to find, watch, and listen to birds, how to choose equipment, and how to take photos of birds (including how to "digiscope" with your smartphone).

The second section, **Attracting Birds to Your Backyard,** shares some of our best advice and tools to help you "birdscape" or create bird-friendly habitat outside your home. We begin with the three essential elements that all birds need to thrive—food, water, and shelter—followed by descriptions of different types of bird feeders and information on bird food options and what to look for when buying or building nest boxes. We also equip you with the things you need to know to attract the birds you want to see at home, and how you can protect and keep them safe while enjoying them.

The third section, **Getting Involved**, shares information about citizen science and how you can participate and contribute to important scientific studies at the Cornell Lab.

The fourth section is the bird field guide, covering 213 species of commonly seen birds in the northwestern United States and Canada. Each species page features easy-to-use sections with graphics, cool facts, backyard tips, and more. The diagram on the following page will show you how to navigate the species field guide pages.

SAMPLE PAGE

*Common and
scientific names*

*Category for
easier searching*

MOUNTAIN BLUEBIRD *(Sialia currucoides)* THRUSHES

ADULT MALE

ADULT FEMALE

*Photos may
include
immature
and adult
birds, and
breeding and
nonbreeding
plumages
for easier
identification
year-round.*

JUVENILE

ADULT FEMALE

RANGE MAP

*nge
Map*

- Breeding
- Nonbreeding
- Year-round

SIZE & SHAPE Mountain Bluebirds are fairly small thrushes with round heads and straight, thin bills. Compared with other bluebirds, they are lanky and long-winged, with a long tail.

*Size &
Shape*

COLOR PATTERN Male Mountain Bluebirds are sky blue, a bit darker on wings and tail and paler below, with white under the tail. Females are mostly gray brown with tinges of pale blue in the wings and tail. They occasionally show a suffusion of orange brown on the breast. Mountain Bluebirds' bills are black. Juveniles have fewer spots than the young of other bluebirds and lack spotting on the back.

*Color
Pattern*

BEHAVIOR Unlike other bluebirds, they often hover while foraging and pounce on insect prey from elevated perches. In winter, they occur in large flocks, wandering the landscape and feasting on berries.

Behavior

HABITAT Mountain Bluebirds are common in the West's wide open spaces, particularly at middle and higher elevations.

Habitat

Male **Mountain Bluebirds** lend a bit of cerulean sparkle to open habitats across much of western North America. These cavity nesters flit between perches in mountain meadows, in burned or cut-over areas, or where prairie meets forest—especially in places where people have provided nest boxes.

All About Birds Northwest **231**

BIRDING
101

FOUR KEYS TO BIRD IDENTIFICATION

To identify an unfamiliar bird, first focus on four keys to identification.

With more than 800 species of birds in the U.S. and Canada, it's easy for a beginning bird watcher to feel overwhelmed by possibilities. Field guides often look crammed with similar birds arranged in seemingly haphazard order. We can help you figure out where to begin.

White-throated Sparrow

First we share where *not* to start. Many ID tips focus on very specific details of plumage called field marks, such as the eyering of a Ruby-crowned Kinglet, or the double breast band of a Killdeer. While these tips are useful, they assume you've already narrowed down your search to just a few similar species. Instead, start by learning how to recognize the group a mystery bird belongs to. You may still need to look at field marks to clinch some IDs. But these four keys—**Size and Shape**, **Color Pattern**, **Behavior**, and **Habitat**—will quickly get you to the right group of species, so you'll know exactly which field marks to look for.

1 SIZE AND SHAPE

Birds are built for what they do. Every part of the bird you're looking at is a clue to what it is.

The combination of size and shape is one of the most powerful tools to identification. Though you may be drawn to watching birds because of their wonderful colors or fascinating behavior, when it comes to making identifications, size and shape are the first pieces of information you should examine. With just a little practice and observation, you'll find that differences in size and shape will jump out at you. The first steps are to learn typical bird silhouettes, find reliable ways to gauge the size of a bird, and notice differences in telltale parts of a bird such as the bill, wings, and tail. Soon, you'll know the difference between Red-winged Blackbirds and European Starlings while they're still in flight, and be able to identify a Red-tailed Hawk or Turkey Vulture without taking your eyes off the road.

Become Familiar with Silhouettes

Often you don't need to see any color at all to know what kind of bird you're looking at.

Silhouettes quickly tell you a bird's size, proportions, and posture, and quickly rule out many groups of birds—even ones of nearly identical overall size.

House Finch

A small-bodied finch with a fairly large beak and somewhat long, flat head. The House Finch has a relatively shallow notch in its tail.

Beginning bird watchers often get sidetracked by a bird's bright colors, only to be frustrated when they search through their field guides. Finches, for example, can be red, yellow, blue, brown, or green, but they're still always shaped like finches. Learn silhouettes, and you'll always be close to an ID.

Judge Size Against Birds You Know Well

Size is trickier to judge than shape.

You never know how far away a bird is or how big that nearby rock or tree limb really is. Throw in fluffed-up or hunkered-down birds and it's easy to get fooled. But with a few tricks, you can still use size as an ID key. Compare your mystery bird to a bird you know well. It helps just to know that your bird is larger or smaller than a sparrow, a robin, a crow, or a goose, and it may help you choose between two similar species, such as Downy and Hairy woodpeckers or Sharp-shinned and Cooper's hawks.

Sometimes you need two reference birds for comparison. A crow is bigger than a robin but smaller than a goose.

Judge Against Birds in the Same Field of View

Your estimate of size gets much more accurate if you can compare one bird directly against another.

When you find groups of different species, you can use the ones you recognize to sort out the ones you don't.

Use size and shape to find the full range of species hiding in a large flock. Amid these Caspian Terns are some smaller Common Terns. You'll also notice a Ring-billed Gull in the front on the left and a larger Herring Gull near the center.

For instance, if you're looking at a gull you don't recognize, you can start by noticing that it's larger than a more familiar bird, such as a Ring-billed Gull, that's standing right next to it. For some groups of birds, including shorebirds, seabirds, and waterfowl, using a known bird as a ruler is a crucial identification technique.

Apply Your Size and Shape Skills to the Parts of a Bird

After you've taken note of a bird's overall size and shape, there's still plenty of room to hone your identification.

Turn your attention to the size and shape of individual body parts. Here you'll find clues to how the bird lives its life: what it eats, how it flies, and where it lives.

Start with the bill—that all-purpose tool that functions as a bird's hands, pliers, knitting needles, knife-and-fork, and bullhorn. A flycatcher's broad, flat, bug-snatching bill looks very different from the thick, conical nut-smasher of a finch. Notice the slightly downcurved bills of the Northern Flickers in your backyard. That's an unusual shape for a woodpecker's bill, but perfect for a bird that digs into the ground after ants, as flickers often do.

Bills are an invaluable clue to identification, but tail shape and wing shape are important, too. Even subtle differences in head shape, neck length, and body shape can all yield useful insights if you study them carefully.

Noticing details like these can help you avoid classic identification mistakes. For example, the Ovenbird is a common eastern warbler that has tricked many a bird watcher into thinking it's a thrush. The field marks are certainly thrushlike—warm brown above, strongly streaked below, even a crisp white eyering. But look at overall shape and size rather than field marks, and you'll see the body plan of a warbler—plump, compact body, short tail and wings, thin, pointed, insect-grabbing bill.

Measure the Bird Against Itself

This is the most powerful way to use a bird's size for identification.

It's hard to judge a lone bird's size, and an unusual posture can make shape hard to interpret. But you can always measure key body parts (e.g., wings, bill, tail, legs) against the bird itself.

Look for details such as how long the bird's bill is relative to the head. That's a great way to tell apart Downy and Hairy woodpeckers as well as Greater and Lesser yellowlegs, but it's useful with other confusing species, too. Judging how big the head is compared to the rest of the body helps separate Cooper's Hawks from Sharp-shinned Hawks in flight. Get in the habit of using the bird itself as a ruler, and you'll be amazed at how much information you can glean from each view. Good places to start include noting how long the legs are; how long the neck is; how far the tail extends past the body; and how far the primary feathers of the wing end compared to the tail.

Hairy vs. Downy Woodpeckers

The Hairy Woodpecker (L) is quite a bit larger than the Downy Woodpecker (R), but this is not obvious unless they are side by side. Looking at relative bill size is a way to distinguish between the two when they are not together. The Downy Woodpecker's bill is proportionally smaller than the Hairy Woodpecker's when compared to head size.

2 COLOR PATTERN

When identifying a bird, focus on patterns instead of trying to match every feather.

A picture, even a fleeting glimpse, can be worth a thousand words. As soon as you spot a bird, your eyes take in the overall pattern of light and dark. And if the light allows, you'll probably glimpse the main colors as well. This is all you need to start your identification.

Use these quick glimpses to build a hunch about what your mystery bird is, even if you just saw it flash across a path and vanish into the underbrush. Then, if the bird is kind enough to hop back into view, you'll know what else to look for to settle the identification.

Imagine that you're on vacation in Yosemite National Park. You see a small, bright-yellow bird flitting into the understory. Yellow immediately suggests a warbler (or the larger Western Tanager). Did you pick up a hint of grayness to the head? Or perhaps some glossy black? Just noticing that much can put you on track to identifying either a MacGillivray's Warbler or a Wilson's Warbler.

Wilson's Warbler

Some birds have very fine differences that take practice even to see at all. But don't start looking for those details until you've used overall patterns to let the bird remind you what it is. Read on for a few tips about noticing patches of light and dark, and the boldness or faintness of a bird's markings.

Light and Dark

When you're trying to make an ID, keep in mind that details can change, but overall patterns stay the same.

Remember that birds molt and their feathers wear. Their appearance can vary if the bird is old or young, or by how well it had been eating last time it molted. And of course, the light the bird is sitting in can have a huge effect on the colors you see.

At a distance and in very quick sightings, colors fade and all that's left are light and dark. It helps to familiarize yourself with common patterns. For example, American White Pelicans are large white birds with black trailing edges to their wings. Snow Geese are similarly shaped and colored, but the black in their wings is confined to the wingtips.

Lesser Scaup

Greater and Lesser scaups are dark ducks with a pale patch on the side; Northern Shovelers are the opposite: light-bodied ducks with a dark patch on the side.

Many birds are dark above and pale below—a widespread pattern in the animal world that helps avoid notice by predators. By reversing this pattern, male Bobolinks, with their dark underparts and light backs, look conspicuous even from all the way across a field.

Other birds seem to be trying to call attention to themselves by wearing bright patches of color in prominent places. Male Red-winged Blackbirds use their vivid shoulder patches to intimidate their rivals (notice how they cover up the patches when sneaking around off their territory). American Redstarts flick bright orange patches in their wings and tail, perhaps to scare insects out of their hiding places.

Red-winged Blackbird

Many birds, including Dark-eyed Juncos, Spotted and Eastern towhees, American Robins, and several hummingbirds, flash white in the tail when they fly, possibly as a way of confusing predators. White flashes in the wings are common, too: look for them in Northern Mockingbirds; Acorn, Golden-fronted, and Red-bellied woodpeckers; Common and Lesser nighthawks; and Phainopeplas.

Bold and Faint

Notice strong and fine patterns.

There are some confusing bird species that sit side by side in your field guide, wearing what seems like the exact same markings and defying you to identify them. Experienced birders can find clues to these tricky identifications by noticing how boldly or finely patterned their bird is. These differences can take a trained eye to detect, but the good news is that there's a great trial case right outside at your backyard feeder.

Male Purple Finch

Male House Finch

House Finches are common across most of temperate North America. Much of the continent also gets visits from the very similar Purple Finch. Males of the two species are red on the head and chest and brown and streaky elsewhere. The females are both brown and streaky. So how do you tell them apart? Look at how strongly they're marked.

Male House Finches tend to be boldly streaked down the flanks, whereas male Purple Finches are much paler and more diffusely streaked. Even the red is more distinct, and more confined to the head and breast, in a male House Finch. Male Purple Finches look washed all over, even on the back, in a paler raspberry red.

The all-brown females of these two species are an even better way to build your skills. The streaks on female House Finches are indistinct, brown on brown, with little actual white showing through. If a female Purple Finch lands next to it, she'll stand out with crisply defined brown streaks against a white background, particularly on the head.

3

Once you've had some practice, these small differences can be very useful. Similar degrees in marking can be seen between the coarsely marked Song Sparrow and finely painted Lincoln's Sparrow, and between immature Sharp-shinned and Cooper's hawks.

BEHAVIOR

There's what birds wear, and then there's how they wear it. A bird's attitude goes a long way in identification.

Bird species don't just look unique, they have unique ways of acting, moving, sitting, and flying. When you learn these habits, you can recognize many birds the same way you notice a friend walking through a crowd of strangers.

Chances are you'll never see a Cedar Waxwing poking through the underbrush for seeds, or a Wood Thrush zigzagging over a summer pond catching insects. But similar-sized birds such as towhees and swallows do this all the time. Behavior is one key way these birds differ.

Because so much of a bird's identity is evident in how it acts, behavior can lead you to an ID in the blink of an eye, in bad light, or from a quarter-mile away. Before you even pick up your binoculars, notice how your bird is sitting, how it's feeding or moving, whether it's in a flock, and if it has any nervous habits such as flicking its wings or bobbing its tail.

And remember that to get good at recognizing birds by their behavior, you must spend time watching them. It's tempting to grab your field guide as soon as you see a field mark. Or, after identifying a common bird, you might feel rushed to move on and find something more unusual. Resist these urges. Relax and watch the bird for as long as it will let you. This is how you learn the way a bird acts, how you discover something new...and let's face it, it's probably why you went out bird watching in the first place.

Posture

The most basic aspect of behavior is posture, or how a bird presents itself.

You can learn to distinguish many similarly proportioned birds just from the poses they assume. It's a skill that includes recognizing a bird's size and shape, and adds in the impression of the bird's habits and attitude.

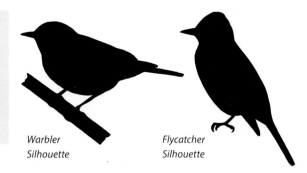

Warblers and flycatchers can be distinguished by posture.

Warbler Silhouette

Flycatcher Silhouette

For example, in the fall season, the small, drab-green Pine Warbler looks similar to the Acadian Flycatcher, right down to the two wingbars and the straight bill. But you're unlikely to confuse the two because their postures are so different. Pine Warblers hold their bodies horizontally and often seem to crouch. Flycatchers sit straight up and down, staying on alert for passing insects.

Horizontal versus vertical posture is the first step. Next, get an impression of the how the bird carries itself. Does it seem inquisitive like a chickadee or placid like a thrush? Does it lean forward, ready for mischief, like a crow? Or is it assertive and stiff, like a robin? Do the bird's eyes dart around after targets, like a flycatcher, or methodically scan the foliage like a vireo? Is the bird constantly on alert, like a finch in the open? Nervous and skittish like a kinglet?

Movement

As soon as a sitting bird starts to move, it gives you a new set of clues about what it is.

You'll not only see different parts of the bird and new postures, you'll sense more of the bird's attitude through the rhythm of its movements. There's a huge difference between the bold way a robin bounces up to a perch, a mockingbird's showy, fluttering arrival, and the meekness of a towhee skulking around.

On the water, some ducks, such as Mallard and Northern Pintail, tip up (or "dabble") to reach submerged vegetation. Others, including scaup and Redhead, disappear from view as they dive for shellfish and other prey. Among the divers, you'll notice that some species, such as eiders, open their wings just before they dive. These ducks flap their wings for propulsion underwater, and they almost always begin a dive this way.

Flight Pattern

Certain birds have flight patterns that give them away.

Almost nothing flaps as slowly as a Great Blue Heron—you can see this from miles away. Learn the long swooping flight of most woodpeckers and you'll be able to pick them out before they've even landed.

Many small birds, particularly finches, have bouncy, roller-coasterlike trajectories caused by fluttering their wings and then actually folding them shut for a split second.

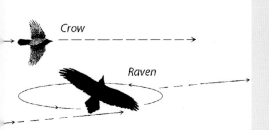
Crow

Raven

Crows and Ravens

Flight style can be a great way to identify birds at a distance. Although crows and ravens look very similar, they fly quite differently. American Crows flap slowly and methodically, whereas Common Ravens take frequent breaks from flapping to soar or glide.

Birds of prey have their own distinct styles. Red-tailed Hawks and other buteos fly with deep, regular wingbeats or soar in circles on broad wings. Falcons fly with powerful beats of their sharply pointed wings.

Feeding Style

Much of the time that you watch birds on the move, you'll be watching them feed, so it pays to become familiar with foraging styles.

Some are obvious: the patient stalking of a heron; the continual up-and-back sprints of Sanderlings; the plunge of a kingfisher. But you can develop a surprisingly specific impression of almost any bird just from a few seconds of watching it forage.

For example, swallows, flycatchers, vireos, finches, and thrushes are all roughly the same size, but they feed in totally different manners: swallows eat on the wing; flycatchers dart out from perches and quickly return; vireos creep through leaves; finches sit still and crush seeds; and thrushes hop low to the ground eating insects and fruit.

Flocking

A flock of kingfishers? A single starling all on its own? Some species seem to be born loners, and others are never found solo.

Even among flocking birds, there are those content to travel in threes and fours, and others that gather by the dozens and hundreds. A noisy group of yellow birds in a treetop is much more likely to be a flock of American Goldfinches than a group of Yellow Warblers. A visit to northern coasts in winter might net you several thousand Brant, but you'll probably only see Harlequin Ducks by the handful.

You'll often see gulls in flocks on a beach, in a parking lot, or wheeling overhead.

Learning the tendencies of birds to flock and their tolerance for crowding is one more aspect of behavior you can use. Just remember that many species get more sociable as summer draws to a close. After nesting is over and young are feeding themselves, adults can relax and stop defending their territories.

4   HABITAT

A habitat is a bird's home, and many birds are choosy. Narrow down your list by keeping in mind where you are.

Identifying birds quickly and correctly is often about probability. By knowing what's likely to be seen you can get a head start on recognizing the birds you run into. And when you see a bird you weren't expecting, you'll know to take an extra look.

Habitat is both the first and last question to ask yourself when identifying a bird. Ask it first, so you know what you're likely to see, and last as a double-check. You can fine-tune your expectations by taking geographic range and time of year into consideration.

Birding by Probability

We think of habitats as collections of plants—grassland, cypress, pine woods, broadleaf forest. But they're equally collections of birds. By noting the habitat you're in, you can build a hunch about the kinds of birds you're most likely to see.

Of course, if you only let yourself identify birds you expect to see, you'll have a hard time finding unusual birds. The best way to find rarities is to know your common birds first (the ones left over are the rare ones). Birding by probability just helps you sort through them that much more quickly.

Use Range Maps

You don't have to give yourself headaches trying to keep straight every last bird in your field guide. They may all be lined up next to each other on the pages, but that doesn't mean they're all in your backyard or local park.

Make it a habit to check the range maps before you make an identification. For example, you can strike off at least half of the devilishly similar *Empidonax* flycatchers at once, just by taking into account where you are when you see one. Similarly, North America has two kinds of small nuthatches with brown heads, but they don't occur within about 800 miles of each other.

Of course, birds do stray from their home ranges, sometimes fantastically, and that's part of the fun. But remember that you're birding by probability, so first compare your bird against what's likely to be present. If nothing matches, then start taking notes.

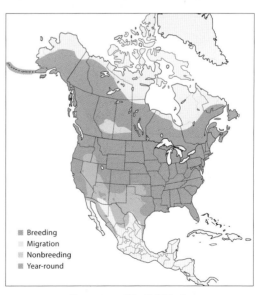

Breeding
Migration
Nonbreeding
Year-round

Range map of the Bald Eagle

Check the Time of Year

Range maps hold another clue to identification—they tell you when a bird is likely to be around.

Ruby-throated Hummingbird

Many of summer's birds, including most of the warblers, flycatchers, thrushes, hummingbirds, and shorebirds, are gone by late fall. Other birds move in to replace them. This mass exodus and arrival is part of what makes bird watching during migration so exciting.

Use eBird to Help

eBird's online species maps are a great way to explore both range and season. You can zoom in to see bird records from your immediate surroundings, and you can filter the map to show you just sightings from a particular month or season.

Another way to focus on the most likely birds near you is to use our free Merlin® Bird ID app for iOS and Android. Merlin takes your location and date, asks you a few simple questions, and gives you a short list of matching possibilities. See page 30 for more on Merlin.

USING FIELD MARKS TO IDENTIFY BIRDS

Once you've looked at Size and Shape, Color Pattern, Behavior, and Habitat to decide what general type of bird you're looking at, you may still have a few similar birds to choose between. To be certain of your identification, you'll need to look at field marks.

Birds display a huge variety of patterns and colors, which they have evolved in part to recognize other members of their own species. Birders use these features (called "field marks") to help distinguish species. Pay particular attention to the field marks of the head and the field marks of the wing.

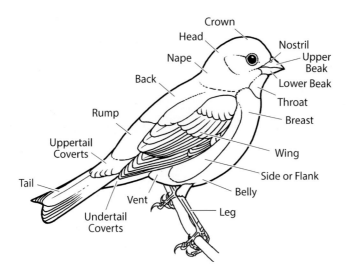

Ornithologists divide a bird's body into topographical regions: beak (or bill), head, back, wings, tail, breast, belly, and legs. To help with identification, many of these regions are divided still further. This diagram shows some of the commonly used descriptive terms.

Field Marks of the Head

When identifying an unknown bird, markings on the head are particularly important, as are beak shape and size. Here are head markings visually displayed to help you along.

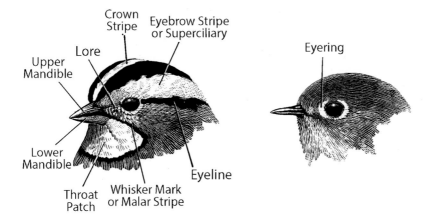

Field Marks of the Wing

A bird's wings are another great place to pick up clues about its identity. In a few groups, notably warblers and vireos, the presence of wingbars and patches of color on the wing can give positive identification even when the bird is in nonbreeding plumage. In other groups, such as flycatchers and sparrows, the absence of wing markings may be important. It also pays to learn the main feather groups, such as primaries, secondaries, tertials, and coverts, and to look for "feather edging"—a different color running along the edges of feathers.

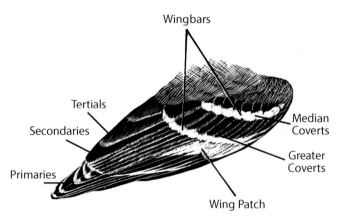

USE MERLIN TO SEE THE POSSIBILITIES

Merlin®, an instant bird identification app from the Cornell Lab of Ornithology, can make many identifications simple. It works by narrowing down your choices, prompting you to enter the date, location, and the bird's size, colors, and behavior.

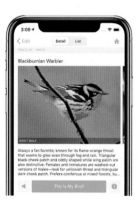

Merlin was designed to be a birding coach for beginning and intermediate bird watchers. Merlin asks you the same questions that an expert birder would ask to help solve a mystery bird sighting. Notice that date and location are Merlin's first and most important questions.

It takes years of experience in the field to know what species are expected at a given location and date. Merlin shares this knowledge with you based on more than one billion sightings submitted to eBird from birders across the world.

Merlin also asks you to describe the color, size, and behavior of the bird you saw. Because no two people describe birds exactly the same way, Merlin presents a shortlist of matching species based on descriptions from Cornell Lab experts as well as thousands of bird enthusiasts who helped "teach" Merlin by participating in online activities.

If you photograph a bird and aren't sure what it is, Merlin can help identify that as well. Using a computer vision system trained on millions of images from the Macaulay Library, the Photo ID tool will help guide you to the right answer.

Much like a modern field-guide app, Merlin also provides world-class photos, ID text, sounds, and range maps. You can browse thousands of stunning images taken by top photographers and listen to a selection of songs and calls for each species. Merlin works all over the world, so no matter where you live or might be traveling, download Merlin for FREE (see page 30 for details).

THE RIGHT STUFF

10 TIPS FOR BEGINNING BIRD WATCHERS

Birding mainly involves patience, careful
the wonder and beauty of the natural world overtake you. But having the right equipment can help too:

1 Binoculars
Your enjoyment of birds depends hugely on how great they look through your binoculars, so make sure you're getting a big, bright, crisp picture through yours. In recent years excellent binoculars have become available at surprisingly low prices. So, while binoculars under $100 may seem tempting, it's truly worth it to spend $250 to $300 for vastly superior images as well

as lifetime warranties, waterproof housing, and lighter weight. We suggest getting 7-power or 8-power binoculars—they're a nice mix of magnification while still allowing you a wide enough view that your bird won't be constantly hopping out of your image.

2 Field Guides

Field guides like this one focus on the most common species in your area and are meant to be portable. Unlike their digital counterparts, they often earn a special place on windowsills, providing a ready resource at home for hours of study and daydreaming.

3 Bird Feeders

With binoculars for viewing and a guide to help you figure out what's what, the next step is to attract birds to your backyard, where you can get a good look at them. Bird feeders come in all types, but we recommend starting with a black-oil sunflower feeder, adding a suet feeder in winter and a hummingbird feeder in summer (or all year in parts of the continent). From there you can diversify to feeders that house millet, thistle seeds, mealworms, and fruit to attract other types of species. In sections that follow, we describe the main types of bird feeders along with images of what they look like, to help you choose the right feeders for your yard and to attract the birds you want to see.

4 Spotting Scopes

By this point in our list, you've got pretty much all the gear you need to be a birder—that is, until you start looking at those ducks on the far side of the pond, or shorebirds in mudflats, or that Golden Eagle perched on a tree limb a quarter-mile away. Though they're not cheap, spotting scopes are indispensable for seeing details at long range—or simply reveling in intricate plumage details that can be brought to life only with a 20x to 60x zoom. The fact that they are mounted on a stable tripod also helps you see details that can be challenging to appreciate while hand-holding binoculars. And scopes, like binoculars, are coming down in price while going up in quality.

5 Cameras

Affordable modern digital cameras allow even novice photographers to take great photos anywhere, anytime. And even if you don't get a great shot every time, even a blurry photo of a bird can help you or others clinch its ID. Birds are inherently artistic creatures, and more and more amateur photographers are connecting with birds through taking gorgeous pictures. If you don't want to invest in a camera with a big lens or long zoom right away, you can also try digiscoping—fitting your point-and-shoot camera or your smartphone's camera up to a spotting scope or binoculars to get a magnified view.

6 Keeping a List

"Listing" doesn't have to be for hardcore birders only; it's fun to record special moments from your days of birding. Many people save their records online using eBird. A Cornell Lab project, eBird allows you to keep track of every place and day you go bird watching, enter notes, share sightings with friends, and explore the data other eBirders have entered. Learn more about eBird and how to use it for free on pages 59–61.

7 Birding by Ear

Many people love bird sounds—calls, songs, and other avian utterances that fill the air. You can use these sounds as clues to identify species. When you are out in the field, use Merlin® to identify bird song.

8 Visual Bird Identification Skills

Now that we've covered the physical tools that equip you for bird watching, let's loop back to your mental tools. Once you're outside and surrounded by birds, practice the four-step approach to identification that we shared earlier in Birding 101: Size and Shape; Color Pattern; Behavior; and Habitat.

9 Birding Apps and Digital Field Guides

If you have a smartphone, you can carry a bookshelf in your pocket. You've already learned about the free Merlin® Bird ID app, but there are many other resources at your disposal. Download the eBird app to keep track of your bird observations in the field, as well as explore recent sightings and bird lists for nearby hotspots. There are also digital field guides—most of the major printed field guides have an app or eBook version. Some specialized apps cover specific groups of species, such as the Warbler Guide and Raptor ID apps. Others, like LarkWire, focus on helping you learn bird song. Search for them in Apple and Android stores. Our All About Birds species guide (*AllAboutBirds.org*) works on mobile devices, giving you access to free ID information and sound recordings straight from your smartphone's internet browser.

10 Connect with Other Birders

Bird watching can be a relaxing solo pursuit, like a walk in the woods decorated with bird sightings. But birding can also be a social endeavor, and the best way to learn is from other people. A great way to connect with people and birds in your area is to look on ***birding.aba.org/***. You'll get emails that will tell you what people have been seeing, announce local bird outings,

and connect you with members of your local birding club. Most regions also have Facebook groups where people share what they've been seeing and welcome newcomers. There's a decent chance that someone's leading a bird walk near you this weekend—and they'd love to have you come along.

LISTENING TO BIRDS

When a bird sings, it's telling you what it is, where it is, and often what is happening.

You can only see straight ahead, but you can hear in all directions at once. Learning bird songs is a great way to identify birds hidden by dense foliage, birds far away, birds at night, and birds that look identical to each other.

And then there's the "dawn chorus," that time as the sun begins to light up the world, when birds join together in a symphony of sound. When you first listen to a dawn chorus in full swing, the sheer onslaught of bird song can be overwhelming. How does anyone begin to pick apart the chirps, whistles, and trills that are echoing out of the woods? The answer, of course, is to concentrate on one bird at a time—and that approach holds true when you're trying to learn individual songs, too. Don't try to memorize each entire song you hear; instead, focus on one quality of the sound at a time. Many birds have a characteristic rhythm, pitch, or tone to their song. Here's how to use them:

Rhythm

Get used to a bird's characteristic tempo as well as the number of distinct sections to its song. Marsh Wrens sing in a hurry, while White-throated Sparrows are much more leisurely.

Repetition

Some birds characteristically repeat syllables or phrases before moving on to a new sound. Northern Mockingbirds do this many times in a row. Though Brown Thrashers sound similar, they typically repeat only twice before changing to a new syllable.

Wood Thrush

Pitch

Most birds sing in a characteristic range, with smaller birds (such as the Cedar Waxwing) typically having higher voices and larger birds (such as the Common Raven) usually having deeper voices. Many bird songs change pitch, so it helps to pay attention to the overall pitch trend in a song. Some birds are distinctive for having steady voices, such as the Chipping Sparrow's trill.

| Rising | Falling | Steady | Variable |

Tone

The tone of a bird's song is sometimes hard to describe, but it can be very distinctive. As a start, pay attention to whether a bird's voice is a clear whistle, harsh or scratchy, liquid and flutelike, or a clear trill. If you can remember the quality of a bird's voice, it can give you a clue to the bird's identity even if the bird doesn't sing the same notes every time.

- **Buzzy:** Like a bee–a good example would be Townsend's Warbler song.

Buzzy

- **Clear:** Something you could whistle. Northern Cardinals have a clear song, as do Yellow Warblers.

Clear

- **Trilled:** A lot of sounds in a row that are too fast to count (technically, more than 11 sounds per second). Chipping Sparrows and Dark-eyed Juncos sing trills.

Trilled

PHOTOGRAPHING BIRDS

5 BASICS OF GOOD BIRD PHOTOGRAPHY

With the explosion in availability and design of digital cameras, it's now possible for hobbyists to take amazingly good photos. Though your photos may not show up on the cover of *National Geographic*, you can up the "wow" factor by paying attention to a few basics.

Beyond the mechanical aspects of shutter speed, aperture, and ISO (which digital cameras increasingly handle automatically), there is an indefinable something that transforms an image into a work of art. Often thought of as talent, just as often it's the result of hours of practice and attention to detail. Here are five basics of good bird photography to bear in mind:

1 Lighting
The best times to shoot are morning and late afternoon when the light is angled, warmer, and more subdued. It's harder to take a good picture in the middle of a bright, clear day because images end up with too much contrast, where light areas get washed out and shadows turn inky black.

Having the source of light behind and slightly to one side of you creates a more three-dimensional subject. Having your subject backlit rarely works well unless you're deliberately going after a silhouette.

2 Framing
Professionals usually avoid placing any subject in the exact center of a photograph. It tends to be more visually stimulating to see the bird off to one side, facing inward. Our own eyes naturally follow the same trajectory. Luckily, it's easy to crop your image later on to get the framing how you want it, so framing in the field is less important unless you're very close to your subject.

3 Composition
Non-bird elements in your picture can add or detract from a pleasing composition. Branches, shrubbery, rocks, and flowers can be a distraction—or they can be used artfully to frame the bird within the picture. Although you want to avoid having a branch right behind the bird looking like it's growing

out of its head, incorporating some part of the bird's habitat often makes a shot better. If the background is too busy, try opening the aperture to blur the background and make your subject stand out.

4 Angle
You can shoot from a position that is higher than your subject, lower, at eye level, or somewhere in between. Each situation can be different—but adjusting your height to shoot the bird at eye level is often a good choice, as it puts the viewer on the same plane as the bird. To get closer to wary birds, you can wear muted clothing, hide behind vegetation, and move slowly and calmly in a zigzag pattern. It is never a good idea to bait a bird or to approach so closely that you flush the bird or alter its behavior.

Sanderling

5 Knowledge of Your Subject
To be the best bird photographer you can be, you really have to know birds. For example, knowing the habitat and behavior of a species allows you to predict where you're likely to find them and anticipate what they might do next. For example, berry bushes attract Cedar Waxwings; herons haunt the edges of marshes and ponds; waterfowl often rest and preen in the same spot every day. Study your subject and you'll know when and where to get the shot.

What Kind of Camera?
We're in a golden age of camera design and there are great options at every level of interest. Serious enthusiasts tend toward DSLR (digital single-lens reflex) or mirrorless cameras with interchangeable lenses, but these can be expensive. At the entry level, so-called "superzoom" cameras can produce surprisingly good results while remaining compact and fairly inexpensive.

DIGISCOPING

Placing the lens of a digital camera to the eyepiece of a spotting scope is called "digiscoping." It's an inexpensive way to take decent pictures without a heavy, expensive telephoto lens.

Both scopes and digital cameras have improved tremendously since the dawn of digiscoping. One of the most significant advances has been the advent of smartphones, which are now arguably the best tool for digiscoping and certainly the most convenient. Scopes, too, have come down in price.

Digiscoped Rose-breasted Grosbeak

There can be different goals in digiscoping. It can be practiced slowly and patiently to capture frame-worthy photos, whether detail-rich or artistically blurred. More often, it's a handy way to capture shots to remind yourself of a special moment or to back up a rare bird report. It's even becoming common for people to record video while digiscoping.

Granted, digiscoping does require a spotting scope, which can cost as much as a camera and telephoto lens—but some birders are happy to put their money toward a scope that can do double duty in both bird watching and photography.

Getting a good image when digiscoping comes down to gathering plenty of light, getting the camera lens the correct distance from the scope's eyepiece, and holding everything steady.

Getting Connected

There are a variety of ways to bring the camera lens and scope eyepiece together. For smartphones, the earliest method involved placing a finger between phone and eyepiece both to steady the lens and keep it at the correct distance. Today you can find phone adapters custom-sized to hold a phone in the proper position—greatly cutting down on fiddling and frustration.

If you don't line up camera and eyepiece perfectly, you may get uneven focus, part of the image cut off, or shadows creeping in as light leaks in between scope and camera lenses. Remember that the many commercial adapters are not universal, so make sure you get what fits your gear.

Standing Steady

The magnification produced by digiscoping is just what you need to pull your subject in close, but it also magnifies small movements from wind or a shaky trigger finger. Keeping extraneous motion to a minimum is of paramount importance. A quality tripod for your scope will provide stable support and prevent your photos from turning into a blurry mess. You'll find that a rock-steady tripod will be well worth it anyway—even in routine bird watching without attaching a camera.

5 TIPS FOR SUCCESSFUL DIGISCOPING

1 Let There Be Light

One cause of blurry photos is low light coming through the scope, which forces a slower shutter speed and increases the effect of motion. Using larger, brighter scopes, such as 85-mm models rather than 65-mm models, results in noticeably better digiscoped photos. If you can change your camera's ISO (a feature

Digiscoped American Goldfinch

becoming more common on smartphones), setting it higher can get you a faster shutter speed.

2 Resist the Zoom

For scopes with a zoom, bear in mind that you quickly lose light as you zoom in. The human eye is good at compensating for this; cameras less so. Take advantage of your camera's many megapixels by shooting at a lower, brighter zoom setting and then cropping later.

3 Capture the Motion

Many cameras and phones have a continuous shooting feature that takes photos one after another. This setting can help you catch birds in just the right pose. As an alternative, consider shooting video of a fast-moving subject—this can be more helpful than still photos when trying to identify a bird later.

4 Try It with Your Binoculars

Sometimes called "digibinning," this advanced technique can sometimes produce decent photos. If you don't already have a spotting scope, it's a less expensive way to get into digiscoping. But be warned: it's hard to hold the binocular-phone combination steady. It's a good idea to start with large, stationary birds such as herons.

5 Practice, Practice, Practice

Fortunately, once you've got the equipment, taking digital photos is virtually free. It may seem impossible at first, but you'll quickly improve as you become comfortable with setting up the scope and handling your camera's controls. Don't be afraid to experiment—you never know what you'll come away with.

ATTRACTING BIRDS TO YOUR YARD

Cedar Waxwing ©Jay McGowan/Macaulay Library

BIRDSCAPING

You can watch birds anywhere.

Parks, nature preserves, and wildlife refuges provide some of the most diverse species, but the easiest place to watch birds is your own backyard. Enhancing your yard to attract and support birds is called "birdscaping."

American Goldfinch

Putting up a feeder is an easy way to attract birds. But if you'd prefer a more natural approach or you want to satisfy more than birds' nutritional needs, consider landscaping your yard—even just a part of it—to be more bird friendly. Even a small yard can provide vital habitat. The core concept is simple—all birds need three basic things from their habitats.

1 Food

Your birds can get food from feeders that you put up. Landscaping your yard to provide the fruit, seeds, beneficial insects, and other small animals that birds feed on adds natural food sources for birds, too.

2 Water

All living things need water to survive. Providing this habitat necessity is one of the quickest ways to attract birds to your property. If there is a water source in your yard, such as a pond, creek, birdbath, or even a puddle, you've probably noticed birds using it. If you don't have a water feature yet, a birdbath is an easy way to provide this habitat need.

3 Shelter

Whether it's protection from the elements, safe places to hide from predators, or secure locations to hide nests, providing shelter is one of the best ways to make your property bird-friendly.

Improve Your Yard

Take a "bird's-eye" look at your backyard. Does it provide those things? If not, there are plants you can grow and many other ways you can enhance your yard to make it safe and inviting for birds. Here are some tips to help you:

1 Evaluate Your Yard

First, take stock of what you already have. Draw a map of your property including buildings, sidewalks, fences, trees, shrubs, feeders, and nest boxes. Note sunny or shady sites, low or wet areas, sandy sites, and plants you want to keep.

2 Start With a Plan

Before you start digging holes and rearranging your yard, develop a planting plan. Draw each new plant onto a piece of tracing paper, then place that over the map of your yard. Once your plants are in, use your map as a reminder about which ones need to be watered and weeded, especially in the first year after planting. Mulch is great for keeping moisture in and weeds out.

3 Think Variety

Try to include variety and year-round value in your planting plan. Look for places to include grasses, legumes, hummingbird flowers, plants that fruit in summer and fall, winter-persistent plants, and conifers for shelter. Plant native species instead of exotics, and look for places to create shelter with a brush pile or standing dead tree.

BIRD FEEDERS

Fifty million people in North America feed birds and it's a great way to attract birds to your backyard. But feeders are not one size fits all—different species are attracted to different designs. Here are the main types of feeders and the types of birds they attract.

Ground

Many species of birds, including sparrows and doves, prefer to feed on large, flat surfaces and may not visit any type of elevated feeder. Song Sparrows and many towhee species, for instance, will rarely land on a feeder, but they will readily eat fallen seed from the ground beneath your feeders. To attract these species, try spreading seed on the ground or on a large surface such as the top of a picnic table. Ground feeders that sit low to the ground with mesh screens for good drainage can also be used. Make sure that there are no predators around, including outdoor cats.

Large and Small Hopper

A hopper feeder is a platform on which walls and a roof are built, forming a "hopper" that protects seed against the weather. Large hoppers attract most species of feeder birds and will allow larger species, such as doves and grackles, to feed. Small hoppers will attract smaller birds while preventing those larger species from comfortably perching and monopolizing the feeder.

Large and Small Tube

A tube feeder is a hollow cylinder, often made of plastic, with multiple feeding ports and perches. Tube feeders keep seed fairly dry. Feeders with short perches accommodate small birds such as finches but exclude larger birds such as grackles and jays. The size of the feeding ports varies as well, depending on the type of seed to be offered. Note that special smaller feeding ports are required for nyjer (thistle) seed to prevent spillage.

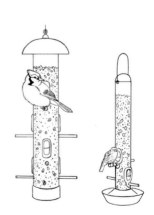

Sugar Water

Sugar-water feeders are specially made to dispense sugar water through small holes. Choose a feeder that is easy to take apart and clean, because the feeder should be washed or run through the dishwasher frequently.

Platform

A platform feeder is any flat, raised surface onto which bird food is spread. The platform should have plenty of drainage holes to prevent water accumulation. A platform with a roof will help keep seeds dry. Trays attract most species of feeder birds. Placed near the ground, they are likely to attract juncos, doves, and sparrows.

Suet Cage

Suet or suet mixes can be placed in a specially made cage, tied to trees, or smeared into knotholes. Cages that are only open at the bottom tend to be starling-resistant but allow woodpeckers, nuthatches, and chickadees to feed by clinging upside down.

Thistle Sock

Thistle "socks" are fine-mesh bags to which birds cling to extract nyjer or thistle seeds. Seed within thistle socks can become quite wet with rain, so only use large ones during periods when you have enough finches to consume the contents in a few days.

Window Feeder

Small plastic feeders affixed to window glass with suction cups, and platform feeders hooked into window frames, attract finches, chickadees, titmice, and some sparrows. They afford wonderful, close-up views of birds, and their placement makes them the safest of all feeder types for preventing window collisions.

FEEDER PLACEMENT & SAFETY

Place feeders in a quiet area where they are easy to see and convenient to refill. Place them close to natural cover, such as trees or shrubs. Evergreens are ideal, as they provide thick foliage that hides birds from predators and buffers winter winds. Be careful not to place feeders too close to trees with strong branches that can provide jump-off points for squirrels and cats. A distance of about 10 feet is a good compromise.

Hummingbird Feeders

Place hummingbird feeders in the shade if possible, as sugar solution spoils quickly in the sun. Don't use honey, artificial sweeteners, or food coloring. If bees or wasps become a problem, try moving the feeder.

Clean and refill hummingbird feeders every few days in a dishwasher or very hot water to prevent dangerous mold. Keep seed and suet feeders clean by washing them periodically in a dishwasher, with soap and very hot water, or with a diluted bleach or vinegar solution.

Window Strikes

Ornithologists estimate that up to *one billion* birds are killed by hitting windows in the United States and Canada each year. Placing feeders close to your windows (ideally closer than three feet) can help reduce this problem. When feeders are close, a bird leaving the feeder cannot gain enough momentum to do harm if it strikes the window.

You can prevent more window strikes by breaking up reflections of trees and open space, which birds perceive as a flight path through your home. Techniques include attaching streamers, suction-cup feeders, or decals to windows, crisscrossing branches within the window frames, or installing awnings or screens. Acopian Bird Savers are closely spaced ropes that hang down over windows. They do the work of tape or decals but are easier to install and can be aesthetically pleasing.

Another method is to attach netting to the outside of the window to buffer the impact. Deer netting (the kind used to keep deer from eating plants in your yard) works well, pulled taut to prevent any entanglements.

To learn more about window crashes, how to prevent them, and more specific solutions to this problem, visit ***https://tinyurl.com/preventing-window-crashes***.

BIRD FOOD

Sunflower seeds attract the widest variety of birds and are the mainstay food used in most bird feeders. Other varieties of seed can help attract different types of birds to your feeders and yard and this section highlights many of them. When buying mixtures, note that those that contain red millet, oats, and other fillers are not attractive to most birds and can lead to a lot of waste.

Sunflower Seeds

There are two kinds of sunflower—black oil and striped. The black oil seeds ("oilers") have very thin shells, easy for virtually all seed-eating birds to crack open, and the kernels within have a high fat content, which is extremely valuable for most winter birds. Striped sunflower seeds have a thicker shell, much harder for House Sparrows and blackbirds to crack open. So, if you're inundated with species you'd rather not subsidize at your feeder, before you do anything else, try switching to striped sunflower. Sunflower in the shell can be offered in a wide variety of feeders, including trays, tube feeders, hoppers, and acrylic window feeders. Sunflower hearts and chips shouldn't be offered in tube feeders where moisture can collect. Since squirrels love sunflower seeds, be prepared to take steps to squirrel-proof your feeder if needed.

Safflower

Safflower has a thick shell, hard for some birds to crack open, but is a favorite among cardinals. Some grosbeak chickadees, doves, and native sparrows also eat it. According to some sources, House Sparrows, European Starlings, and squirrels don't like safflower, but in some areas they seem to have developed a taste for it. Cardinals and grosbeaks tend to prefer tray and hopper feeders, which ma these feeders a good choice for offering safflower.

Nyjer or Thistle

Small finches including American Goldfinches, Lesser Goldfinches, Indigo Buntings, Pine Siskins, and Common Redpolls often devour these tiny, black,

needlelike seeds. As invasive thistle plants became a recognized problem in North America, suppliers shifted to a daisylike plant, known as *Guizotia abyssinica*, that produces a similar type of small, oily, rich seed. The plant is now known as niger or nyjer, and is imported from overseas. The seeds are heat-sterilized during importation to limit their chance of spreading invasively, while retaining their food value.

White Proso Millet

White millet is a favorite with ground-feeding birds including quails, native sparrows, doves, towhees, juncos, and cardinals. Unfortunately, it's also a favorite of House Sparrows, which are already subsidized by human activities and supported at unnaturally high population levels by current agricultural practices and habitat changes. When these species are present, you may want to stop offering millet; virtually all the birds that like it are equally attracted to black

oil sunflower. Because white millet is so preferred by ground-feeding birds, scatter it on the ground or set low platform feeders with excellent drainage.

Shelled and Cracked Corn

Corn is eaten by grouse, pheasants, turkeys, quail, cardinals, grosbeaks, crows, ravens, jays, doves, d cranes, and other species. Unfortunately, corn has two serious problems. First, it's a favorite of House Sparrows, starlings, geese, bears, raccoons, and deer. Second, corn is the bird food most likely to be contaminated with aflatoxins, which are extremely toxic even at low levels. Nev buy corn in plastic bags, never allow it to get wet, never offer it in amounts that can't be consumed in a

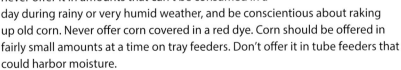

day during rainy or very humid weather, and be conscientious about raking up old corn. Never offer corn covered in a red dye. Corn should be offered in fairly small amounts at a time on tray feeders. Don't offer it in tube feeders that could harbor moisture.

Peanuts

Peanuts are very popular with jays, crows, chickadees, titmice, woodpeckers, and many other species, but are also favored by squirrels, bears, raccoons, and other animals. Like corn, peanuts have a high likelihood of harboring aflatoxins, so must be kept dry and used up fairly quickly. Peanuts in the shell can be set out on platform feeders or right on a deck railing or windo feeder as a special treat for jays. If peanuts, peanut hearts, or mixtures of peanuts and other seeds are offered in tube feeders, make sure to change the seed frequently, especially during rainy or humid weather, and be sure to completely empty out and clean the tube every time you do so.

Milo or Sorghum

Milo is a favorite with many western ground-feeding birds. On Cornell Lab of Ornithology seed-preference tests, Steller's Jays, Curve-billed Thrashers, and Gambel's Quails preferred milo to sunflower. In another study, House Sparrows did not eat milo. Milo should be scattered on the ground or on low tray feeders.

Golden Millet, Red Millet, Flax, and Others

These seeds are often used as fillers in packaged birdseed mixes, but most birds shun them. Waste seed becomes a breeding ground for bacteria and fungus, contaminating fresh seed more quickly. Make sure to read the ingredients list on birdseed mixtures, avoiding those with these seeds. If a seed mix has a lot of small, re seeds, make sure they're milo or sorghum, not red millet.

Mealworms

Mealworms ae the larvae of the mealworm beetle, *Tenebrio molitor*, and they provide a high-protein treat for many birds. Some people provide live mealworms, while others prefer offering dried larvae. Birds such as chickadees, titmice, wrens, and nuthatches relish this fc and mealworms are one of the few food items that relia attracts bluebirds. Offer mealworms on a flat tray or in a specialized mealworm feeder.

Fruit

Various fruits can prove quite attractive to many species of birds. Oranges cut in half will often attract orioles which will sip the juice and eat the flesh of the orange. Grapes and raisins are a favorite of many fruit-eating birds such as mockingbirds, catbirds, bluebirds, robins, and waxwings. You can also provide a dish of grape jelly for these species, but be sure to avoid jellies containing artificial ingredients  like preservatives or sweeteners. Several species are also attracted to the dried seeds of fruits such as pumpkins or apples. Be sure to dispose of any fruit that becomes moldy because some molds create toxins that are harmful to birds.

Sugar Water or Nectar

To make nectar for hummingbirds, add one part table sugar to four parts boiling water and stir. A slightly more diluted mixture can be used for orioles (one part sugar to six parts water). You may want to use regular granulated white sugar rather than raw or cane sugar, which may contain additional ingredients that have unknown effects on hummingbirds. Allow the mixture to cool before  filling the feeder. Store extra sugar water in the refrigerator for up to one week (after that it may become moldy, which is dangerous for birds). Adding red food coloring is unnecessary and possibly harmful to birds. Red portals on the feeder, or even a red ribbon tied on top, will attract the birds just as well.

Grit

Birds "chew" their food in the muscular part of their stomac' called the gizzard. To aid in the grinding, birds swallow small, hard materials such as sand, small pebbles, ground eggshells, and ground oyster shells. Grit, therefore, attracts many birds as a food supplement or even by itself. Oyster shells and eggshells have the added benefit of being a good source of calcium, something birds need during egg laying. If you decide to provide eggshells, be sure to sterilize them first. You can boil them for 10 minutes or heat them in an oven (20 minutes at 250°F). Let the eggshells cool, then crush them into pieces about the size of sunflower seeds. Offer the eggshell in a dish or low platform feeder.

WATER SOURCES

Like all animals, birds need water to survive. Though they can extract some moisture from their food, most birds drink water every day. Birds also use water for bathing, to clean their feathers and remove parasites. After splashing around in a bath for a few minutes, a bird usually perches in a sunny spot and fluffs its feathers out to dry. Then it carefully preens each feather, adding a protective coating of oil secreted by a gland at the base of its tail.

Because birds need water for drinking and bathing, they are attracted to water just as they are to feeders. A dependable supply of fresh, clean water is very important. In fact, a birdbath may even bring in birds that don't eat seeds and won't visit your feeders otherwise. Providing water for birds can improve the quality of your backyard bird habitat and should provide you with a fantastic opportunity to observe bird behavior.

Blackburnian Warbler

Birds seem to prefer baths that are at ground level, but raised baths will attract birds as well and may make birds less vulnerable to predators. Change the water daily to keep it fresh and clean. You can also arrange a few branches or stones in the water so that birds can stand on them and drink without getting wet (this is particularly important in winter). Birdbaths should be only an inch or two deep, with a shallow slope.

One of the best ways to make your birdbath more attractive is to provide dripping water. You can buy a dripper or sprayer, or you can recycle an old bucket or plastic container by punching a tiny hole in the bottom, filling it with water, and hanging it above the birdbath so the water drips out. In freezing climates, a birdbath heater will keep ice from freezing. Don't add antifreeze; it is poisonous to all animals, including birds.

To learn more about birdbaths: *https://tinyurl.com/learn-more-birdbaths.*

FEATURES OF A GOOD BIRDHOUSE

IT'S WELL CONSTRUCTED

Untreated Wood – Use untreated, unpainted wood, preferably cedar, pine, cypress, or for larger boxes (owls) non-pressure-treated CDX exterior grade plywood.

Galvanized Screws – Use galvanized screws for the best seal. Nails can loosen over time, allowing rain into the nest box. Screws are also easier to remove for repairs or maintenance. Do not use staples.

IT KEEPS BIRDS DRY

Sloped Roof – A sloped roof that overhangs the front by 2–4″ and the sides by 2″ will help keep out driving rain, while also thwarting predators. Add 1/4″-deep cuts under the roof on all three edges to serve as gutters that channel rain away from the box.

Recessed Floor – A recessed floor keeps the nest from getting wet and helps the box last longer. Recess the floor at least 1/4″ up from the bottom.

Drainage Holes – Add at least four drainage holes (3/8″ to 1/2″ diameter) to the floor to allow any water that enters the box to drain away. Alternatively, you can cut away the corners of the floorboard to create drainage holes.

IT HELPS REGULATE TEMPERATURE

Thick Walls – Walls should be at least 3/4″ thick to insulate the nest properly. (Note that boards sold as 1″ are actually 3/4″ thick.)

Ventilation Holes – For adequate ventilation, there should be two 5/8″-diameter holes on each of the side walls, near the top (four total).

IT KEEPS OUT PREDATORS

No Perches – A perch is unnecessary for the birds and can actually help predators gain access to the box.

Types of Predator Guards – Although predators are a natural part of the environment, birdhouses are typically not as well concealed as natural nests and some predators can make a habit of raiding your boxes. Adding a baffle or guard helps keep nestlings and adults safe from climbing predators. Below are some time-tested options.

←Collar Baffle
A metal collar of about 3 feet in diameter surrounding the pole underneath the nest box.

Stovepipe Baffle→
A more complex pole-mounted baffle. These baffles are generally 8" in diameter and 24"–36" long.

←Hole Guard
A wooden block over the entrance hole that extends the depth of the entrance hole. You can also use an entrance hole guard in combination with a pole-mounted baffle (preferred), or attach it to boxes installed on trees.

Noel Guard→
A wire mesh tube attached to the front of the nest box.

IT HELPS FLEDGLINGS LEAVE THE NEST

Rough Interior Walls – The interior wall below the entrance hole should be rough to help nestlings climb out of the box. For small boxes (wrens and chickadees), plain wood is usually rough enough, but you can roughen smooth boards with coarse sandpaper.

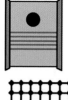

Interior Grooves – A series of shallow horizontal cuts, like a small ladder, works well in medium-sized boxes meant for swallows and bluebirds. Swallows, in particular, need a little help climbing out of boxes.

Duck Boxes – For duck boxes, staple a strip of 1/4"-mesh hardware cloth from floor to hole to help ducklings escape deep boxes.

IT HAS THE RIGHT ENTRANCE SIZE FOR THE RIGHT BIRD

By providing a properly sized entrance hole, you can attract desirable species to your birdhouses while excluding predators and unwanted occupants. Below are the requirements for entrance-hole size for some common species that nest in boxes.

HOLE SIZE	SPECIES
3"	Screech-owls, American Kestrel
$2^1/_2$"	Northern Flicker
$1^9/_{16}$"	Ash-throated Flycatcher, Great Crested Flycatcher, Mountain Bluebird
$1^1/_2$"	Eastern Bluebird, Western Bluebird, Bewick's Wren, Carolina Wren
$1^3/_8$"	White-breasted Nuthatch, Tree Swallow, Violet-green Swallow
$1^1/_4$"	Prothonotary Warbler, Red-breasted Nuthatch, Tufted Titmouse
$1^1/_8$"	House Wren, chickadees

IT MAKES PLACEMENT AND MAINTENANCE EASY

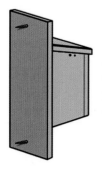

Extended Back

A few extra inches at the top and bottom of your birdhouse can make it easier to mount on a metal pole. Alternatively, you can predrill mounting holes in the back panel before assembly and use a short-handled screwdriver to install the box.

Hinged Door with a Sturdy Closing Mechanism

A hinged side gives you access for cleaning and monitoring your nest box, both of which are important for a successful nesting season. A latch or nail keeps the box securely closed until you are ready to open it.

COMMON NEST BOX PREDATORS

SNAKES – Many snakes are excellent climbers and can easily surmount an unguarded pole. Snakes most likely to climb into birdhouses are generally nonvenomous (such as racers and rat snakes) and helpful at controlling rodents. Avoid installing nest boxes next to brush piles or trees.

RACOOONS – Raccoons are intelligent and can remember nest box locations from year to year. They can be abundant in populated areas. Mount nest boxes on a metal pole equipped with a baffle; avoid mounting them on trees or fence posts.

CHIPMUNKS / MICE – Chipmunks and mice are both nest predators and competitors for nest boxes. To keep chipmunks and mice out, mount boxes away from trees on a metal pole equipped with a baffle.

CATS – Cats are excellent jumpers and can leap to the top of a nest box from a nearby tree or from the ground. Mount your box high enough and far enough from trees so cats cannot spring to the top of the box in a single leap. Keep pet cats indoors for their own safety and that of birds.

INTO DIY?

Visit *nestwatch.org/birdhouses* to get FREE downloadable nest-box plans.

Marbled Godwit ©Luke Seitz/Macaulay Library

GETTING INVOLVED

CITIZEN SCIENCE

Each month, bird watchers report millions of bird observations to citizen-science projects at the Cornell Lab of Ornithology, contributing to the world's most dynamic and powerful source of information on birds.

The Cornell Lab of Ornithology has been at the forefront of citizen science since 1966. Today, the birding community can use our innovative online tools to tap into millions of records and see how their own sightings fit into the continental picture. Scientists can analyze the same data to reveal striking changes in the movements, distributions, and numbers of birds across time,

and to determine how birds are affected by habitat loss, pollution, and disease.

If you enjoy watching birds, you can help and contribute to science, whether you are a beginner or a seasoned birder. Participating can take as little or as much time as you want—you decide!

There's a Project for Every Bird Watcher

Our fun and meaningful citizen-science projects enable people to watch birds at their favorite locations and share their sightings:

- **eBird** is a powerful tool for keeping track of your sightings and for exploring what others have seen—with global coverage and millions of sightings recorded per month for science and conservation.

- **Great Backyard Bird Count** is possibly the easiest project of all and the best one to start with—a global effort to count birds over one long weekend each February.

- **Project FeederWatch** is a winter project where you count birds at your feeders to help track bird populations and distributions.

- **NestWatch** asks you to report on the nests of birds breeding around you—training and best practices for visiting nests are provided.

- **Celebrate Urban Birds** combines art and science, and encourages participants in urban and rural settings to share their knowledge of local birds and culture.

eBIRD

Since its inception in 2002, eBird has grown into one of the world's largest data sources about living things—thanks to birders contributing a billion or more sightings of birds.

eBird gives birders a convenient, free way to enter, store, and organize their sightings. And it makes those sightings available to others, turning it into a useful resource for studying or finding birds anywhere in the world. Not only that, your sightings power science and conservation, helping scientists identify which species are declining and where best to direct conservation efforts.

Use eBird to start or maintain your birding lists—or use it to find out where and when to go birding. It works all over the world and provides endless ideas about what to do and where to go next. And it's free.

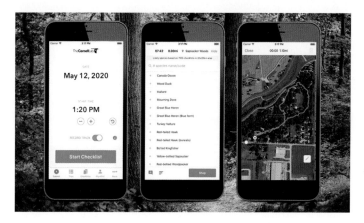

eBird provides easy-to-use online tools for birders and critical data for science. With eBird, you can:

- Record the birds you encounter
- Keep track of birding activity and lists
- Learn where to find birds near you
- Share sightings with other birders
- Contribute to science and conservation

Record and Store Sightings in eBird

eBird allows you to easily record the birds you find. Simply enter when, where, and how you went birding, then fill out a checklist of all the birds you identified with confidence by sight or sound. A free mobile app allows you to create and share checklists faster than ever. Data quality filters check all submissions automatically and local experts review unusual records before they enter the database.

eBird automatically organizes your bird observations into local and national lists, year lists, and more. You can also add photos and sound recordings to your checklists, so you can share your experiences with friends while also powering Merlin Bird ID, an automatic bird identification tool that can help you build skills for better birding. All these features work in any country in the world and are available in many languages.

Explore Data and Learn with eBird

One of eBird's greatest strengths is its ability to show you where and when birds occur, using innovative visualization tools. These free tools are used annually by millions of birders, scientists, and conservationists worldwide. Here are a few:

- **Species Maps:** Choose a species, then explore a map of everywhere it has been reported. Filter the map by date or zoom in to anywhere in the world with pinpoint precision.

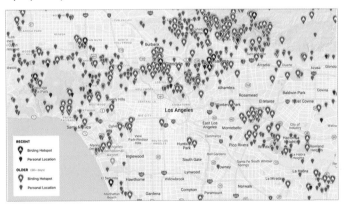

- **Photo and Sound Archive:** Each month, eBirders upload thousands of images and sounds. All of them are searchable in the Macaulay Library archive, so you can explore birds both familiar and new.

- **Explore a Region:** See the full species list, plus recent sightings, photo and audio recordings, best hotspots, and top birders for any county, state, province, or country. The Illustrated Checklist is a living field guide for any region!

- **Seasonal Occurrence Graphs:** Create a customized species list for any region and season. This tool tells you which species to expect when; bars tell you how rare or common each bird is throughout the year.

Seasonal abundance
TheCornellLab Data provided by eBird

Cedar Waxwing (*Bombycilla cedrorum*) © Brian Sullivan / Macaulay Library

- **Hotspot Explorer:** Use an interactive map to explore popular birding spots anywhere in the world—a great tool for travelers looking for local tips on where to go birding.

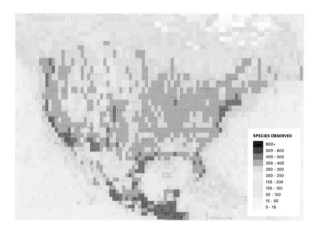

SPECIES OBSERVED
600+
500 - 600
400 - 500
300 - 400
250 - 300
200 - 250
150 - 200
100 - 150
50 - 100
15 - 50
0 - 15

Your Sightings Support Science and Conservation

Every checklist you submit helps scientists better understand when and where birds occur, helping pinpoint where conservation is likely to have the greatest impact on bird populations. Your checklists also help scientists track the health of our bird populations; eBird data helps identify which species may be in trouble and in need of attention. Learn more about eBird and the birds recently seen in your area at *eBird.org*.

GREAT BACKYARD BIRD COUNT

In 1998, the annual four-day Great Backyard Bird Count (GBBC) began in the United States and Canada. It was the first citizen-science program to collect and display bird observation data online on a large scale. Today, the GBBC is one of the most popular annual events among bird watchers and has expanded to include the whole world. More than 200,000 people of all ages and walks of life take part. In 2020, 249,444 counts flooded in, recording a total of 6,942 species of birds—more than half of all bird species in the world!

Why Count Birds?

Scientists and bird enthusiasts can learn a lot by knowing where the birds are. No single scientist or team of scientists could hope to document and understand the complex distribution and movements of so many species in such a short time. Scientists use information from the GBBC, along with observations from other citizen-science projects, to see the big picture about what is happening to bird populations. You can help scientists investigate far-reaching questions, such as these:

- How does weather and climate change influence bird populations?

- Some birds appear in large numbers during some years but not others. Where are these species from year to year, and what can we learn from these patterns?

- How does the timing of bird migrations compare across years?

- What kinds of differences in bird diversity are apparent in cities versus suburban, rural, and natural areas?

Why Is the GBBC in February?

Originally the GBBC was held in the U.S. and Canada each February to create a snapshot of the distribution of birds just before spring migrations ramped up in March. Scientists at the Cornell Lab of Ornithology, National Audubon Society, Birds Canada, and elsewhere can combine this information with data from surveys conducted at different times of the year. In 2013, the count went global, creating snapshots of birds wherever they are in February, regardless of seasons across the hemispheres.

How to Participate

We invite you to participate! Visit *birdcount.org* to find out when the next GBBC is happening (it falls in February during the U.S. Presidents' Day weekend). If you're new to citizen science, you'll need to register for a free online account to enter your checklist counts. If you have already participated in another Cornell Lab citizen-science project, you can use that login information for GBBC.

Once registered, simply tally the numbers and kinds of birds you see for at least 15 minutes on one or more days of the count every February. You can count from any location, anywhere in the world, for as long as you wish. During the count, you can explore what others are seeing in your area or around the world.

To learn more and participate in the Great Backyard Bird Count, visit *birdcount.org*.

The Great Backyard Bird Count is led by the Cornell Lab of Ornithology and National Audubon Society, with Birds Canada and many international partners. The Great Backyard Bird Count is powered by eBird.

BIRD ACADEMY

Whether you're newly curious about the bird songs in your backyard, an avid birder with a life list to tend, or a budding ornithologist, Bird Academy has a course for every bird enthusiast.

Bird Academy courses are entirely online. You can learn at your own pace, return to the material as often as you wish, and there is no deadline to complete them. Take advantage of exclusive learning tools and friendly video tutorials created by our team of expert birders, ornithologists, and educational designers. *The Wonderful World of Owls*, *How to Identify Bird Songs*, *Nature Journaling and Field Sketching*, *Understanding Bird Behavior*, and *Sparrow Identification* are just a few of the courses on offer.

To find out more, visit *Academy.AllAboutBirds.org.*

Barn Owl

PROJECT FEEDERWATCH

Northern Cardinal

Project FeederWatch is a survey of birds that visit feeders in backyards, nature centers, community areas, and other locales in North America. Each year, tens of thousands of people participate in Project FeederWatch. Annually, FeederWatchers report more than 7 million birds, providing valuable data for monitoring changes in the distribution and abundance of backyard birds. Participants gain from the rewarding experience of learning about birds at their feeders and contributing their own observations to reveal larger patterns in bird populations across the continent.

Why Are FeederWatch Data Important?

With each season, FeederWatch increases in importance as a unique tool to monitor bird species in North America. What sets FeederWatch apart from other monitoring programs is the detailed picture that FeederWatch data provide about weekly changes in bird distribution and abundance. Because participants count and identify all their birds multiple times from the same location, FeederWatch data are extremely powerful for detecting gradual changes in bird populations and ranges through time. FeederWatch data tell us where birds are as well as where they are not, which enables people to piece together accurate population maps. Finally, FeederWatch data provide information on a spatial and temporal scale that could not be collected by any other method than through the efforts of many participants over many years.

How Are FeederWatch Data Used?

The massive amounts of data collected by FeederWatchers across the continent help people understand:

- Long-term trends in bird distribution and abundance
- Invasive species dynamics continent-wide
- Behavioral interactions of birds at feeders
- The timing and extent of winter irruptions of winter finches and other species

- Expansions or contractions in ranges of feeder birds

- How supplementary food and backyard habitat affect birds

- How disease is spread among birds that visit feeders

How to Participate

Anyone interested in birds can participate, including people of all skill levels and backgrounds. FeederWatch is a great project for children, families, individuals, classrooms, retirees, youth groups, nature centers, and bird clubs. You can count birds as often as every week, or as infrequently as you like—the schedule is very flexible. All you need is a bird feeder, birdbath, or plantings that attract birds.

Participants submit their counts using the FeederWatch mobile app or website (*FeederWatch.org*) and have access to a variety of digital resources including detailed counting instructions; information about birds and bird feeding; tools to explore personal and continental data; Winter Bird Highlights, FeederWatch's year-end report; and the digital version of Living Bird, the Cornell Lab's award-winning magazine. There is a small annual participation fee for U.S. residents, and Canadians can join by making a donation of any size to Birds Canada. The participation fee covers staff support, web design, data analysis, and the year-end report. Without the support of our participants, this project wouldn't be possible.

To learn more about Project FeederWatch, visit *FeederWatch.org*.

Project FeederWatch is operated by the Cornell Lab of Ornithology and Birds Canada.

NESTWATCH

NestWatch is a nationwide monitoring program designed to track status and trends in the reproductive biology of birds, including when nesting occurs, how many eggs are laid, how many hatch, and how many young survive. The database is used to study the current condition of breeding bird populations and how they may be changing over time.

Nest of a Song Sparrow.

By finding and monitoring bird nests, NestWatch participants help scientists track the breeding success of birds across North America. Participants witness fascinating behaviors of birds at the nest, and collect information on the location, habitat, species, number of eggs, and number of young. Launched in 2007 with funding from the National Science Foundation, NestWatch has collected more than 400,000 nesting records. Combined with historic data, this information will help scientists address how birds are affected by large-scale changes such as global climate change, urbanization, and land conversion.

How to Participate

Participating in NestWatch is free and just about anyone can do it (children should always be accompanied by an adult when observing bird nests). Simply follow the directions on the website to become a certified NestWatcher, find a bird nest using the helpful tips, visit the nest every 3–4 days to record what you see, and then report this information on the website, or use the mobile app. Your observations will be added to those of thousands of other NestWatchers in a continually growing database used by researchers to understand and study birds. While you contribute extremely valuable information to science, you will also learn firsthand about the breeding behaviors of birds.

To learn more about NestWatch, visit **NestWatch.org**.
Download the mobile app on Google Play or the App Store.

CELEBRATE URBAN BIRDS

Celebrate Urban Birds is a year-round project developed by the Cornell Lab for people in cities, suburbs, and rural areas. It is an easy, fun project for the entire family; no prior knowledge of birds is required, and your data will help scientists understand how birds use green spaces in cities. Since 2007, Celebrate Urban Birds has partnered with 11,000 community organizations and distributed 400,000 educational kits. Educational materials and online trainings are offered in both English and Spanish.

How to Participate

1. Visit *CelebrateUrbanBirds.org* and click "Get Started Now."

2. Learn to identify 16 focal species. You can get additional species lists online at *CelebrateUrbanBirds.org/regional*.

3. Pick a place to watch birds in an area that is 50 feet by 50 feet (the size of half a basketball court).

4. Spend 10 minutes watching birds in the selected area.

5. Repeat observations three times in the same area in one month.

6. Share data online or send to the Cornell Lab by mail.

Every year Celebrate Urban Birds awards dozens of mini-grants to community organizations, including Alzheimer's support groups, youth clubs, oncology centers, businesses, and rehabilitation centers throughout the Americas to lead community activities focused on birds, greening, and the arts. Any community-based organization, especially those led by minoritized communities, are encouraged to apply for a grant. Visit *CelebrateUrbanBirds.org* to order educational materials, apply for a community grant, or find hundreds of fun, creative activities that involve the arts, greening, and birds for people of all ages.

To learn more about CUBs, visit *CelebrateUrbanBirds.org*.

SEVEN SIMPLE ACTIONS TO HELP BIRDS

In 2019, scientists documented North America's staggering loss of nearly three billion breeding birds since 1970. Helping birds can be as simple as making changes to everyday habits.

1 Make Windows Safer, Day and Night
The challenge: Up to one billion birds are estimated to die each year after hitting windows in the United States and Canada.

The cause: By day, birds perceive glass reflections in glass as habitat they can fly into. By night, migratory birds drawn in by city lights are at high risk of colliding with buildings.

These simple steps save birds: On the outside of the window, install screens or break up reflections using film, paint, Acopian BirdSavers or other string spaced no more than two inches high or four inches wide.

2 Keep Cats Indoors
The challenge: Cats are estimated to kill more than 2.6 billion birds annually in the U.S. and Canada. This is the #1 human-caused reason for the loss of birds, aside from habitat loss.

The cause: Cats can make great pets, but more than 110 million feral and pet cats now roam in the United States and Canada. These nonnative predators instinctively hunt and kill birds even when well fed.

A solution that's good for cats and birds: Save birds and keep cats healthy by keeping cats indoors or creating an outdoor "catio." You can also train your cat to walk on a leash.

3 Reduce Lawn, Plant Natives
The challenge: Birds have fewer places to safely rest during migration and to raise their young: More than 10 million acres of land in the United States were converted to developed land from 1982 to 1997.

The cause: Lawns and pavement don't offer enough food or shelter for many birds and other wildlife. With more than 40 million acres of lawn in the U.S. alone, there's huge potential to support wildlife by replacing lawns with native plantings.

Add native plants, watch birds come in: Native plants add interest and beauty to your yard and neighborhood, and provide shelter and nesting areas for birds. The nectar, seeds, berries, and insects will sustain birds and diverse wildlife.

4 Avoid Pesticides

The challenge: More than one billion pounds of pesticides are applied in the United States each year. The continent's most widely used insecticides, called neonicotinoids or "neonics," are lethal to birds and to the insects that birds consume. Common weed killers used around homes, such as 2, 4-D and glyphosate (used in Roundup), can be toxic to wildlife, and glyphosate has been declared a probable human carcinogen.

The cause: Pesticides that are toxic to birds can harm them directly through

contact, or if they eat contaminated seeds or prey. Pesticides can also harm birds indirectly by reducing the number of available insects, which birds need to survive.

A healthy choice for you, your family, and birds: Consider purchasing organic food. Nearly 70% of produce sold in the U.S. contains pesticides. Reduce pesticides around your home and garden.

Orange-crowned Warbler

5 Drink Coffee That's Good for Birds

The challenge: Three-quarters of the world's coffee farms grow their plants in the sun (source), destroying forests that birds and other wildlife need for food and shelter. Sun-grown coffee also often requires using environmentally harmful pesticides and fertilizers. On the other hand, shade-grown coffee preserves a forest canopy that helps migratory birds survive the winter.

The cause: Too few consumers are aware of the problems of sun coffee. Those who are aware may be reluctant to pay more for environmentally sustainable coffee.

Enjoy shade-grown coffee: It's a win-win-win: it's delicious, economically beneficial to coffee farmers, and helps more than 42 species of North American migratory songbirds, including orioles, warblers, and thrushes, that winter in coffee plantations.

6 Protect Our Planet from Plastics

The challenge: It's estimated that 4,900 million metric tons of plastic have accumulated in landfills and in our environment worldwide, polluting our oceans and harming wildlife such as seabirds, whales, and turtles that mistakenly eat plastic, or become entangled in it.

The cause: Plastic takes more than 400 years to degrade, and 91% of plastics created are not recycled. Studies show that at least 80 seabird species ingest plastic, mistaking it for food. Cigarette lighters, toothbrushes, and other trash have been found in the stomachs of dead albatrosses.

Reduce your plastics: Avoid single-use plastics including bags, bottles, wraps, and disposable utensils. It's far better to choose reusable items, but if you do have disposable plastic, be sure to recycle it.

7 Watch Birds, Share What You See

The challenge: The world's most abundant bird, the Passenger Pigeon, went extinct, and people didn't realize how quickly it was vanishing until it was too late. Monitoring birds is essential to help protect them, but tracking the health of the world's 10,000 bird species is an immense challenge.

The cause: To understand how birds are faring, scientists need hundreds of thousands of people to report what they're seeing in backyards, neighborhoods, and wild places around the world. Without this information, scientists will not have enough timely data to show where and when birds are declining around the world.

Enjoy birds while helping science and conservation: Join a project such as eBird, Project FeederWatch, Breeding Bird Survey, or the International Shorebird Survey to record your bird observations. Your contributions will provide valuable information to show where birds are thriving—and where they need our help.

If you don't yet know how to use eBird, we have a free course to help you get the most out of the project and its tools: *https://academy.allaboutbirds.org/product/ebird-essentials/.*

GUIDE TO NORTHWEST SPECIES

Lincoln's Sparrow ©Linda Petersen

JUVENILE (WHITE MORPH)

ADULTS (WHITE MORPH)

IMMATURE (DARK MORPH)

ADULT (DARK MORPH)

SIZE & SHAPE The Snow Goose is a medium-sized goose with a hefty bill and long, thick neck. Juveniles are slightly smaller than adults in the fall, and this can be noticeable in flocks during fall and early winter.

COLOR PATTERN The white morph of the Snow Goose is white with black wingtips that are barely visible on the ground but more noticeable in flight. You may also see a dark morph Snow Goose, or "Blue Goose," with a white face, dark brown body, and white under the tail.

BEHAVIOR Snow Geese don't like to travel alone and can form flocks of several hundred thousand. Family groups forage together on wintering grounds, digging up roots and tubers from muddy fields and marshes. In flight, they are steady on the wing with even wingbeats.

HABITAT Snow Geese use agricultural fields, which is one reason their populations are doing so well. During winter and migration, look for them in plowed cornfields, wetlands, lakes, ponds, and marshes where they roost and bathe along shorelines and in open water.

RANGE MAP

■ Breeding
■ Migration
■ Nonbreeding

Watching huge flocks of **Snow Geese** swirl down from the sky, amid a cacophony of honking, is a little standing inside a snow globe. These loud, white-and-black geese can cover the ground in a snowy blar as they eat their way across fallow cornfields or wetlands.

ADULT (BLACK)

ADULT (BLACK)

ADULT (GRAY-BELLIED)

JUVENILE (BLACK)

RANGE MAP

Breeding
Migration
Nonbreeding

SIZE & SHAPE The Brant is a small, compact goose with a short neck and small head and bill.

COLOR PATTERN The Brant has a black head, neck, and chest with a distinctive white, partly broken collar. Young birds are similar to adults, but without the collar and with white scaling on the back. The Brant's body is overall darkish brownish gray. Two forms appear in the Northwest. "Black" Brant is widespread; "Gray-bellied" Brant is mostly restricted to Puget Sound.

BEHAVIOR Brant frequently walk while feeding on upland fields, tundra, or salt marsh. They swim year-round and feed on submerged seagrasses while swimming, especially during the nonbreeding season. Despite their reliance on seagrasses, they do not dive to feed, rather they tip up while feeding.

HABITAT In the summer, Brant breed in both grassland habitats in the High Arctic and wetlands of the Low Arctic. They overwinter around bays and coastlines, congregating in groups just offshore to forage. The Pacific form winters along the Pacific Coast, the Gray-bellied along the Washington Coast.

compact, short-necked **Brant** is an attractive small goose with a black head, white necklace, and rich vn body brightening to white under the tail. They winter in flocks in bays, estuaries, and lagoons, eating rass and other aquatic vegetation. Flocks give pleasing calls, the sound of which carries for long distances.

ADULT

ADULTS

ADULT AND DOWNY YOUNG

ADULTS

SIZE & SHAPE The Canada Goose is a big waterbird with a long neck, large body, large, webbed feet, and a wide, flat bill. Adult Canada Geese can vary widely in size.

COLOR PATTERN Canada Geese have a black head with a white chinstrap, black neck, tan breast, and brown back. At least 11 subspecies of Canada Goose have been recognized. They tend to be smaller as you move northward in summer; plumage is darker as you move westward.

BEHAVIOR Canada Geese feed by dabbling in the water or grazing in fields and large lawns. They are known for their honking call and are often very vocal in flight. They often fly together in pairs or in V formation in flocks, which reduces wind resistance and conserves energy.

HABITAT Canada Geese can be found just about anywhere in the U.S. and Canada, near lakes, rivers, ponds, or other small or large bodies of water, and also in yards, parks, lawns, and farm fields.

RANGE MAP

■ Breeding
■ Nonbreeding
■ Year-round

The large **Canada Goose**, with its signature white chinstrap, is a familiar and widespread bird of fields a parks. Thousands of "honkers" migrate north and south each year, filling the sky with long V-formations Every year, more of these grassland-adapted birds are staying put, and some people regard them as pe

ADULTS

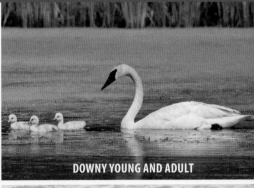

DOWNY YOUNG AND ADULT

JUVENILES

ADULT (L) AND IMMATURE (R)

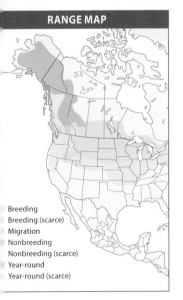

RANGE MAP

Breeding
Breeding (scarce)
Migration
Nonbreeding
Nonbreeding (scarce)
Year-round
Year-round (scarce)

SIZE & SHAPE Trumpeter Swans are our biggest native waterfowl. They have heavy bodies and long necks typically held straight both on the water and in flight. The large bill slopes gradually down from the forehead.

COLOR PATTERN Adult Trumpeter Swans are entirely white with a black bill with a broad area of black facial skin in front of the eye, and black legs. The white head can be stained rusty. Older juveniles are mostly pale, dusky gray with white highlights.

BEHAVIOR Trumpeter Swans forage in shallow water, reaching under the surface for vegetation and, at times, tipping up in the manner of a dabbling duck. They also visit agricultural fields to eat spilled or leftover grains and crops.

HABITAT Trumpeter Swans breed in open habitats near shallow water bodies. They winter on estuaries, large lakes, and rivers that remain at least partially ice-free year-round. They sometimes forage in fields.

mpeter Swans are impressively large; males average over 26 pounds, making them North America's viest native flying bird. To get aloft, the swans need a 100-meter long "runway" of open water. Running d across the surface, they almost sound like galloping horses as they generate speed for takeoff.

BREEDING MALE

BREEDING MALE

DOWNY YOUNG (L) AND ADULT FEMALE (R)

NONBREEDING MALE

SIZE & SHAPE The Wood Duck has a unique shape among ducks—a boxy, crested head; thin neck; and long, broad tail. In flight, they hold their heads up high, sometimes bobbing them.

COLOR PATTERN The male Wood Duck is a gorgeous duck with intricate plumage. In good light, males have a glossy green head with white stripes, a chestnut breast, and buffy sides. The female is gray brown with a white-speckled breast and a white teardrop around the eye.

BEHAVIOR Unlike most waterfowl, Wood Ducks perch and nest in trees and are comfortable flying through woods. Their broad tail and short, broad wings help make them maneuverable. When swimming, the head jerks back and forth much as a walking pigeon's does. You often see Wood Ducks in small groups (fewer than 20), keeping apart from other waterfowl.

HABITAT Look for Wood Ducks in wooded swamps, marshes, streams, beaver ponds, and small lakes. As cavity nesters, Wood Ducks take readily to nest boxes.

RANGE MAP

■ Breeding
■ Nonbreeding
■ Year-round

Wood Ducks are one of the few duck species equipped with strong claws that can grip bark and perch branches. Soon after hatching, the mother duck leaves the nest and calls to her ducklings to jump down and join her in the water. Ducklings can jump from heights of over 50 feet without injury.

BREEDING MALE

BREEDING MALES

NONBREEDING MALE

ADULT FEMALE

RANGE MAP

Breeding
Migration
Nonbreeding
Year-round

SIZE & SHAPE The aptly named Northern Shoveler has a shovel-shaped bill that quickly sets it apart from other dabbling ducks, even at a considerable distance. It is a medium-sized duck that tends to sit tilted forward in the water, as if its large bill is pulling its front half down.

COLOR PATTERN Breeding male shovelers are bold white, blue, green, and rust, but their most notable feature is their white chest and white lower sides. In flight, males flash blue on the upper wing and green on the secondaries (the speculum). Female and immature shovelers are mottled brown and have powdery blue on the wings (sometimes visible on resting birds), and a very large orange bill. Nonbreeding males sometimes show a white facial crescent near the bill.

BEHAVIOR Northern Shovelers often have their heads down in shallow wetlands, busily sweeping their bills side to side, filtering out aquatic invertebrates and seeds from the water.

HABITAT Northern Shovelers forage in shallow wetlands, coastal marshes, flooded fields, lakes, and sewage lagoons. They nest along the margins of wetlands or in neighboring grassy areas.

...aps the most distinctive of the dabbling ducks thanks to its large spoon-shaped bill, the **Northern** **...veler** busily forages, head down, in shallow wetlands. The edges of its uniquely shaped bill have ...blike projections, which filter out tiny crustaceans and seeds from the water.

MALE

BREEDING MALE

ADULT FEMALE

ADULT FEMALE

SIZE & SHAPE Gadwall are about the same size as Mallards, but the bill is noticeably thinner. Gadwall have a fairly large, square head with a steep forehead. In flight, the neck is slightly thinner and the wings slightly more slender than those of a Mallard.

COLOR PATTERN Male Gadwall are gray brown with a black patch at the tail. Females are patterned with brown and buff and have variably orange to black bills. In flight, both sexes have a white wing patch that is sometimes visible while swimming or resting.

BEHAVIOR Gadwall feed with other dabbling ducks, tipping forward to reach submerged vegetation. They sometimes steal food from diving ducks or coots. In winter, you'll often see them in pairs; mates are selected for the breeding season as early as late fall.

HABITAT Gadwall breed mainly in the Great Plains and prairies. On migration and in winter, look for them in reservoirs, ponds, freshwater and saltwater marshes, city parks, or muddy edges of estuaries.

RANGE MAP

- Breeding
- Breeding (scarce)
- Migration
- Nonbreeding
- Year-round

The **Gadwall**'s understated elegance makes this common duck easy to overlook. Males are intricately patterned with gray, brown, and black; females resemble female Mallards, although with a thinner bill a different head shape and wing pattern. Gadwall sometimes snatch food from diving ducks and coots.

BREEDING MALE

BREEDING MALE

ADULT FEMALE

NONBREEDING MALE

RANGE MAP

Breeding
Migration
Winter
Year-round

SIZE & SHAPE American Wigeons are medium-sized, compact ducks with a short bill and a round head. They tend to sit on the water with their heads pulled down. They are larger than Green-winged Teal and smaller than Mallards.

COLOR PATTERN Breeding males have a grayish head with a white cap and a wide green stripe behind the eye. A pinkish cinnamon body with white patches on the sides of the rump contrasts with black undertail feathers. Females and nonbreeding males are brown with a dark smudge around the eye. Both sexes have a black-tipped gray bill.

BEHAVIOR American Wigeons congregate on lakes and wetlands, nibbling aquatic vegetation on the surface or tipping up for submerged plants. They also waddle through fields, plucking at plants. They are more vocal than many ducks, especially during the nonbreeding season.

HABITAT At all times of year, American Wigeons can be found in freshwater wetlands, lakes, slow-moving rivers, impoundments, flooded fields, estuaries, bays, and marshes.

t lakes and wetlands come alive with the breezy whistle of the **American Wigeon**, a dabbling duck pizzazz. Noisy groups congregate during fall and winter, plucking plants with their short gooselike from wetlands and fields or nibbling plants from the water's surface.

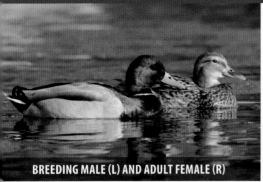

BREEDING MALE (L) AND ADULT FEMALE (R)

BREEDING MALE

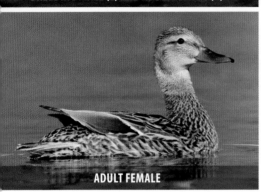

ADULT FEMALE

NONBREEDING MALE

SIZE & SHAPE Mallards are large ducks with hefty bodies, rounded heads, and wide, flat bills. Like many dabbling ducks, the body is long, and the tail rides high out of the water, giving a blunt shape. In flight, their wings are broad and set back toward the rear.

COLOR PATTERN Male Mallards have a dark, iridescent green head and bright yellow bill. The gray body is sandwiched between a brown breast and black rear. Females and juveniles are mottled brown with orange-and-blackish bills. Both sexes have a white-bordered, blue speculum patch in the wing.

BEHAVIOR Mallards are dabbling ducks and almost never dive. They can be very tame, especially in city ponds, and often group together with other Mallards, other species of dabbling ducks, or even farm ducks.

HABITAT Mallards can live in almost any wetland habitat. Look for them on lakes, ponds, marshes, rivers, and coastal habitats, as well as city and suburban parks and residential backyards.

RANGE MAP

■ Breeding
■ Winter
■ Year-round

Perhaps the most familiar of all ducks, **Mallards** occur throughout the U.S. and Canada in ponds and pa as well as wetlands and estuaries. The male's gleaming green head, gray flanks, and black tail-curl argu; make it the most easily identified duck. Almost all domestic ducks come from this species.

BREEDING MALE

BREEDING MALE

ADULT FEMALE

NONBREEDING MALE

RANGE MAP

Breeding
Migration
Nonbreeding
Year-round

SIZE & SHAPE Northern Pintails are elegant, long-necked ducks with a slender profile. The tail is long and pointed, but it is much longer and more prominent on breeding males than on females and nonbreeding males. In flight, wings are long and narrow.

COLOR PATTERN Breeding males stand out with a white breast and white line down their rich brown head and neck. When molting, both sexes are mottled brown and white with a tan face and a dark bill. In flight, males flash a green speculum and females a bronzy speculum.

BEHAVIOR These dabbling birds use their bills to filter out seeds and insects on the water's surface. They feed on grain and insects in wetlands and agricultural fields. They form groups, often with other ducks, in the nonbreeding season.

HABITAT Northern Pintails nest in wetlands, croplands, grasslands, wet meadows, and shortgrass prairies, and forage in lakes and ponds. When not breeding, look for them in wetlands, ponds, lakes, bays, tidal marshes, and flooded agricultural fields.

ant **Northern Pintails** swim through wetlands and lakes with their long, pointed tails held high. These r breeders head to the Prairie Pothole Region of the Great Plains, as well as Alaska and other parts of da, to nest as soon as the ice breaks up. Though still common, their populations are declining.

BREEDING MALE

BREEDING MALE

ADULT FEMALE

JUVENILE

SIZE & SHAPE Canvasbacks are big-headed diving ducks with a gently sloping forehead and a stout neck. The long bill meets a sloping forehead, creating a seamless look. On the water, the Canvasback has an oval body and a short, sloping tail.

COLOR PATTERN Breeding males have a chestnut head and neck set off against a black chest, whitish body, and black rear. Females are pale brown where males are chestnut and black, and have a grayish rather than white body. In late summer and early fall, males have brown heads and necks with a paler body. Males have red eyes, and females have dark eyes.

BEHAVIOR Diving ducks that are gregarious during the nonbreeding season, Canvasbacks form large single-species rafts or mix with Redheads and scaups. They dive underwater to feed on plant tubers, seeds, and clams.

HABITAT Canvasbacks breed in lakes, deep-water marshes, bays, and ponds. In winter, look for them in deep freshwater lakes and coastal waters.

RANGE MAP

■ Breeding
■ Migration
■ Nonbreeding
■ Year-round

Often called the aristocrat of ducks, the **Canvasback** holds its long sloping forehead high with a distinguished look. This diving duck eats plant tubers at the bottom of lakes and wetlands. It breeds in lakes and marshes and winters by the thousands on freshwater lakes and coastal waters.

BREEDING MALE

BREEDING MALE

NONBREEDING MALE

ADULT FEMALE

RANGE MAP

reeding
reeding (scarce)
igration
onbreeding
ear-round

SIZE & SHAPE Redheads are medium-sized diving ducks with a smoothly rounded head and a moderately large bill. They are slightly larger than Ring-necked Ducks and slightly smaller than Canvasbacks.

COLOR PATTERN Male Redheads are a mixture of cinnamon head, black breast and tail, and gray body. Females and immatures are a plain, mostly uniform brown. Redheads have black-tipped, gray bills, and gray flight feathers.

BEHAVIOR In migration and winter, look for Redheads in large rafts, often with other duck species. They usually dive for their food, although they use shallower water than other diving ducks and may feed by tipping up, like a dabbling duck.

HABITAT Redheads breed mainly in seasonal wetlands such as the Prairie Pothole Region of the Great Plains. In migration and winter, they form large flocks on the Gulf Coast, as well as on lakes, reservoirs, bays, and along the Great Lakes and coastlines across the southern U.S.

a gleaming cinnamon head setting off a body marked in black and gray, adult male **Redheads** light e open water of lakes and coastlines. These sociable ducks molt, migrate, and winter in sometimes flocks, particularly along the Gulf Coast, where winter numbers can reach the thousands.

BREEDING MALE

BREEDING MALE

ADULT FEMALE AND DOWNY YOUNG

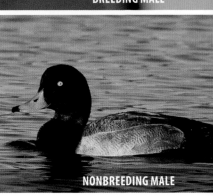

NONBREEDING MALE

SIZE & SHAPE The Greater Scaup is a medium-sized diving duck with an evenly rounded head. It is larger than a Green-winged Teal and smaller than a Canvasback.

COLOR PATTERN At a distance, breeding male Greater Scaup are black and white, but closer views reveal an iridescent green sheen on the head, super thin black barring on the back, a bluish bill, and a yellow eye. Females are brown overall with a darker brown head and a white patch next to the bill, but the size of the white patch varies. Nonbreeding males look like a cross between a female and a breeding male: a mottled brown-and-gray body and a blackish head.

BEHAVIOR During migration and winter, these diving ducks form large flocks on bays, lakes, and larger wetlands. They tend to form tight groups with each other and sometimes mix with other diving ducks.

HABITAT Greater Scaup breed in shallow lakes and ponds in treeless wetlands in the tundra. During winter, look for Greater Scaup on coastal bays, lakes, and reservoirs.

RANGE MAP

■ Breeding
▦ Migration
▦ Nonbreeding
▦ Nonbreeding (scarce)

The only circumpolar diving duck, the **Greater Scaup** breeds across the tundra. They congregate by the hundreds and thousands along both coasts during winter. Remarkably similar to the Lesser Scaup, the Greater Scaup has a rounded head, the Lesser Scaup a peaked head.

BREEDING MALE

BREEDING MALE

IMMATURE MALE

ADULT / IMMATURE FEMALE

RANGE MAP

Breeding
Migration
Nonbreeding
Year-round

SIZE & SHAPE The Lesser Scaup is a medium-sized diving duck with a small peak at the back of the head. Behind the small peak, the back of the head and neck is mostly flat, not strongly rounded as it is on Greater Scaup.

COLOR PATTERN Breeding males are black and white with an iridescent purple-to-green head sheen, a delicately patterned black-and-white back, a bluish bill, and a yellow eye. Females are brown with a darker brown head and a white patch by the bill.

BEHAVIOR During migration and winter, Lesser Scaup form large flocks on lakes, bays, rivers, and larger wetlands. They tend to form tight groups and mix with other diving ducks such as Canvasbacks and Greater Scaup.

HABITAT During winter, look for Lesser Scaup on inland lakes, reservoirs, coastal bays, and estuaries. During the breeding season, they are more commonly found nesting in marshes of northern North America.

ps of **Lesser Scaup** congregate on bodies of water during migration and winter, sometimes by the sands. Look for them floating on the surface or diving to eat aquatic invertebrates and plants. Unlike reater Scaup's rounded head, the Lesser Scaup's tiny, peaked hat sits near the back of the head.

BREEDING MALE

BREEDING MALE

NONBREEDING MALES

ADULT FEMALE

SIZE & SHAPE Harlequin Ducks are small, compact waterfowl with a large, rounded head with a steep forehead, and a small bill.

COLOR PATTERN Breeding male Harlequin Ducks are a spectacular slate blue with white stripes and chestnut sides. The head is elaborately marked with a white crescent in front of the eye, and chestnut highlights on the brow. Females are overall grayish brown, with white around the bill and eye, and a neat white spot on the rear of the cheek. Juveniles are similar to adult females, but with darker bellies.

BEHAVIOR A powerful swimmer, the Harlequin Duck navigates rapidly-moving water to breed and forage, gleaning prey from the rocky bottom. In winter, groups of Harlequin Ducks idle near the shore or on rocks, feeding.

HABITAT During the breeding season, look for Harlequin Ducks in mountain streams and rivers, usually in forested regions. In winter, they primarily keep to turbulent coastal waters, especially in rocky regions.

RANGE MAP

■ Breeding
■ Nonbreeding

The **Harlequin Duck** is known for the male's striking plumage and the dramatic landscapes that it calls home. They breed mainly along whitewater rivers and winter on rocky coasts. Their lifestyle is rough o their bodies, and many endure broken bones from a lifetime of being tossed around in the rough wate

BREEDING MALE

NONBREEDING MALE

JUVENILE

ADULT FEMALE

RANGE MAP

Breeding
Migration
Nonbreeding
Year-round

SIZE & SHAPE Ruddy Ducks are small and compact with stout, scoop-shaped bills, and long, stiff tails they often hold cocked upward. They have slightly peaked heads and fairly short, thick necks.

COLOR PATTERN Male Ruddy Ducks have blackish caps and white cheeks. In summer, they have chestnut bodies with bright blue bills. In winter, they are dull gray brown with gray bills. Females are brownish with a blurry cheek stripe.

BEHAVIOR Ruddy Ducks dive to feed on aquatic invertebrates, especially midge larvae. They feed most actively at night, so you'll often see them sleeping during the day, head tucked under a wing and tail cocked up.

HABITAT Ruddy Ducks nest in marshes adjacent to lakes and ponds, primarily in the Prairie Potholes Region. In migration, they flock to large rivers, ponds, lakes, and coastal estuaries, frequently mixing with other diving ducks.

right colors and odd behavior of male **Ruddy Ducks** drew attention from early naturalists, though didn't pull any punches. One 1926 account states, "Its intimate habits, its stupidity, its curious ng customs and ludicrous courtship performance place it in a niche by itself…"

ADULT MALE

ADULT FEMALE

JUVENILES

ADULT FEMALE

SIZE & SHAPE California Quail are plump, short-necked game birds with a small head and bill. They fly on short, very broad wings. The tail is fairly long and square. Both sexes have a comma-shaped topknot of feathers projecting forward from the forehead, longer in males than females.

COLOR PATTERN Adult males are rich gray and brown, with a black face outlined with bold white stripes. Females are a plainer brown and lack the facial markings. Both sexes have a pattern of white, creamy, and chestnut scales on the belly. Young birds look like females but have a shorter topknot.

BEHAVIOR Mainly a seedeater, this little quail also eats leaves, flowers, catkins, manzanita and poison oak berries, acorns, and invertebrates such as caterpillars, beetles, millipedes, and snails. Their diet is about 70% vegetarian.

HABITAT You'll find California Quail in chaparral, sagebrush, and oak and foothill forests of California and the Northwest. They're tolerant of people and common in city parks, suburban gardens, and agricultural areas.

RANGE MAP

■ Year-round

The **California Quail** is a soccer ball of a bird with a stiffly accented *Chi-ca-go* song—a common sound brushy areas in California and the Northwest. Often seen scratching at the ground in large groups or dashing forward, they are common but unobtrusive. They flush to cover if scared, so approach gently.

DISPLAYING ADULT MALE

ADULT MALE

ADULT FEMALE

JUVENILE

RANGE MAP

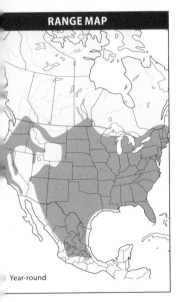

Year-round

SIZE & SHAPE Wild Turkeys are very large, plump birds with long legs, wide, rounded tails, and small heads on long, slim necks.

COLOR PATTERN Turkeys are dark with a bronze-green iridescence to their plumage. Their wings are barred with white. Their rump and tail feathers are tipped rusty or white. The bare skin of the head and neck varies from red to blue to gray.

BEHAVIOR Turkeys travel in flocks and search the ground for nuts, berries, insects, and snails, using their strong feet to scratch leaf litter out of the way. In early spring, males perform courtship displays in clearings. They puff up their body feathers, flare their tails into a vertical fan, and strut slowly while giving a gobbling call. At night, they roost in trees in groups.

HABITAT Wild Turkeys live in mature forests, particularly those with oak, hickory, or beech trees, interspersed with edges and fields. You may see them along roads and in woodsy backyards.

k for flocks of **Wild Turkeys** striding around woods and clearings like the miniature dinosaurs they are. rting males puff themselves up and fill the air with gobbling. The bird's popularity at the Thanksgiving e led to a drastic decline in numbers, but they now occur in every U.S. state except Alaska.

BREEDING MALE

BREEDING MALE

ADULT

ADULT

SIZE & SHAPE Ruffed Grouse are fairly small grouse with a short, triangular crest and a long, fan-shaped tail. They have short legs and often look slimmer than other grouse species.

COLOR PATTERN Ruffed Grouse are intricately patterned with dark bars and spots on either a reddish brown or grayish background. Dark bars down the side of the neck widen on the belly. The tail is barred, with one wide, black band near the tip.

BEHAVIOR Look for Ruffed Grouse foraging on the forest-interior floor for seeds and insects. Displaying males stand atop logs and beat their wings to make a deep, airy drumming sound. In spring, you'll likely see lone birds; in summer, look for females with broods of chicks. In winter, they form flocks and often eat buds of broadleaf trees.

HABITAT Ruffed Grouse usually occupy mixed broadleaf and coniferous forest interiors with scattered clearings. They also live along forested streams and in areas growing back from burning or logging.

RANGE MAP

■ Year-round

The **Ruffed Grouse** is hard to see, but its "drumming on air" display is a fixture of many spring forests. It can come as a surprise to learn this distant sound, like an engine trying to start, comes from a bird at all. Displaying males expose a rich black ruff of neck feathers, giving them their name.

ADULT MALE

ADULT MALE

ADULT FEMALE

ADULT FEMALE

RANGE MAP

Year-round

SIZE & SHAPE The Spruce Grouse is a stout chickenlike bird with a small bill, short but thick legs, and medium-length tail that can be fanned into a semicircle. They are about the same size as Ruffed Grouse and considerably smaller than Dusky and Sooty grouse.

COLOR PATTERN Females are mottled in brown, gray, gold, black, and white. Males are similarly patterned above but have a slate-gray head and neck, a red eyebrow, a black chest, and white spots on the lower belly. Adult males of the Franklin's subspecies, found in British Columbia and the northwestern Lower 48, have an all black tail with white spots on the tail coverts.

BEHAVIOR Spruce Grouse forage on the ground for small plants, fungi, and insects; or in coniferous trees, where they nibble fresh needles—their primary diet. They are almost always seen walking rather than flying. Displaying males strut to entice females.

HABITAT Spruce Grouse occur only in coniferous forests. They prefer younger, regenerating tracts with a dense understory more than old growth.

the chickenlike **Spruce Grouse** in coniferous forests in northern and western North America, eating tly the needles of fir, spruce, and pine—a diet that makes them unpalatable to many hunters. etimes known as "fool hens," these birds are famous for their tameness around humans.

ADULT MALE DISPLAYING

ADULT MALE DISPLAYING

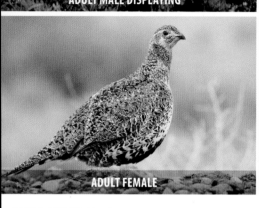

ADULT FEMALE

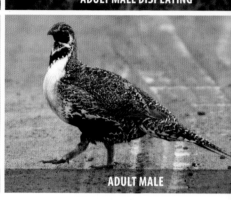

ADULT MALE

SIZE & SHAPE The Greater Sage-Grouse is a very large grouse with a chubby body, small head, and long tail. Males change shape dramatically when they display, puffing up their chest, drooping their wings, and fanning their tail into a starburst.

COLOR PATTERN Sage-grouse are mottled gray brown with a black belly. Males have a black head and throat. The male's breast has a fluffy white ruff that, during displays, surrounds a pair of inflatable yellow air sacs. Females have a dusky cheek patch and white markings behind the eye.

BEHAVIOR For most of the year, sage-grouse are inconspicuous, eating sagebrush and other plants at ground level. In spring, males perform elaborate strutting displays for females. Females evaluate the males and choose which ones to mate with.

HABITAT Sage-grouse are emblematic of the sagebrush steppe of the intermountain West, which is their only habitat. They are widespread across the sagebrush plains but are sensitive to disturbance. In early spring, they gather on patches of open ground known as leks, where males display to females.

RANGE MAP

■ Year-round

In spring, at dawn, the sagebrush plains of western North America fill with leks of dozens of male **Greater Sage-Grouse** puffing their chests, tails fanned. They inflate yellow air sacs and thrust their heads, producing pops and whistles. Habitat fragmentation has caused severe declines for this spectacular bird.

ADULT MALE DISPLAYING

ADULT MALE

ADULT FEMALE

IMMATURE MALE

RANGE MAP

■ Year-round

SIZE & SHAPE The Dusky Grouse is a large, heavyset, chickenlike bird with a short bill, short, strong legs, and a medium-length tail that can be fanned into a semicircle.

COLOR PATTERN Both sexes are mottled in patterns of brown, gray, white, and black. Males have blue-gray underparts and blackish tails with gray tips of variable width. In display, they reveal purplish red air sacs on the neck, and their eye combs swell to a rich golden color or red.

BEHAVIOR Dusky Grouse spend much of the day resting or foraging on the ground for plants and insects, as well as in trees for leaves, needles, and buds. In early spring, males display from perches in trees or near the ground, and perform strutting displays on the ground.

HABITAT During the breeding season, Dusky Grouse are usually found in or near mountain forests. In summer, their foraging takes them out of the forests into surrounding grasslands and shrub-steppe habitats, and high-elevation subalpine and alpine habitats.

e large **Dusky Grouse** lives in mountain forests of ponderosa and lodgepole pine, aspen, and fir. The species ges from sunbaked bitterbrush steppe to the twisted "krummholz" trees of frigid mountaintops, thriving plants and insects. This species was once combined with the Sooty Grouse and called the Blue Grouse.

ADULT MALE

ADULT MALE DISPLAYING

JUVENILE

ADULT FEMALE

SIZE & SHAPE The Sooty Grouse is a heavyset, chickenlike bird with a short bill, short, strong legs, and a medium-length tail that can be fanned into a semicircle.

COLOR PATTERN Both male and female are camouflaged with patterns of brown, gray, white, and black. Males have blackish tails with gray tips and paler gray underparts. In display, males reveal yellowish or pinkish air sacs on the neck, and their eye combs swell and become yellow, orange, or red.

BEHAVIOR Sooty Grouse spend most of their time on the ground foraging but will also forage for buds in broadleaf trees. In winter, they spend most of their time in coniferous trees eating needles. Males vocalize often while perched in trees.

HABITAT During breeding season, Sooty Grouse can be found in forested habitats from sea level to thousands of feet in elevation. Lowland forest is the preferred habitat for this species. In winter, they are most often found in coniferous forests.

RANGE MAP

■ Year-round

Sooty Grouse are large game birds of the wet mountain forests of the Pacific Coast. Unlike their close relative the Dusky Grouse of the Rockies, Sooty Grouse display from perches high up in trees. Their deep owl-like, rhythmic hooting calls are loud but ventriloquial, making the birds difficult to locate.

ADULT MALE

ADULT MALE

IMMATURE MALE

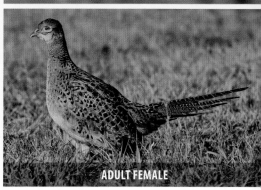

ADULT FEMALE

RANGE MAP

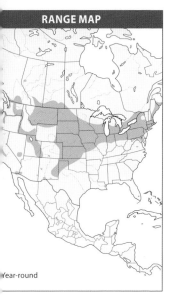

Year-round

SIZE & SHAPE The Ring-necked Pheasant is a large, chicken-like bird with a long, pointed tail. It has fairly long legs, a small head, long neck, and plump body. Juveniles have short tails.

COLOR PATTERN Male Ring-necked Pheasants are gaudy birds with red faces and an iridescent green neck with a bold white ring. The male's very long tail is coppery with thin, black bars. Females are brown with paler scaling on the upperparts; buff or cinnamon underparts with black spotting on the sides; and thin, black bars on their tails.

BEHAVIOR They forage on the ground in fields, where they eat waste grain, other seeds, and insects when available. Ring-necked Pheasants usually walk or run and only occasionally resort to flying, usually when disturbed at close range by humans or other predators. Males give a loud, cackling display that can be heard over long distances.

HABITAT Ring-necked Pheasants frequent agricultural areas mixed with taller vegetation, which they use for cover. Look for them along rural roadsides, and in overgrown fields and brushy areas.

Ring-necked Pheasant was introduced from Asia and has a deleterious effect on some native species, as prairie-chickens. It has powerful breast muscles that allow the birds to escape trouble in a hurry, ing vertically into the air and reaching running speeds of nearly 40 miles per hour.

ADULT

ADULT

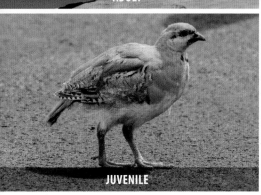
JUVENILE

ADULT

SIZE & SHAPE Chukars are chickenlike game birds with a plump body, short legs, and a small round head. In flight, the tail is square and the wings are broad and rounded.

COLOR PATTERN Chukars are sandy brown overall with bold, vertical black bars on the sides. A dark band through the eyes wraps around the white cheek and throat. A red bill and eyering top off the look.

BEHAVIOR Chukars are ground-dwelling birds that would rather walk or run than fly. They run up rocky slopes with ease and hop from rock to rock, easily outpacing a human. When frightened they explode into the air with a piercing squeal.

HABITAT Chukars occupy steep rocky grasslands and shrublands in remote and rugged areas that are difficult to traverse. They also use dry pasture lands and sagebrush flats in the West. Chukars were introduced to the United States (including Hawaii) from southern Eurasia.

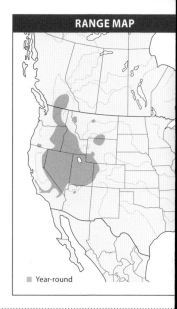

RANGE MAP

■ Year-round

The **Chukar** is a game bird that lives in high desert plains of western North America, Hawaii, and New Zealand. Its namesake call echoes across dry rocky slopes. It runs up steep terrain with the agility and speed of a mountain goat, prompting hunters to nickname it the "devil bird" for the brutal chase it give

BREEDING ADULT

BREEDING ADULT

JUVENILE

NONBREEDING ADULT

RANGE MAP

Breeding
Nonbreeding
Year-round

SIZE & SHAPE Pied-billed Grebes are small, chunky, swimming birds. They have compact bodies and slender necks, with relatively large, blocky heads and short, thick bills. They have virtually no tail.

COLOR PATTERN These brown birds are darker above and lighter below. In spring and summer, the crown and nape are dark, and the throat is black. While breeding, the bill is whitish with a black band, but yellowish brown the rest of the year. Juveniles have striped faces.

BEHAVIOR Pied-billed Grebes can adjust their buoyancy, using this ability to float with just the upper half of the head above water. They catch small fish and invertebrates by diving or slowly submerging.

HABITAT Look for Pied-billed Grebes on small, quiet ponds and marshes where thick vegetation grows out of the water. In winter, they are found on larger water bodies, occasionally in large groups.

bird, part submarine, the **Pied-billed Grebe** is common across much of North America. These expert s inhabit sluggish rivers, freshwater marshes, lakes, and estuaries. Rarely seen in flight and often en amid vegetation, Pied-billed Grebes announce their presence with loud, far-reaching calls.

BREEDING ADULTS

BREEDING ADULT

NONBREEDING ADULT

JUVENILE

SIZE & SHAPE A thickset waterbird, the Red-necked Grebe is similar in size to many ducks, but with a longer neck and a heavy, pointed bill.

COLOR PATTERN Nonbreeding birds are mostly dark gray above, paler below, with pale cheeks and sides of neck. Breeding adults have a rusty red breast and foreneck, with a smart black cap and sharply defined white cheek. Immatures are similar to nonbreeding adults but head pattern is less distinct. Juveniles have striped faces and reddish chestnut necks.

BEHAVIOR In the nonbreeding season, Red-necked Grebes are generally quiet and found singly or in small, loose groups. During the nesting season, pairs perform elaborate, noisy courtship rituals and aggressively defend territories, even against other species of waterfowl.

HABITAT Red-necked Grebes have numerous aquatic habitats during migration and the nonbreeding season, from rivers to lakes, and bays to open ocean. Nesting birds select mostly larger lakes.

RANGE MAP

■ Breeding
■ Breeding (scarce)
■ Migration
■ Nonbreeding

Red-necked Grebes are boldly plumaged waterbirds that breed on northerly lakes and winter mainly along ocean coastlines, sometimes in small groups. During spring migration, flocks may form on large lakes, and pairs begin their boisterous courtship displays well before reaching breeding lakes farther n

NONBREEDING ADULT

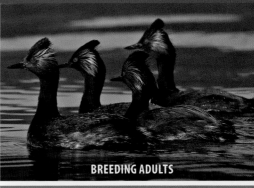
BREEDING ADULTS

NONBREEDING ADULT

NONBREEDING ADULT / IMMATURE

RANGE MAP

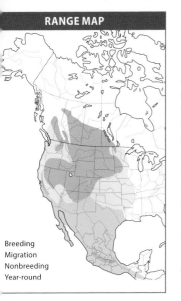

Breeding
Migration
Nonbreeding
Year-round

SIZE & SHAPE The Eared Grebe is a small waterbird with an even smaller head, a thin neck, and a thin bill. It has a sleek back and a tailless, fluffy rear. Breeding birds have a crested or peaked head.

COLOR PATTERN Breeding birds are mostly black with chestnut flanks and golden plumes fanning out from behind the bright red eye. Nonbreeding birds are grayish black overall. The cheeks are smudgy gray and the dark crown extends down past the red eye. A whitish patch on the throat scoops under and up behind the ears.

BEHAVIOR This social bird breeds in colonies and gathers in flocks from the hundreds to the thousands on lakes and ponds during migration and winter. They swim gracefully and jump up slightly before diving underwater for aquatic invertebrates.

HABITAT Eared Grebes breed in shallow lakes and ponds. During migration and in winter, they prefer saltwater habitats and can be found in great numbers in super salty waters with an abundant supply of brine shrimp and flies.

most abundant grebe in the world, the **Eared Grebe** breeds in colonies in shallow wetlands in western h America and heads by the thousands to salty inland waters to feast on brine shrimp before heading er south. In summer, golden wisps fan out from their cheeks. In fall and winter, the wisps are absent.

BREEDING ADULT AND DOWNY YOUNG

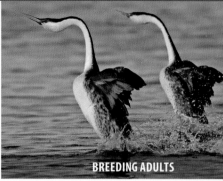

BREEDING ADULTS

NONBREEDING ADULT / IMMATURE

NONBREEDING ADULT / IMMATURE

SIZE & SHAPE The Western Grebe is a large, slender waterbird with a very long neck, a large head that may show a peak, and a long, slender, pointed bill.

COLOR PATTERN Western Grebes are crisp black and white, with a sharp transition between black and white extending down the neck. The head and most of the face are black, with white below the eye. The bill is yellowish or greenish yellow and the eye is red at close range.

BEHAVIOR Western Grebes are almost always in the water, where they dive for prey or rest on the surface. They can disappear for long periods during dives. Courting birds have a memorable display in which the pair races side by side across the water, their necks gracefully curved and bills pointed to the sky.

HABITAT Western Grebes breed on freshwater lakes and marshes with extensive open water bordered by emergent vegetation. In winter, they move to saltwater or brackish bays, estuaries, or sheltered seacoasts.

RANGE MAP

- Breeding
- Migration
- Nonbreeding
- Year-round

Find the elegant **Western Grebe** on lakes and ocean coasts of western North America. It's renowned fo ballet-like courtship display in which male and female "run" across the water in synchrony, their long ne in an S-curve. These waterbirds rarely come ashore, instead taking long dives to catch prey.

ADULT

ADULT

ADULT

ADULTS

RANGE MAP

Year-round
Year-round (scarce)

SIZE & SHAPE Larger and plumper than Mourning Doves, Rock Pigeons are tubby birds with small heads and short legs. Their wings are broad but pointed and their tails are wide and rounded.

COLOR PATTERN Since pigeons are derived from domestic birds, their plumage is wildly variable, but usually they are a combination of gray, black, white, and/or rusty. Many birds are bluish gray with two black bands on each wing, a black tip to the tail, a white rump, and iridescent neck feathers.

BEHAVIOR Pigeons often gather in flocks, walking or running on the ground and pecking for food. When alarmed, the flock may suddenly fly into the air and circle several times before coming down again.

HABITAT Familiar birds of cities and towns, Rock Pigeons were introduced from Europe in the early 1600s as a food source. They also live on farmlands, and near rocky cliffs. They may gather in large flocks in urban parks where people feed them.

...mon in cities around the world, **Rock Pigeons** were introduced to North America in the early 1600s and crowd streets and public squares, where they live off discarded food and birdseed. City pigeons nest on ...ings and window ledges. In the countryside, they nest on barns, grain towers, natural cliffs, and bridges.

ADULT

ADULTS

JUVENILE

JUVENILE

SIZE & SHAPE Band-tailed Pigeons are large, stocky pigeons with small heads, long, rounded tails, and thick-based, pointed wings.

COLOR PATTERN Band-tailed Pigeons are soft blue gray above and purplish gray below, with a white crescent on the back of the neck. The upper half of the tail is gray, fading to a pale gray band at the tip. The wings are unmarked pale gray with dark wingtips noticeable in flight. The bill and feet are yellow. Young birds lack the white crescent on the neck and have light scalloping on the back.

BEHAVIOR These forest pigeons spend much of their time traveling in groups to search for nuts, fruits, and seeds on the ground and in trees. They typically travel and feed in flocks of dozens to hundreds of individuals. Their call is a slow one- or two-syllable coo, sounding somewhat owl-like.

HABITAT Band-tailed Pigeons live in mature coniferous forests in the mountains and conifer-oak woodlands of the West. They also visit forested parks, fields, orchards, and backyard birdfeeders to forage.

RANGE MAP

■ Breeding
■ Nonbreeding
■ Year-round

The sociable **Band-tailed Pigeon** is common in forests of the Pacific Coast and the Southwest, forming large flocks in mountain forests where it feeds on seeds and fruits. These large, swift-flying pigeons can resemble Rock Pigeons, so look for the long tail with a wide, pale band at the tip.

RANGE MAP

Year-round
Year-round (scarce)

SIZE & SHAPE Eurasian Collared-Doves have plump bodies, small heads, and long tails. The wings are broad and slightly rounded. The broad tail is squared off at the tip, rather than pointed like a Mourning Dove's.

COLOR PATTERN Eurasian Collared-Doves are chalky light brown to gray buff birds with broad white patches in the tail. The collar is a narrow black crescent around the nape of the neck. In flight and when perched, the wingtips are darker than the rest of the wing. Adult and immature birds look alike.

BEHAVIOR These doves perch on telephone poles, wires, and in large trees while giving incessant three-syllable coos. Their flight pattern features bursts of clipped wingbeats and looping glides. When walking, these doves bob their heads and flick their tails.

HABITAT Eurasian Collared-Doves live in urban and suburban areas throughout much of the U.S. except the Northeast. In rural settings, look for them on farms and in livestock yards where grain is available.

the **Eurasian Collared-Dove** on phone wires and fence posts, giving its rhythmic three-parted coo. chunky bird gets its name from the black half-collar at the nape of the neck. Introduced to the mas in the 1970s, they made their way to Florida by the 1980s, then colonized much of North America.

ADULT

ADULT MALE

JUVENILE

ADULT

SIZE & SHAPE Mourning Doves are plump-bodied and long-tailed, with short legs, a small bill, and a head that looks tiny in comparison to the body. The long, pointed tail is unique among North American doves.

COLOR PATTERN Mourning Doves often match their open-country surroundings in color. They're a delicate brownish gray to buffy tan overall, and a pale peach color below, with pink legs. They have large black spots on their wings and black-bordered white tips to the outer tail feathers.

BEHAVIOR Mourning Doves fly fast on powerful wingbeats, sometimes making sudden ascents, descents, and dodges, their pointed tails stretching behind them.

HABITAT You can see Mourning Doves nearly anywhere except the deep woods. Mourning Doves prefer open fields, areas with scattered trees, and woodland edges, but many roost in woodlots during winter. They feed on the ground in grasslands, agricultural fields, backyards, and roadsides.

RANGE MAP

- Breeding
- Year-round
- Nonbreeding

The **Mourning Dove's** soft, drawn-out coos sound like laments. Common across much of the continent, this graceful dove perches on telephone wires and forages for seeds on the ground; its flight is fast and straight. When taking off, its wings make a sharp whistling or whinnying sound.

ADULT FEMALE

ADULT MALE

ADULT MALE

JUVENILE

RANGE MAP

Breeding
Migration

SIZE & SHAPE Common Nighthawks are medium-sized, slender birds with very long, pointed wings and medium-long tails. Only the small tip of the bill is usually visible, and this combined with the large eye and short neck gives the bird a big-headed look.

COLOR PATTERN Common Nighthawks are camouflaged in gray, white, buff, and black. The long, dark wings have a white blaze about two-thirds of the way out to the tip. In flight, a pale, V-shaped throat patch contrasts with the rest of the plumage.

BEHAVIOR Look for Common Nighthawks flying in the early morning and evening. During the day, they roost motionless on branches, fence posts, or the ground, and can be hard to see. Their buzzy *peent* call is distinctive.

HABITAT Common Nighthawks are most visible when they forage on the wing over cities and open areas near woods or wetlands. They migrate over fields, river valleys, marshes, woodlands, towns, and suburbs.

warm summer evenings, **Common Nighthawks** roam the skies, giving a sharp, electric *peent* call. These -winged birds fly in graceful loops, chasing insects. They are fairly common but declining birds that e no nest. Their young are highly camouflaged, and even the adults seem to vanish as soon as they land.

SIZE & SHAPE Chimney Swifts are very small birds with slender bodies and very long, narrow, curved wings. They have a round head, short neck, and short, tapered tail that gives them the appearance of a flying cigar. The wide bill is so short that it is hard to see.

COLOR PATTERN Chimney Swifts are dark gray brown all over, slightly paler on the throat. They can appear to be all black from a distance and when backlit against the sky. Adult and immature birds look similar.

BEHAVIOR Chimney Swifts fly rapidly with nearly constant wingbeats, and often twist from side to side and bank erratically. Their wingbeats are stiff, with very little flex at the wrists. They often give a high, chattering call while they fly.

HABITAT Chimney Swifts forage widely, feeding on flying insects. They gather to nest and roost in chimneys and other dim, enclosed areas with a vertical surface on which to cling, like air vents, wells, hollow trees, and caves. They forage over urban and suburban areas, rivers, lakes, forests, and fields.

RANGE MAP

■ Breeding
  Migration

Best identified by silhouette, the **Chimney Swift** spends almost its entire life airborne. Its tiny body, curving wings, and stiff, shallow wingbeats give it a flight style as distinctive as its fluid, chattering call. I can't perch, clinging instead to vertical walls. This species has sharply declined as chimneys fall into disu

RANGE MAP

Breeding
Nonbreeding
Year-round

SIZE & SHAPE This is a fairly large swift with a long, slim body and very long, narrow wings that curve like a scimitar. The overall slim outline can make it appear small, especially at a distance.

COLOR PATTERN A blackish brown bird with a white throat and a white stripe down the center of the breast and belly. Upperparts are blackish with white flanks and a white trailing edge to the secondaries (the inner part of the wing). Juvenile coloring is similar to that of an adult but duller.

BEHAVIOR The White-throated Swift catches tiny aerial insects, usually high in the sky. The fast, erratic flight and high-pitched calls are distinctive even when the plumage pattern is hard to see.

HABITAT This swift nests in natural crevices on rocky cliffs or canyon walls, from sea level to high mountain peaks. They forage over virtually any terrestrial habitat that features small aerial insects. They will nest in buildings, bridges, and overpasses, and sometimes in cities.

for **White-throated Swifts** on cliffs and canyon walls in western North America. They fly at incredible ds, pursuing insects. Courting birds dive toward earth, one clinging to the back of the other, rating just above the ground. In cliff crevices, they use saliva to glue their nests to the vertical wall.

ADULT MALE

ADULT MALE

ADULT FEMALE / IMMATURE

IMMATURE MALE

SIZE & SHAPE The Black-chinned Hummingbird is a small, fairly slender hummingbird with a fairly straight bill.

COLOR PATTERN Males have a velvety black throat which, in perfect light, has an iridescent purple base. Females have a pale throat. In both sexes, the flanks are a dull metallic green, and the bill is black. The female's three outer tail feathers have broad white tips.

BEHAVIOR Black-chinned Hummingbirds hover at flowers and feeders, darting erratically to take tiny swarming insects. They perch atop high snags to survey their territory, watching for competitors to chase off and for flying insects to eat. During courtship and territorial defense, males display by diving 66-100 feet.

HABITAT Look for Black-chinned Hummingbirds at feeders or perched on dead branches in tall trees. They are habitat specialists, found in lowland deserts and mountainous forests, and in natural habitats and very urbanized areas, as long as there are tall trees and flowering shrubs and vines.

RANGE MAP

■ Breeding
  Migration
  Nonbreeding
■ Year-round

Black-chinned Hummingbirds are exceptionally widespread, from deserts to mountain forests, often perc at the top of a bare branch. The adult male has no brilliant colors on its throat except a thin strip of iridesc purple bordering the black chin, only visible when light hits it just right. Some winter along the Gulf Coa:

ADULT MALE

ADULT MALE

ADULT FEMALE / IMMATURE

ADULT FEMALE / IMMATURE MALE

RANGE MAP

Breeding
Nonbreeding
Nonbreeding (scarce)
Year-round

SIZE & SHAPE Though tiny among birds, Anna's Hummingbirds are medium-sized and stocky for a hummingbird. They have a straight, shortish bill and a fairly broad tail. When perched, the tail extends beyond the wingtips.

COLOR PATTERN Anna's Hummingbirds are mostly green and gray, without any rufous or orange marks on the body. The male's forehead and throat are covered in iridescent reddish pink feathers that can look dull brown or gray without direct sunlight. Females and immatures have white in the tail.

BEHAVIOR Anna's Hummingbirds are a blur of motion as they hover before flowers looking for nectar and insects. Listen for the male's scratchy metallic song and look for him perched above head level in trees and shrubs.

HABITAT Anna's Hummingbirds are common in yards, parks, eucalyptus groves, riverside woods, savannas, and coastal scrub. They readily come to hummingbird feeders and flowering plants.

gh no larger than a ping-pong ball and no heavier than a nickel, **Anna's Hummingbirds** make an ssion, with their iridescent emerald feathers and sparkling rose-pink throats. Courting males climb up 0 feet in the air, then swoop to the ground with a burst of noise produced through their tail feathers.

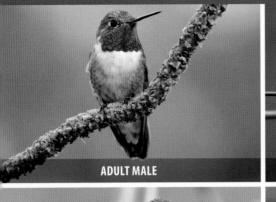

ADULT MALE

IMMATURE MALE

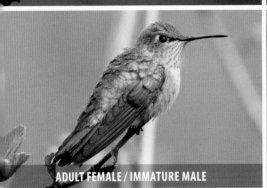

ADULT FEMALE / IMMATURE MALE

ADULT FEMALE / IMMATURE

SIZE & SHAPE Broad-tailed Hummingbirds, though tiny, are medium-sized for a North American hummingbird. They have a slender body, big head, and long straight bill. The tail extends beyond the wingtips when perched.

COLOR PATTERN The Broad-tailed Hummingbird is iridescent green above with greenish or buffy flanks and a white chest and line down the belly. Adult males have a rose-magenta throat patch (gorget) and green crown. Adult females and juveniles have a pale eyering and green spots on their throats and cheeks; when spread, their tails show green, black, rufous, and white.

BEHAVIOR Broad-tailed Hummingbirds zip from flower to flower, hovering above flowers to drink nectar. When zipping around, males make a loud metallic-sounding trill with their wings. Males also perform aerial displays, flying high into the sky and rapidly diving towards the ground making a shrill metallic trill with their wings.

HABITAT Broad-tailed Hummingbirds breed in high-elevation meadows and shrubby habitats near forests in the western United States.

RANGE MAP

- Breeding
- Migration
- Winter
- Year-round

Broad-tailed Hummingbirds breed at elevations up to 10,500 feet, where nightly temperatures plun below freezing. To survive, they slow their heart rate and drop their body temperature, entering a stat torpor. At sunrise, males show off rose-magenta throats while diving. Females raise young alone.

ADULT MALE

ADULT MALE

ADULT FEMALE / IMMATURE

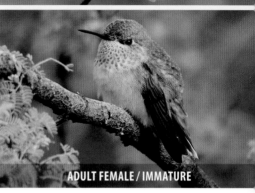
ADULT FEMALE / IMMATURE

RANGE MAP

Breeding
Migration
Nonbreeding

SIZE & SHAPE The Calliope Hummingbird is small even for a hummingbird, and its hunched posture makes it look even smaller. It has a short tail, and the wings barely extend past the end of the tail. The bill is thin and short for a hummingbird.

COLOR PATTERN The standout feature of an adult male Calliope Hummingbird is the magenta rays on the male's throat. Both sexes are greenish above, but males wear a greenish vest below while females have peachy underparts.

BEHAVIOR These birds take nectar from flowering plants and eat flying insects in midair. They often forage low to the ground. In defense of their breeding territory, they perch on high branches. Displaying males dive in a U-shape.

HABITAT Calliope Hummingbirds breed in mountain meadows, aspen thickets near streams, and open forests that are regenerating from a forest fire or logging. They spend winters in pine-oak forests and scrubby edges in Mexico.

nta rays burst from the throat of the male **Calliope Hummingbird** as it performs U-shaped display for females, tail feathers buzzing. This is the smallest bird in the United States, yet it breeds high in the mountains of the Northwest, and travels more than 5,000 miles each year to Mexico and back.

ADULT MALE

ADULT MALE

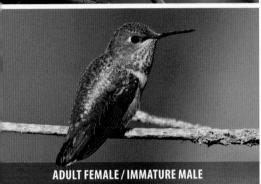

ADULT FEMALE / IMMATURE MALE

ADULT FEMALE / IMMATURE FEMALE

SIZE & SHAPE The Rufous Hummingbird is fairly small with a slender, nearly straight bill, a tail that tapers to a point when folded, and fairly short wings that don't reach the end of the tail when the bird is perched.

COLOR PATTERN Male Rufous Hummingbirds are bright rufous on the back and belly, with an iridescent throat that can appear red, orange, gold, or even greenish. Females are green above with rufous-washed flanks, rufous patches in the green tail, and a dark spot on the throat. Adult males have rufous and black tails. Females and immatures also have green and white in the tail.

BEHAVIOR Look for their fast, darting flight and pinpoint maneuverability. They tirelessly chase away other hummingbirds, even in places they're only visiting on migration. Like other hummers, they eat insects as well as nectar.

HABITAT Rufous Hummingbirds breed in open areas, yards, parks, and forests up to treeline. On migration, they pass through mountain meadows as high as 12,600 feet, where nectar-rich, tubular flowers bloom. Their winter habitat in Mexico includes shrubby openings and oak-pine forests at middle to high elevation.

RANGE MAP

- ■ Breeding
- Migration
- ---- Migration (scarce)
- ■ Nonbreeding
- Nonbreeding (scarce)

One of the feistiest hummingbirds in North America, the brilliant rufous male and the green-and-rufous female **Rufous Hummingbird** are relentless attackers at flowers and feeders, going after (if not always defeating) even the large hummingbirds of the Southwest, which can be double their weight.

ADULT MALE

ADULT MALE

ADULT MALE

ADULT FEMALE / IMMATURE

RANGE MAP

Breeding
Migration
Winter
Year-round

SIZE & SHAPE Allen's Hummingbirds are small, compact, and stocky hummingbirds. The bill is straight and about as long as the head. The tail extends past the wings when perched and the outermost tail feather is narrower than the rest.

COLOR PATTERN Adult males have a rufous tail, face, and flanks that contrast with a bronze-green back and deep red-orange gorget. Females and immatures are bronze green above with paler coppery sides. They are essentially identical to Rufous Hummingbirds.

BEHAVIOR Allen's Hummingbirds zip from flower to flower hovering above them to drink the nectar, ticking as they go. They also flycatch for insects or pluck them from vegetation. Males display by flying side to side or in wide arcs while emitting a bumblebee-like buzz with their wings.

HABITAT Allen's Hummingbirds breed in coastal forest, scrub, backyards, and chaparral along a narrow strip that stretches up the coast from California to southern Oregon.

rly spring, find the **Allen's Hummingbird** in scrub and chaparral along the Pacific Coast. Males put on w for the females, swinging in pendulous arcs before climbing high in the sky and diving down, tails ly squealing. They mostly winter in Mexico, but some stay in southern California year-round.

BREEDING ADULT

BREEDING ADULT

JUVENILE

NONBREEDING ADULT

SIZE & SHAPE Soras are small, chubby, chickenlike rails with long toes. They have stubby bills and frequently hold their tails cocked up.

COLOR PATTERN Soras are mottled gray and brown with white-edged feathers, and a candy-corn-shaped bill. They have a black mask and throat patch, white side lines, and a white patch under the tail. Females are duller than males.

BEHAVIOR Soras walk through shallow wetlands, pushing their head forward with every step while nervously flicking the tail upward. They forage in dense vegetation but may venture into open areas from time to time. Their long toes help them walk on top of floating mats of vegetation.

HABITAT Soras make their homes in shallow freshwater wetlands with dense emergent vegetation. During migration and winter, they also use brackish marshes, flooded fields, and wet pastures.

RANGE MAP

■ Breeding
Migration
Nonbreeding
■ Year-round

Its descending whinny emanates from the depths of cattails and rushes, but the secretive **Sora** rarely shows itself. When it finally appears, the Sora walks slowly through shallow wetlands, a bit like a chicke that has had too much coffee, nervously flicking its tail and exposing the white feathers below.

ADULT

ADULT

JUVENILE

ADULT

RANGE MAP

Breeding
Breeding (scarce)
Migration
Nonbreeding
Year-round

SIZE & SHAPE American Coots are plump, chickenlike birds with a rounded head and a sloping bill. Their tiny tail, short wings, and large feet are visible on the rare occasions they take flight.

COLOR PATTERN Coots are dark gray to black birds with a bright white bill and forehead. The legs are yellow green. At close range, you may see a small patch of red on the forehead.

BEHAVIOR You'll find coots eating aquatic plants on almost any body of water. When swimming, they look like small ducks (and often dive), but on land they look more chickenlike, walking rather than waddling. An awkward and often clumsy flier, the American Coot requires long running takeoffs to get airborne.

HABITAT Look for American Coots at ponds in city parks, in marshes, at reservoirs, along the edges of lakes and in roadside ditches, at sewage treatment ponds, along saltwater inlets, and in saltmarshes.

waterborne **American Coot** is a reminder that not everything that floats is a duck. A close look at the 's small head and scrawny legs reveals a very different kind of bird. Common in nearly any open water ss the continent, they're closer relatives of the Sandhill Crane and rails than of Mallards or teal.

ADULT

ADULT

JUVENILE

ADULT

SIZE & SHAPE Sandhill Cranes are large, tall birds with a long neck, long legs, and broad wings. The short tail is covered by drooping feathers that form a "bustle." The head is small and the bill is straight and longer than the head. In flight, the straight neck sets cranes apart from herons.

COLOR PATTERN Both sexes are pale gray. Adults have a pale cheek and red skin on the crown. Their legs are black. Juveniles are gray without the pale cheek or red crown. Some birds are stained with rust.

BEHAVIOR Sandhill Cranes forage for grains and invertebrates in prairies, grasslands, and marshes. They do not hunt in open water or hunch their necks the way herons do. Sandhill Cranes form extremely large flocks—into the tens of thousands—on their wintering grounds and during migration. They often migrate very high in the sky.

HABITAT Sandhill Cranes breed and forage in open prairies, grasslands, and wetlands. Outside of the breeding season, they often roost in deeper water of ponds or lakes, where they are safe from predators.

RANGE MAP

■ Breeding
■ Migration
■ Nonbreeding
■ Year-round

The crimson-capped **Sandhill Crane** has an elegance that draws attention. It breeds in open wetlands, fields, and prairies and forms large groups, filling the air with rolling cries. While populations are genera strong, some isolated populations in Mississippi and Cuba are endangered.

ADULT MALE

ADULT FEMALE

IMMATURE

JUVENILE

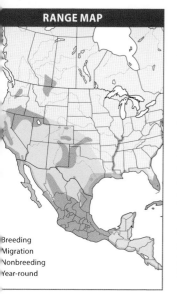

RANGE MAP

Breeding
Migration
Nonbreeding
Year-round

SIZE & SHAPE The Black-necked Stilt is a tall and lanky shorebird with a delicate-looking body. It has very long legs, a long neck, a small head, and a thin, straight bill. It is larger than a Lesser Yellowlegs.

COLOR PATTERN These birds are black above and white below, with white around the eye and rosy pink legs. In females and immatures, the black areas can be brownish.

BEHAVIOR Black-necked Stilts wade into shallow bodies of water in pursuit of tiny aquatic invertebrates. Adults defending nests or chicks fly around and call loudly, sometimes performing a distraction display by feigning injury.

HABITAT Black-necked Stilts are almost always seen near shallow water, including both salt and fresh waters, especially mudflats, salt pans, saltmarshes, and human-modified habitats like sewage ponds, evaporation pools, and flooded fields.

k-necked Stilts are among the most stately of the shorebirds, with long rosy pink legs and elegant age. They move deliberately when foraging, walking slowly through wetlands in search of tiny aquatic When disturbed, stilts are vociferous, and their high, yapping calls carry for some distance.

ADULT

ADULT

JUVENILE

ADULT

SIZE & SHAPE The Black Oystercatcher is a large, heavyset shorebird with a very long, thick straight bill. The neck is heavy and the legs are long and thick.

COLOR PATTERN Adults are blackish with a brilliant orange-red bill and yellow eye ringed with red that appears orange from a distance. At close range, the wings, tail, and back are dark brown. Juveniles are brownish overall, with the outer portion of the bill dusky.

BEHAVIOR Black Oystercatchers remain paired year-round, and often fly in pairs over water and shore giving their pleasant whistling calls. They walk slowly along rocky shores at lower tides looking for shellfish, and pry them open with their heavy bills. During high tide, they rest and preen, often in roosts of a dozen or more.

HABITAT Look for Black Oystercatchers along the rocky seacoasts and islands of the Pacific Coast. They forage in tidepools, sometimes on open tidal flats, but rarely in grassy areas.

RANGE MAP

■ Nonbreeding
■ Year-round

Among the mussel- and barnacle-covered rocks of the Pacific Coast lives this stout shorebird with a gleaming reddish bill, yellow eyes, and pink legs. The **Black Oystercatcher** forages on falling tides, whe exposed marine organisms are vulnerable to quick strikes from its sharp, stout bill.

BREEDING MALE

NONBREEDING ADULT

JUVENILE

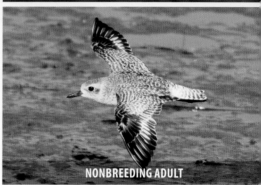

NONBREEDING ADULT

RANGE MAP

Breeding
Migration
Nonbreeding

SIZE & SHAPE The Black-bellied Plover is a medium-sized to large shorebird. It has moderately long legs, a short neck and bill, and a large, rounded head.

COLOR PATTERN Breeding males are a dazzling mix of black and white: checkered upperwings, a black face and belly, a white crown, nape, and undertail, and dark legs and bill. Adult females in breeding plumage are similar but with less contrast. Nonbreeding adults are pale gray above and grayish or whitish below. Juveniles are more scaly looking on the back. All plumages show black "armpits" in flight.

BEHAVIOR Black-bellied Plovers move by stop-run-stop, or stop-run-peck, scanning and capturing prey at stops with a single peck or series of pecks. Worms and clams may be shaken vigorously in nearby shallow water to remove mud.

HABITAT Black-bellied Plovers nest in Arctic lowlands on dry tundra. In winter, find them on coastal lagoons and estuaries. Migrants stop along coastlines and in harvested agricultural areas, sod farms, and muddy edges of lakes and rivers.

k-bellied Plovers are supreme aerialists, and are readily identified at great distance by black axillaries pit" feathers) and their mournful-sounding call. The largest of North America's migratory plovers, it ds farther north than other species, at the very top of the world, and occurs on six continents.

ADULT

ADULT

DOWNY YOUNG

ADULT IN PREDATOR DISTRACTION DISPLA

SIZE & SHAPE Killdeer have the characteristic large, round head, large eye, and short bill of all plovers. They are especially slender and lanky, with a long, pointed tail and long wings.

COLOR PATTERN Both sexes of the Killdeer are brownish tan on top and white below. The white chest is crossed with two black bands, and the brown face is marked with black-and-white patches. The bright orange-buff rump is conspicuous in flight. Downy young have just one black band on the breast.

BEHAVIOR These tawny birds run across the ground in spurts, stopping with a jolt every so often to check their progress, or to see if they've startled up any insect prey. When disturbed, they break into flight and circle overhead, calling repeatedly. Their flight is rapid, with stiff, intermittent wingbeats. To lure predators away from a nest, Killdeer will feign injury with a broken-wing display.

HABITAT Look for Killdeer on open ground with low vegetation (or no vegetation at all), such as lawns, golf courses, driveways, parking lots, and gravel-covered roofs, as well as pastures, fields, sandbars, and mudflats. This species is one of the least water-associated of all shorebirds.

RANGE MAP

■ Breeding
■ Nonbreeding
■ Year-round

The **Killdeer's** broken-wing act leads predators away from a nest, but it doesn't keep cows or horses fr stepping on eggs. To guard against large hoofed animals, the Killdeer uses quite a different display: flu itself up, displaying its tail over its head, and running at the beast to attempt to make it change its path

RANGE MAP

Breeding
Migration

SIZE & SHAPE The Upland Sandpiper is a shorebird with unusual proportions: long legs, a long, thin neck, a small dovelike head, large eyes, and a thin, straight bill. The tail and the wings are long.

COLOR PATTERN Upland Sandpipers are marbled golden brown and blackish above. They are white below, with dark streaks and chevron-shaped markings on the breast and sides. Their throats are white, and they have a white eyering. Adult and immature birds look similar.

BEHAVIOR Upland Sandpipers walk briskly through shortgrass habitats, picking insects and seeds from the ground and vegetation. In breeding season, males perch on fence posts and make circular song flights over the breeding territory, sometimes accompanied by females.

HABITAT Upland Sandpipers nest in grasslands and are most numerous in native prairies in the Great Plains. They also nest in pastures and agricultural fields. During migration and in winter, look for them in shorter vegetation.

all short-billed curlew, the elegant **Upland Sandpiper** paces across grassland habitats throughout ear. It is considered to be an "indicator species" for the quality of native prairie. Unlike most North rican shorebirds, it avoids wetlands, instead hunting insects with jerky steps and quick jabs at prey.

SIZE & SHAPE The Long-billed Curlew is a large, long-legged shorebird with a very long, thin, curved bill. It has a heavy football-shaped body, a long neck, and a small round head. It is larger than a Whimbrel and smaller than a Cattle Egret.

COLOR PATTERN Long-billed Curlews are speckled and barred in browns above with a pale cinnamon wash throughout and a plain cinnamon belly. The head and neck are pale with faint streaks, and the lower bill is pink at the base. In flight, the wings are mostly cinnamon. Adult and immature birds look similar.

BEHAVIOR The Long-billed Curlew forages for earthworms and other deep-burrowing prey in soft muddy substrates using its long, curved bill. In drier grassland habitats, it pecks at insects. It walks with a strut, pushing its head forward.

HABITAT Long-billed Curlews breed in sparse grasses, including shortgrass and mixed-grass prairies and agricultural fields. In the nonbreeding season, look for them in wetlands, tidal estuaries, mudflats, shallow flooded fields, beaches, and even lawns.

RANGE MAP

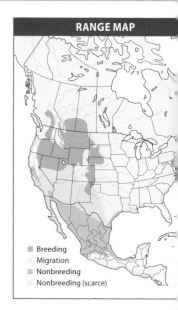

- Breeding
- Migration
- Nonbreeding
- Nonbreeding (scarce)

North America's largest shorebird, the **Long-billed Curlew** is a graceful creature with an almost imposs long, thin, and curved bill. While the pair works together to incubate the eggs and care for the brood, th female typically leaves 2–3 weeks after the eggs hatch, and her mate is left to care for the young.

BREEDING ADULT

BREEDING ADULT

NONBREEDING ADULT / IMMATURE

BREEDING ADULT

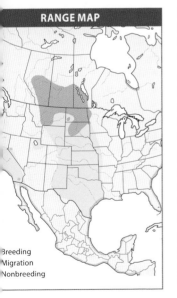

RANGE MAP

Breeding
Migration
Nonbreeding

SIZE & SHAPE The Marbled Godwit is a large, long-legged shorebird with an extremely long, slightly upturned bill. A small round head sits atop a thin neck. In flight, its legs stick out beyond the tail.

COLOR PATTERN Marbled Godwits are barred above and below in brown, white, and cinnamon during the breeding season. The bill is black at the tip and orange at the base during the breeding season, and pink during the nonbreeding season, but this distinction can be difficult to see.

BEHAVIOR The Marbled Godwit probes into sand or mud with its long bill for aquatic invertebrates. It sometimes walks while probing or takes a few steps before burying its bill in the mud. It is social outside of the breeding season and forages in groups.

HABITAT Marbled Godwits breed in northern shortgrass prairies near wetlands. During migration and on the wintering grounds, look for them on mudflats, salt ponds, beaches, estuaries, and wetlands.

ebirds have some of the most interesting bill shapes, and the **Marbled Godwit** is no exception with vordlike bill. This well-camouflaged speckled brown bird is especially noticeable on the prairie when it ads its long and pointed wings to take flight.

BREEDING ADULTS

BREEDING ADULT

JUVENILE

NONBREEDING ADULT

SIZE & SHAPE Ruddy Turnstones are short, stocky, oval-shaped shorebirds with stout, slightly upturned bills. They are larger than Spotted Sandpipers but smaller than Willets.

COLOR PATTERN Breeding males have black-and-white markings on the head and throat and a chestnut and black pattern on the back. Breeding females are paler. Both have orange legs that are brighter in the breeding season.

BEHAVIOR Ruddy Turnstones flip rocks, pebbles, and seaweed along shorelines in search of food. They rarely wade in waters more than a few inches deep, generally foraging out of the water. On migration and in winter, they gather in groups of 10 to over 1,000.

HABITAT Ruddy Turnstones breed in the tundra of northern North America. On migration and in winter, they use freshwater shorelines, mudflats, rocky shorelines, and sandy beaches further south.

RANGE MAP

■ Breeding
■ Migration
■ Nonbreeding

A shorebird that looks a bit like a calico cat, the **Ruddy Turnstone's** orange legs and uniquely patterne black-and-white head and chest make this bird easy to pick out of a crowd. Long-distance migrants tha breed in the Arctic tundra, they spend off-seasons on rocky shorelines and sandy beaches on both coas

NONBREEDING ADULT

NONBREEDING ADULT

JUVENILE

BREEDING ADULT

RANGE MAP

Breeding
Migration
Nonbreeding

SIZE & SHAPE Sanderlings are small, plump sandpipers with a stout bill about the same length as the head. Sanderlings are medium-sized members of the genus *Calidris*.

COLOR PATTERN In nonbreeding plumage, they are light gray above and white below, with a blackish shoulder mark. In spring and summer, they are spangled black, white, and rufous on the head, neck, and back. Juveniles have a checkered back and unmarked white underparts. Their legs and bills are black.

BEHAVIOR Sanderlings breed on the High Arctic tundra and migrate south in fall to populate beaches. They gather in loose flocks to probe the sand for marine invertebrates, running back and forth in a perpetual "wave chase."

HABITAT During migration and winter, Sanderlings forage on North American beaches but will also use mudflats in the Midwest. They nest in the High Arctic on gravel patches and low-growing, wet tundra.

Sanderling's black legs blur as it runs back and forth on the beach, picking or probing for tiny prey in wet sand left by receding waves. Sanderlings are medium-sized sandpipers recognizable by their pale breeding plumage, black legs and bill, and obsessive wave-chasing habits.

NONBREEDING ADULT

NONBREEDING ADULT

BREEDING ADULT

JUVENILE

SIZE & SHAPE The Western Sandpiper is a small, portly shorebird with a long, thin bill with a slight droop. It has pointed wings, a short tail, and medium-length legs for its size. Females tend to be larger and have longer bills than males.

COLOR PATTERN Breeding adults have black, brown, rufous, and gold upperparts, with white underparts marked with extensive dark arrow-shaped streaks. They have a rufous crown and ear patch, and dark legs and bill. Nonbreeding adults are pale gray above, whitish below. Juveniles are similar to nonbreeding adults but the upperparts are more vivid in the wings, showing gold and rufous edges to feathers.

BEHAVIOR Western Sandpipers congregate in large flocks on beaches and mudflats. Their toes are adapted for walking and running in short bursts while foraging on beaches. They can often be seen balancing on one leg, or even hopping.

HABITAT Western Sandpipers breed in low coastal tundra with sedges. On migration and in winter, look for them along mudflats, beaches, shores of lakes and ponds, and flooded fields.

RANGE MAP

■ Breeding
Migration
■ Winter
Winter (scarce)

In migration, the **Western Sandpiper** stages in huge, spectacular flocks, particularly along the Pacific Coast at San Francisco Bay and in the Copper River Delta in Alaska. Estimates suggest that nearly the v breeding population passes through the Copper River Delta in a few weeks each spring.

NONBREEDING ADULT

BREEDING ADULT

JUVENILE

JUVENILE

RANGE MAP

Breeding
Migration
Nonbreeding
Year-round

SIZE & SHAPE The Spotted Sandpiper is a medium-sized shorebird with a bill slightly shorter than its head and a body that tapers to a longish tail. They have a rounded breast and usually appear as though they are leaning forward.

COLOR PATTERN In breeding season, Spotted Sandpipers have an orange bill and bold spots on their bright white breast. The back is dark brown. In winter, a Spotted Sandpiper's breast is not spotted; it's plain white, while the back is grayish brown and the bill is pale yellow. In flight, Spotted Sandpipers have a thin white stripe along the wing.

BEHAVIOR Spotted Sandpipers are often solitary and walk with a distinctive teeter, bobbing their tails up and down constantly. When foraging, they walk quickly, crouching low, occasionally darting toward prey, all while bobbing the tail.

HABITAT Find Spotted Sandpipers along streambanks, rivers, ponds, lakes, and beaches. They are one of the most widespread breeding shorebirds in the U.S., commonly seen near fresh water, even in arid or forested regions.

Spotted Sandpiper is the most widespread breeding sandpiper in North America. Female Spotted Sandpipers sometimes practice an unusual breeding strategy called polyandry, where a female mates with four males, each of which then cares for a clutch of eggs.

NONBREEDING ADULT

BREEDING ADULT

JUVENILE

NONBREEDING ADULTS

SIZE & SHAPE Willets are large, stocky shorebirds with long legs and thick, straight bills considerably longer than the head. Their wings are broader and rounder than those of many shorebirds, and the short tail is squared off at the tip.

COLOR PATTERN Willets are gray or brown birds that, when flying, display a striking white stripe between black patches along each wing. In summer, Willets are mottled gray, brown, and black; in winter they are a plain gray. The legs are bluish gray to olive gray.

BEHAVIOR Willets are often seen alone. They walk deliberately, pausing to probe for prey in sand and mudflats. When startled, they react with a piercing call, often opening their wings and running rather than taking flight.

HABITAT In winter, look for Willets on beaches, rocky coasts, mudflats, and marshes. In breeding season, Western birds nest in grasslands and prairies near fresh water. Eastern birds breed on barrier beaches, islands, and in coastal saltmarshes, and spend the winter in South America.

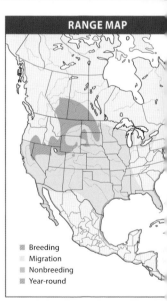

RANGE MAP

- Breeding
- Migration
- Nonbreeding
- Year-round

Like Killdeer, **Willets** will pretend to be disabled by a broken wing in order to draw attention to thems and lure predators away from their eggs or chicks. Because they find prey using the sensitive tips of th bills, and not just eyesight, Willets can feed both during the day and at night.

BREEDING ADULT

BREEDING ADULT

NONBREEDING ADULT

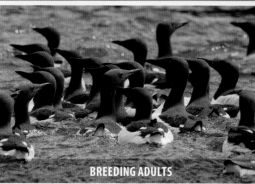

BREEDING ADULTS

RANGE MAP

Breeding
Nonbreeding
Nonbreeding (scarce)
Year-round

SIZE & SHAPE On land, the Common Murre stands upright like a penguin. In water, it looks rather ducklike with a long and slender body, and a long, thin bill.

COLOR PATTERN Breeding Common Murres are neatly marked with blackish head, face, and upperparts (dark brown when seen at close range) and clean white below. Nonbreeding adults have a pale throat and face with a dark line behind the eye.

BEHAVIOR Common Murres are heavy-bodied seabirds that fly with rapid wingbeats. They typically nest in dense, busy colonies crowded onto high cliff ledges, where they constantly make guttural calls. They forage in large groups at sea, often congregating in large rafts.

HABITAT Common Murres spend most of their lives on the open ocean—often far out to sea, although some individuals can often be spotted closer to shore. They breed on oceanside cliffs and islands.

Common Murre egg is so pointed at one end that when placed on a flat surface and pushed, it rolls d in a circle. This may help keep the egg from rolling off of its nesting shelf. Significant variation in and markings of these eggs may allow parent murres to recognize their own egg after time at sea.

BREEDING ADULT

BREEDING ADULT

JUVENILE

NONBREEDING ADULT

SIZE & SHAPE The Pigeon Guillemot is a medium-sized to small seabird with a relatively long, thick neck and a thin, straight bill. It's about the same size as a Green-winged Teal.

COLOR PATTERN In summer, Pigeon Guillemots are black with large, white wing patches and red feet. In winter, they are mostly whitish with a dusky gray back. Juveniles have mottling on the head and neck and black markings on the white wing patches.

BEHAVIOR Pigeon Guillemots fly close to the surface of the water, usually within 10 feet. They dive underwater for prey, using their wings and feet to propel themselves through the water. They are strong swimmers, even in rough seas.

HABITAT Pigeon Guillemots nest on rocky coastlines and offshore islands. They forage in nearshore waters but are occasionally seen much further from the shoreline. In winter, they favor sheltered waters further inshore.

RANGE MAP

■ Year-round

The **Pigeon Guillemot** is one of the few members of the auk and puffin family to lay two eggs—nearly others lay only one egg. The Pigeon Guillemot often scales vertical rock faces by some vigorous flappi its wings combined with its use of sharp claws on webbed feet.

NONBREEDING ADULT

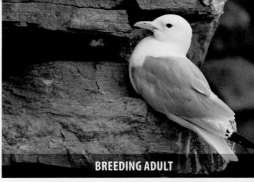

BREEDING ADULT

JUVENILE

NONBREEDING ADULT

RANGE MAP

Breeding
Nonbreeding
Year-round

SIZE & SHAPE The Black-legged Kittiwake is a medium-sized to small gull with a squared-off tail and relatively long and narrow wings.

COLOR PATTERN Adult Black-legged Kittiwakes have a small, yellow bill, gray back, and a white head and underparts; in winter, adults have dark smudging on the head. The legs and wingtips, said to be "dipped in ink," are black. Juveniles have black "eyeshadow," ear spots, and hind collars. Dark bars across the wings combine to make an M-shape when flying.

BEHAVIOR Black-legged Kittiwakes feed in flocks at the water's surface, mostly in the daytime. They may make shallow dives or snatch food from the surface. They nest in mixed-species colonies that can be as large as 100,000 birds.

HABITAT Black-legged Kittiwakes nest on cliff ledges of offshore islands, sea stacks, or inaccessible areas of coastal mainland. They winter at sea.

nty gull of northern oceans, **Black-legged Kittiwakes** nest in colonies on cliffs of the North Atlantic, Pacific, and Arctic. On these sheer, rocky cliffs, their unceasing cries of *kittiwake* join with the crashing o make the classic sound of a seabird colony.

BREEDING ADULT

BREEDING ADULT

IMMATURE (FIRST WINTER)

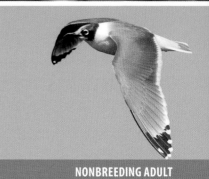

NONBREEDING ADULT

SIZE & SHAPE The Franklin's Gull is a fairly small gull with a short neck and a slim, rather short bill. Like other gulls, the wings are long and the tail is short. It is larger than a Bonaparte's Gull and smaller than a Laughing Gull.

COLOR PATTERN Breeding adult Franklin's Gulls have a black head with white crescents above and below the eye. Upperparts are dark gray; legs and bill are reddish. Nonbreeding adults have a gray half-hood or mask, and bill and legs are dark. In adults, a white crescent separates black wingtips from the gray upperwing.

BEHAVIOR Franklin's Gulls catch insects in the air in flight, or pick prey from the ground as they walk. In the water, they glean prey from the surface while swimming, sometimes swimming in circles to bring prey to the surface.

HABITAT Franklin's Gulls nest in freshwater prairie and open-country marshes with emergent and floating vegetation. They migrate through the continent's center, using agricultural fields, marshes, and reservoirs.

RANGE MAP

■ Breeding
■ Migration

A delicate waterbird that nests by the thousands in North American marshes, the **Franklin's Gull** spen[ds] winters off the coasts of Chile and Peru. Its buoyant, swift, graceful flight is useful for catching both flyi[ng] insects and small fish, as well as for making its long migrations.

BREEDING ADULT

BREEDING ADULT

NONBREEDING ADULT

JUVENILE

RANGE MAP

Nonbreeding
Nonbreeding (scarce)
Year-round

SIZE & SHAPE Heermann's Gull is a medium-sized gull with long wings, a fairly rounded head, and a straight, relatively long bill that is less heavy and angled than bills of larger gulls.

COLOR PATTERN The unpatterned dark gray plumage of the adult Heermann's Gull is unique among gulls. The head is white but becomes gray and speckled during the nonbreeding season. The bill is red and tipped with black. Juvenile birds are sooty brown all over with buff edges to feathers, giving a scaly look. The bill is pale pink with a black tip. Eyes are dark and legs are black.

BEHAVIOR Heermann's Gulls pick food from the surface of the water, hovering and dipping over the waves, then plunging in to pursue fish. They also steal food from marine mammals and other birds. During the nonbreeding season, Heermann's Gulls typically hunt offshore for schooling fish or loaf on beaches, rocky shorelines, or estuaries.

HABITAT The Heermann's Gull nests on arid offshore islands. In winter, look for them along the coast and out to sea. They are rarely found inland.

Heermann's Gull is the only North American gull that breeds south of the U.S. and heads north for nonbreeding season. After breeding is over in July, the gull quickly heads north all the way to southern da. It heads south again by December, and most birds are at breeding islands in Mexico by March.

BREEDING ADULT

NONBREEDING ADULT

JUVENILE

IMMATURE (FIRST WINTER)

SIZE & SHAPE The Mew Gull is a medium- to small-sized gull with a small bill, and a petite, round head.

COLOR PATTERN In breeding plumage, the Mew Gull has a bright-white head, neck, and underparts, and an unmarked yellow bill and yellow legs. The back and wings are dark gray, and the wingtips are black with white spots. The tail is white. Dark eyes are ringed in red in breeding adults. First winter birds have sooty brown flight feathers, a pale rump, and brown tail feathers. Winter adults have dusky streaking on the head and a dusky smudge on the bill. Juveniles are scaly grayish beige overall.

BEHAVIOR The Mew Gull flutters over water, head down and legs dangling, to pick up bits of food from the water's surface. It sometimes paddles against the current, picking up food as it floats past. It will occasionally dive for fish.

HABITAT The Mew Gull breeds in tundra, marsh, ponds, lakes, rivers, streams, islands, and coastal cliffs. It winters in nearshore waters and coasts, river estuaries, beaches, mudflats, harbors, and sewage outfalls and treatment ponds.

RANGE MAP

■ Breeding
■ Migration
■ Nonbreeding
■ Year-round

Although the **Mew Gull** is a common bird along the Pacific Coast, it is a rarity in the East. Birds that app along the Atlantic Coast are likely to be from Europe. The Mew Gull is the only "white-headed" gull that regularly uses trees for nesting.

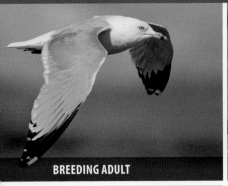

BREEDING ADULT

NONBREEDING ADULT

IMMATURE (FIRST WINTER)

IMMATURE (SECOND WINTER)

RANGE MAP

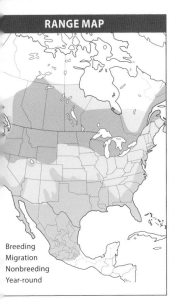

Breeding
Migration
Nonbreeding
Year-round

SIZE & SHAPE The Ring-billed Gull is a medium-sized gull with a fairly short, slim bill. When perched, its long, slender wings extend past its square-tipped tail. In flight, the birds move lightly on easy flaps of their fairly slender wings.

COLOR PATTERN Adults are pale gray above and white below with a white head and tail; their black wingtips are spotted with white. They have yellow legs and eyes, and yellow bills with black bands. Nonbreeding adults have brown-streaked heads. Second-winter birds have a black band on the tail and lack white spots in the black wingtips. First-winter birds have gray backs but are otherwise mottled brown and white; they have black-tipped pink bills and pink legs.

BEHAVIOR These sociable gulls often fly overhead by the hundreds or feed together on golf courses, beaches, and fields. Strong, nimble flyers and opportunistic feeders, Ring-billed Gulls circle and hover acrobatically, looking for food.

HABITAT Ring-billed Gulls are often found in urban, suburban, and agricultural areas. On the coast, they frequent estuaries, beaches, mudflats, and coastal waters. In winter, they're common around docks, wharves, and harbors.

liar acrobats of the air and comfortable around humans, **Ring-billed Gulls** frequent parking lots, age dumps, beaches, and fields, sometimes by the hundreds. You're most likely to see them far away coastal areas—in fact, most Ring-billed Gulls nest in the interior of the continent, near fresh water.

BREEDING ADULT

ADULT

IMMATURE (FIRST WINTER)

IMMATURE (SECOND WINTER)

SIZE & SHAPE The Western Gull is a large and stocky gull with a heavy bill. The rounded head has a slight peak over the eye.

COLOR PATTERN Breeding adult Western Gulls have a white head and underparts, and rich pink legs. Nonbreeding birds have very little streaking on the neck, unlike other gull species. The back is dark slate gray, and the dark eyes are ringed in orange skin. Juvenile birds are dark brown all over, with light edgings to feathers and black legs.

BEHAVIOR Western Gulls capture food near the surface of the water or on the shore, swallowing large prey whole. They steal food from cormorants and other gulls and are common at garbage dumps.

HABITAT Look for Western Gulls foraging at sea, in intertidal areas, along beaches, and at dumps. They roost in fields, dumps, and parking lots, but they breed on rocky offshore islands.

RANGE MAP

■ Nonbreeding
■ Year-round

Like most gulls, the **Western Gull** is an opportunistic feeder, capturing its own live prey, scavenging ref or stealing food from seals and other gulls. It is even known to steal milk from lactating female seals tha are lying on their backs sleeping on the beach.

BREEDING ADULT

NONBREEDING ADULT

IMMATURE (FIRST SUMMER)

NONBREEDING ADULT

RANGE MAP

Breeding
Breeding (scarce)
Migration
Nonbreeding
Year-round

SIZE & SHAPE This is a medium-sized gull with a round head and somewhat slanted forehead. California Gulls have fairly long wings and a long, slim bill. They are smaller than Herring Gulls but larger than Ring-billed Gulls.

COLOR PATTERN Adults have a medium-gray back, black wingtips, white underparts, and a yellow bill with a red spot and dark band near the tip. In winter, dark streaks mark the back of the neck. Juveniles are mottled brown and white.

BEHAVIOR California Gulls are strong, nimble fliers and opportunistic foragers; they forage on foot, from the air, and from the water. These social gulls breed in colonies and mix with other gull species along the coast in winter.

HABITAT California Gulls breed on islands in rivers or lakes (including salty lakes) and forage along lakes, bogs, farm fields, garbage dumps, parking lots, ocean beaches, and open ocean. Most winter along the West Coast.

are often thought of as coastal birds, but **California Gulls** are common in inland areas in the West. e medium-sized gulls breed in colonies on islands and levees in lakes and rivers. You'll also spot them stures, scrublands, and garbage dumps, as they often forage miles from the colony.

HERRING GULL *(Larus argentatus)*

BREEDING ADULT

NONBREEDING ADULT

JUVENILE

IMMATURE (SECOND WINTER)

SIZE & SHAPE Herring Gulls are large gulls with hefty bills and robust bodies. In flight, they look barrel-chested and broad-winged compared to smaller gulls.

COLOR PATTERN Breeding adult Herring Gulls have light gray backs, black wingtips, and white heads and underparts, and a pale eye ringed in red. In winter, dusky brown streaks mark their heads. The legs are dull pink at all ages. Juveniles are tan overall with dark eyes and tan-and-white checkerboarding on the back. Immature plumages are intermediate between juvenile and adult.

BEHAVIOR Herring Gulls patrol shorelines and open ocean, picking scraps off the surface. Rallying around fishing boats or refuse dumps, they are loud scavengers that snatch other birds' meals.

HABITAT Look for Herring Gulls along coasts, and near large lakes and rivers; in summer, look for them as far north as coastal Alaska. They feed in open water, mudflats, plowed fields, and garbage dumps; they gather in open space near food.

RANGE MAP

■ Breeding
  Migration
■ Winter
■ Year-round

Spiraling above a fishing boat or squabbling at a dock or parking lot, **Herring Gulls** are the quintessen gray-and-white, pink-legged "seagulls." They're the most familiar gulls of the North Atlantic and can be found across much of coastal North America in winter.

BREEDING ADULT

NONBREEDING ADULT

IMMATURE (SECOND WINTER)

IMMATURE (FIRST WINTER)

RANGE MAP

Breeding
Nonbreeding
Year-round

SIZE & SHAPE The Glaucous-winged Gull is a large, heavyset gull with a big, somewhat flat head, and a long, heavy bill with a thick tip and pronounced angle along the lower edge.

COLOR PATTERN Breeding adults are medium-gray above, including wingtips, and white below, with a yellow bill and pinkish legs. Wingtips have white spots. Nonbreeding adults have brownish streaking on the head. Juveniles are pale brown overall, including wingtips. Subadult plumages are intermediate between juvenile and adult.

BEHAVIOR Glaucous-winged Gulls pull fish, crabs, mollusks, and sea stars from rocks or pools, often dropping hard prey from the air to break it open on rocks. They will join large flocks of seabirds to feed on schools of small fish, and scavenge near fishing boats, fish-processing plants, and eagles and bears.

HABITAT The Glaucous-winged Gull breeds on rocky islands and coastal cliffs, and sometimes on flat roofs of buildings. It forages at sea, in intertidal areas, along beaches, and at dumps. It roosts in fields, dumps, and parking lots.

Glaucous-winged Gull is a large, pale gull of Pacific shorelines. It's relatively easy to pick out from r gulls—most species have black wingtips, but adult Glaucous-winged Gulls have pearly gray tips that match the color of the rest of the back and upperwing.

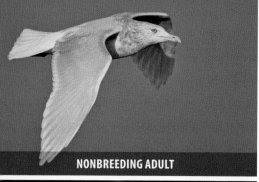

NONBREEDING ADULT

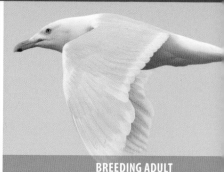

BREEDING ADULT

IMMATURE (FIRST SUMMER)

JUVENILE

SIZE & SHAPE A stocky gull with a deep chest, a heavy bill, and a large head that makes the eye appear small. This can give the impression of a "snowman" of a bird compared to other large gulls. They are larger than Herring Gulls.

COLOR PATTERN Breeding adult Glaucous Gulls have a clean white head, pale gray back, and white wingtips. Underparts are white. Nonbreeding birds have varying amounts of brown streaking on the head and neck. The bill is yellow with a red spot near the tip of the lower bill; eyes are pale yellow. Juveniles are all over light brownish gray or buff, with a pink bill dipped in black. Eyes are dark.

BEHAVIOR The Glaucous Gull captures food near the surface of the water or on the shore. It steals food from other gulls, and swallows large prey whole.

HABITAT Rarely seen far from large bodies of water, this bird breeds along marine and freshwater coasts, tundra, islands, cliffs, shorelines, and ice edges. It winters further south on maritime coasts, freshwater lakes, agricultural fields, urban areas, and garbage dumps.

RANGE MAP

■ Breeding
  Migration
■ Nonbreeding
■ Year-round

Glaucous Gulls are the second biggest gull in the world. Breeding adults are pearly gray and snow white with white wingtips. They often nest near colonies of other birds, where they hunt chicks and eat eggs. Pairs form strong bonds lasting many years, unlike in some gull species.

BREEDING ADULTS

BREEDING ADULT

JUVENILE

NONBREEDING ADULTS

RANGE MAP

Breeding
Migration
Nonbreeding
Year-round

SIZE & SHAPE The Caspian Tern is the largest tern in the world. It has a large bill with a thick base, and a shallow fork in the tail. The large head can look smoothly rounded, squared off, or slightly crested.

COLOR PATTERN Caspian Terns have a black cap, a white body, and a brilliant coral-red bill with a dark band near the tip. Nonbreeding adults and immatures have a grayish crown and forehead. Juveniles have black edging to back feathers.

BEHAVIOR Caspian Terns fly over water with the bill pointing down, then plunge into the water to catch fish.

HABITAT Caspian Terns tend to breed in salt marshes and a range of islands, including barrier, dredge-spoil, and freshwater lake and river islands. In migration and winter, they are found along coastlines, large rivers, and lakes. They roost on islands and isolated spits.

Caspian Tern aggressively defends its breeding colony. It will pursue, attack, and chase predatory and can cause bloody wounds on the heads of people who invade the colony. The entire colony will flight, however, when a Bald Eagle flies overhead, exposing the chicks to predation from gulls.

BREEDING ADULT

BREEDING ADULT

NONBREEDING ADULT / JUVENILE

JUVENILE

SIZE & SHAPE The Black Tern is a small and delicately built waterbird with a thin, pointed bill; long, pointed wings; a shallowly forked tail; and short legs. It is larger than a Least Tern, and smaller than a Common Tern.

COLOR PATTERN Adults in breeding plumage are dark gray above with black heads and black underparts. Underwings and undertail coverts are pale. Nonbreeding adults are gray above, whitish below, with a dusky crown, ear patch, and mark at the side of the breast. Juveniles are similar to nonbreeding adults but with a brown scaled pattern to the upperparts.

BEHAVIOR Black Terns forage by flying slowly and either dipping to the water's surface to pick up small fish or insects, or by catching insects on the wing. They breed in colonies in freshwater lakes, making nests on floating vegetation.

HABITAT Black Terns nest in freshwater marshes and bogs and winter in coastal lagoons, marshes, and open ocean waters. Migrants may stop over in almost any type of wetland.

RANGE MAP

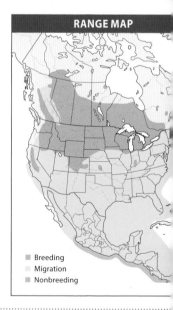

■ Breeding
■ Migration
■ Nonbreeding

An outlier in a world of white seabirds, breeding **Black Terns** are a handsome mix of charcoal gray and black. Their delicate form and neatly pointed wings provide tremendous agility as these birds flutter and swoop to pluck fish from the water's surface or veer to catch flying insects, much as a swallow does.

BREEDING ADULT

BREEDING ADULT

JUVENILE

NONBREEDING ADULT

RANGE MAP

Breeding
Migration
Nonbreeding
Year-round

SIZE & SHAPE The Forster's Tern is a slender, long-tailed, long-winged waterbird with a long, pointed bill and short legs. When perched, the long tail streamers extend past the end of the wings. It is larger than a Black Tern.

COLOR PATTERN Breeding adults are gray above and white below, with a black cap and orange bill with a black tip. They have silvery gray wingtips and orange legs. Nonbreeding adults have a dark bill, white crown, and blackish eye patch. Juvenile birds are a mottled rusty brown, white, and gray with a black eye patch.

BEHAVIOR Forster's Terns forage by flying slowly over the water to scan for fish, then diving to capture prey. Breeding adults perform spiraling courtship flights and also parade through the colony in tandem with raised bills.

HABITAT Forster's Terns breed in marshes, usually in areas with extensive open water and some floating vegetation. They winter in oceans, bays, and estuaries, close to the coast. Some winter inland near the Gulf of Mexico.

ing slender, silvery wings and an elegantly forked tail, **Forster's Terns** cruise above the shallow waters rshes and coastlines. These medium-sized white terns are often confused with the similar Common but Forster's Terns have a longer tail and, in nonbreeding plumage, a distinctive black eye patch.

BREEDING ADULT

BREEDING ADULT

JUVENILE

NONBREEDING ADULT

SIZE & SHAPE The Red-throated Loon is a small loon with a long, sinuous neck, a thin, daggerlike bill, and long, narrow, pointed wings. The legs are set far back on the body, and the feet trail behind the tail in flight. The bill is usually pointed slightly upward.

COLOR PATTERN Breeding adults are dark grayish brown above, pale below, with a pale gray neck and rusty throat patch. The back of the neck is accented with thin black-and-white stripes that extend down the sides of breast. Nonbreeding adults are blackish above and white below, with a mostly white face.

BEHAVIOR Red-throated Loons forage by scanning beneath the water's surface, dipping the head, then diving to pursue fish. They also locate prey in flight, often in large flocks that descend when schools of fish are detected.

HABITAT Red-throated Loons breed in the Arctic in tundra and taiga lakes and along marine coasts. They use large lakes and bays during migration, and coastal ocean waters during winter.

RANGE MAP

■ Breeding
■ Breeding (scarce)
■ Migration
■ Nonbreeding

Red-throated Loons are among the finest fish hunters in North America. They are smaller and more sle than other loons, with a smaller bill tilted slightly upward. Like other loons, they dive for fish from the surface, but they also hunt from the air. They fly swiftly and are able to stall, pivot, and drop with precisi

BREEDING ADULT

NONBREEDING ADULT

NONBREEDING ADULT / IMMATURE

JUVENILE

RANGE MAP

reeding
ligration
lonbreeding

SIZE & SHAPE Common Loons are large, diving waterbirds with rounded heads and daggerlike bills. They have long bodies and short tails that are usually not visible. In flight, they stretch out, with a long, flat body and long neck and bill. Their feet stick out beyond the tail (unlike ducks and cormorants), looking like wedges.

COLOR PATTERN In summer, adults have a black head and bill, a black-and-white spotted back, and a white breast. From September to March, adults are plain gray on the back and head with a white throat. The bill also fades to gray. Juveniles look similar, but with more pronounced scalloping on the back.

BEHAVIOR Common Loons are stealthy divers, submerging without a splash to catch fish. Pairs and groups often call to each other at night. In flight, notice their shallow wingbeats and unwavering, straight flight path.

HABITAT Common Loons breed on quiet, remote freshwater lakes of the northern U.S. and Canada, and they are sensitive to human disturbance. In winter and during migration, look for them on lakes, rivers, estuaries, and coastlines.

erie calls of **Common Loons** echo across the clear lakes of the northern wilderness. In winter, look for along seashores and on inland reservoirs and lakes. These powerful, agile divers catch small fish in water chases. They are less suited to land and typically come ashore only to nest.

BREEDING ADULT

BREEDING ADULTS

JUVENILE

NONBREEDING ADULT

SIZE & SHAPE The Brandt's Cormorant is a large waterbird with an oval body and slender neck. Its medium-sized blunt bill is hooked at the tip. It has a medium-length tail, short legs, and large webbed feet.

COLOR PATTERN Adults in breeding plumage are mostly blackish, with blue eyes, vivid-blue throat skin surrounded by a buffy band, and whiskery white feathers on the head, neck, and shoulders. Nonbreeding adults are uniformly black. Juveniles are brownish overall, with the throat skin surrounded by buffy plumage.

BEHAVIOR Brandt's Cormorants forage by diving and swimming underwater to catch prey by driving it toward the surface, then grasping it with the bill. They also seize prey from the bottom or from undersea structures. They often forage in large flocks of mixed species.

HABITAT Look for Brandt's Cormorants at inshore coastal waters, especially areas with kelp beds. They are also found at large bays, estuaries, or coastal lagoons. Breeding colonies prefer gentle slopes on the windward side of islands, or steep cliffs with ledges.

RANGE MAP

■ Nonbreeding
■ Year-round

The largest cormorant on the Pacific Coast, **Brandt's Cormorant** is an expert diver that can swim deeper than 200 feet in pursuit of fish and shellfish. In addition to standard cormorant black, Brandt's sports a cobalt-blue throat patch and eyes during breeding season, with wispy white feathers on the head.

NONBREEDING ADULT

BREEDING ADULT

VENILES (L) AND NONBREEDING ADULT (R)

JUVENILE

RANGE MAP

Breeding
Migration
Nonbreeding
Year-round

SIZE & SHAPE The Double-crested Cormorant is a large waterbird with a relatively short tail and a small head on a long, kinked neck. The thin, hooked bill is roughly the length of its head. Its heavy body sits low in the water, and it can be mistaken for a loon.

COLOR PATTERN Adults are brownish black with a small patch of yellow-orange skin on the face. Immatures are browner overall, palest on the neck and breast. Breeding adults in the West develop a small double crest of stringy white feathers behind the eyes.

BEHAVIOR Double-crested Cormorants float low in the water and dive to catch small fish. After fishing, they stand on docks, rocks, and tree limbs with wings spread open to dry. In flight, they often travel in V-formation flocks.

HABITAT Double-crested Cormorants are the most widespread cormorants in North America, and they are seen in fresh water. They breed on coastlines and along large inland lakes. They form colonies of stick nests built high in trees on islands or in patches of flooded timber.

prehistoric-looking **Double-crested Cormorant** is a common sight around fresh and salt waters across erate North America—attracting the most attention when standing on docks, rocky islands, and channel ers, wings spread to dry. These solid, heavy-boned birds are experts at diving to catch small fish.

ADULTS / IMMATURES

BREEDING ADULTS

NONBREEDING ADULTS

NONBREEDING ADULT

SIZE & SHAPE The American White Pelican is a huge waterbird with very broad wings, a long neck, and a massive bill that gives the head a unique, long shape. They have thick bodies, short legs, and short, square tails. A yellow plate forms on the upper bill of breeding adults. The large throat pouch, typical of pelicans, isn't usually obvious.

COLOR PATTERN Adults are white with black feathers visible when the wings are spread. A patch of chest feathers can turn yellow in spring. The bill and legs are yellow orange. Immatures are mostly white, but the head, neck, and back are washed with dusky brown and the bill is dull pink.

BEHAVIOR American White Pelicans feed from the water's surface, dipping their beaks in to catch prey. They often upend but do not plunge-dive. They are among the heaviest flying birds in the world and often travel long distances in large flocks.

HABITAT American White Pelicans typically breed on islands in shallow wetlands in the interior of the continent. They spend winters mainly on coastal waters, bays, and estuaries, or a little distance inland.

RANGE MAP

- Breeding
- Migration
- Nonbreeding
- Year-round

One of the largest North American birds, the **American White Pelican** is majestic in the air, soaring with incredible steadiness. On the water, they dip their pouched bills to scoop up fish, or tip-up like dabbling ducks. Sometimes, groups of pelicans work together to herd fish into the shallows for easy feeding.

BREEDING ADULT

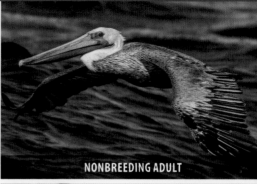

NONBREEDING ADULT

JUVENILE

JUVENILES

RANGE MAP

Breeding
Migration
Year-round
Year-round (scarce)

SIZE & SHAPE Brown Pelicans are huge, stocky seabirds. They have thin necks and very long bills with a stretchy throat pouch used for capturing fish. Their wings are long and broad, often noticeably bowed when the birds are gliding.

COLOR PATTERN Adults are gray brown with pale, yellowish heads and white necks. In breeding plumage, the back and sides of the neck turn a rich, dark reddish brown. Immatures are gray brown above with a pale whitish belly and breast.

BEHAVIOR Brown Pelicans plunge into the water, stunning small fish with the impact of their bodies and scooping them up in their throat pouches. When not feeding, they stand on fishing docks, jetties, and beaches or cruise the shoreline.

HABITAT Brown Pelicans live along seacoasts and are rarely seen inland. An exception is at Salton Sea in California, where they are found in large numbers. They nest in colonies, often on isolated islands free of land predators.

drons of **Brown Pelicans** glide above the surf along coasts and feed by plunge-diving from high up, the force of impact to stun small fish before scooping them up. They are fairly common today—an ple of a species' recovery from pesticide pollution that once placed them at the brink of extinction.

ADULT

ADULT

IMMATURE

JUVENILE

SIZE & SHAPE This largest of North American herons has long legs, a sinuous neck, and a thick, daggerlike bill. Head, chest, and wing plumes give a shaggy appearance. In flight, the Great Blue Heron curls its neck into a tight "S" shape; its wings are broad and rounded, and its legs trail well beyond the tail.

COLOR PATTERN Great Blue Herons appear blue gray from a distance, with a wide black stripe over the eye. In flight, the upper side of the wing is two-toned: pale on the forewing and darker on the flight feathers.

BEHAVIOR Hunting Great Blue Herons wade slowly or stand statuelike, stalking prey in shallow water or open fields. Their very slow wingbeats, tucked-in neck, and trailing legs create an unmistakable silhouette in flight.

HABITAT Look for Great Blue Herons in saltwater and freshwater habitats, from seashores, marshes, sloughs, riverbanks, and lakes to backyard goldfish ponds. They also forage in grasslands and agricultural fields.

RANGE MAP

■ Breeding
■ Nonbreeding
■ Year-round

Whether poised at a river bend or cruising the coastline with slow, deep wingbeats, the **Great Blue Heron** is a majestic sight. It will often stand motionless as it scans for prey or wades belly deep with long, delibe steps. This heron may move slowly, but it can strike like lightning to grab a fish or snap up a gopher.

NONBREEDING ADULT / IMMATURE

BREEDING ADULT

NONBREEDING ADULT / IMMATURE

NONBREEDING ADULT / IMMATURE

RANGE MAP

Breeding
Migration
Nonbreeding
Year-round

SIZE & SHAPE Great Egrets are tall, long-legged wading birds with an S-curved neck and a daggerlike bill. In flight, the long neck is tucked in, and the legs extend far beyond the tip of the short tail. During breeding season, long feathery plumes, called aigrettes, grow from its back. They are held up during courtship displays.

COLOR PATTERN Every feather on a Great Egret is white. The bill is solid yellowish orange, and the legs and feet are entirely black. During courtship, the skin patch between the bill and eyes brightens to lime green.

BEHAVIOR You can find Great Egrets wading in shallow water hunting for food. They typically stand still and watch for prey to pass by, and then, with startling speed, strike with a jab of the long neck and bill.

HABITAT Great Egrets live in freshwater, brackish, and marine wetlands. During the breeding season, they are found in nesting colonies on lakes, ponds, marshes, estuaries, impoundments, and islands.

ristinely white **Great Egret** gets even more dressed up for the breeding season. A patch of skin on its turns neon green, and long plumes grow from its back. Called aigrettes, those plumes were the bane rets in the late 19th century, when such adornments were prized for ladies' hats.

ADULT

ADULT

JUVENILE

ADULT

SIZE & SHAPE Compared with most herons, Green Herons are short and stocky, with relatively short legs and thick necks that are often drawn up against their bodies. They have broad, rounded wings and a long, daggerlike bill. They sometimes raise their crown feathers into a short crest. They are crow-sized—small for a heron.

COLOR PATTERN From a distance, Green Herons look all dark. Up close, they are deep green on the back with a rich chestnut breast and neck. The wings are dark gray. Juveniles are browner, with pale streaking on the neck and wing spots.

BEHAVIOR Green Herons stand very still at the water's edge as they hunt for food, typically on solid ground or vegetation, seldom wading. In flight, they can look ungainly, often partially uncrooking their necks.

HABITAT Green Herons live near wooded ponds, marshes, rivers, reservoirs, and estuaries. They may nest in dry woods and orchards as long as there is water nearby for foraging.

RANGE MAP

Breeding
Migration
Nonbreeding
Year-round

The dark, stocky **Green Heron** often hides behind leaves at the water's edge, patiently crouching on slender yellow legs to surprise fish with a snatch of their daggerlike bill. They sometimes lure in fish using small items such as twigs or insects as bait.

ADULT

ADULT

IMMATURE (FIRST SUMMER)

JUVENILE

RANGE MAP

Breeding
Migration
Nonbreeding
Year-round

SIZE & SHAPE Black-crowned Night-Herons are medium-sized herons with rather squat, thick proportions. They have thick necks, large, flat heads, and heavy, pointed bills. The legs are short, and the wings are broad and rounded.

COLOR PATTERN Adults are light-gray birds with a neatly defined black back and black crown. Immatures are brown with white spots on the wings and blurry streaks on the underparts. Adults have black bills; immatures have yellow-and-black bills. Juveniles are brown and streaky overall.

BEHAVIOR These herons often spend their days perched on tree limbs or concealed among foliage. They forage in the evening and at night, in water, on mudflats, and on land. In flight, they fold their head back against their shoulders.

HABITAT These social birds tend to roost and nest in groups, although they typically forage on their own. Look for them in most wetland habitats across North America, including estuaries, marshes, streams, lakes, and reservoirs.

k-crowned Night-Herons are most active at night or at dusk. Look for their ghostly forms flapping out daytime roosts to forage in wetlands. These social birds breed in colonies of stick nests usually built water. The most widespread heron in the world, it lives in fresh, salt, and brackish wetlands.

BREEDING ADULT

NONBREEDING ADULT

NONBREEDING ADULT / IMMATURE

JUVENILE

SIZE & SHAPE The White-faced Ibis is a large wading bird with a football-shaped body, long legs, and a long, curved bill. It flies with its long neck outstretched and head slightly drooping.

COLOR PATTERN The breeding adult White-faced Ibis is maroon overall with reddish legs and a bare patch of pink skin in front of the eye which is bordered in white. In good light, wings are metallic green and bronze. Nonbreeding and immature birds look like adults but lack the bare skin patch and the white border around the eye. Juveniles have paler cheek patches and white feathers on the neck. Adults have red eyes.

BEHAVIOR Pairs of White-faced Ibises often preen each other during courtship, a behavior known as allopreening. Look for them perching in low trees and shrubs at the edge of wetlands.

HABITAT White-faced Ibises are found in freshwater and saltwater marshes, wetlands, and flooded fields. They often feed in large flocks.

RANGE MAP

- Breeding
- Breeding (scarce)
- Migration
- Nonbreeding
- Year-round

The **White-faced Ibis** looks quite similar to its cousin, the Glossy Ibis. Often found in mixed flocks, immature birds are nearly indistinguishable but may be paler underneath and have more green iridescence on the back and wings. Breeding birds have more white on the face than the Glossy Ibis.

ADULT

ADULT AND IMMATURES (FIRST YEAR)

IMMATURE

ADULT

RANGE MAP

Breeding
Year-round

SIZE & SHAPE Turkey Vultures are large, dark birds with long, broad wings. Bigger than other raptors, except eagles and condors, Turkey Vultures hold their wings slightly raised when soaring, making a V-shape when seen head-on.

COLOR PATTERN Turkey Vultures appear black from a distance but up close are dark brown with a featherless head and pale bill. While most of the body and forewings are dark, the undersides of the flight feathers and wingtips are paler. Adults' heads are red; juveniles' are grayish and become red over time.

BEHAVIOR Turkey Vultures are majestic but unsteady soarers. Their teetering flight with deep but few wingbeats is characteristic. Look for them gliding relatively low to the ground, sniffing for carrion, or riding thermals up to higher vantage points.

HABITAT Turkey Vultures are common around open areas such as roadsides, suburbs, farm fields, countryside, and food sources such as landfills, trash heaps, and construction sites.

u see a large raptor soaring in wobbly circles with its wings raised in a V, it's likely **Turkey Vulture**. e birds ride thermals in the sky and use their keen sense of smell to find fresh carcasses. A consummate nger, it cleans up the countryside one bite at a time, never mussing a feather on its bald head.

ADULT

ADULT

JUVENILE

ADULT

SIZE & SHAPE Ospreys are very large, distinctively shaped hawks. Despite their size, their bodies are slender, with long, narrow wings and long legs. In flight, crooked wings combine with the body to make a distinctive M shape.

COLOR PATTERN Ospreys are brown above and white below, and overall, they are whiter than most raptors. From below, wings are mostly white with darker flight feathers and a prominent dark patch at the wrists. The head is white with a broad brown stripe through the eye. Juveniles have white spots on the back and buffy shading on the breast.

BEHAVIOR Ospreys search for fish by flying on steady wingbeats and bowed wings or circling high in the sky over relatively shallow water. They often hover briefly before diving, feet first, to grab a fish.

HABITAT Look for Ospreys around nearly any body of water: saltmarshes, rivers, ponds, reservoirs, estuaries, and even coral reefs.

RANGE MAP

Breeding
Migration
Winter
Year-round

Novel among North American raptors for its diet of live fish and ability to dive into water to catch them, **Ospreys** are common sights soaring over shorelines, patrolling waterways, and standing on their huge stick nests, white heads gleaming. Their numbers have rebounded since the ban on the pesticide DDT.

ADULT

ADULT

IMMATURE (FIRST YEAR)

IMMATURE (SECOND YEAR)

RANGE MAP

Breeding
Breeding (scarce)
Migration
Nonbreeding
Nonbreeding (scarce)
Year-round

SIZE & SHAPE Golden Eagles are some of the largest birds in North America. Their wings are broad like a Red-tailed Hawk's, but longer. At a distance, the head is relatively small, and the tail is long, projecting farther behind than the head sticks out in front. The wings are held up slightly when soaring and gliding, recalling Turkey Vultures.

COLOR PATTERN Adult Golden Eagles are dark brown with a golden sheen on the back of the head and neck. For their first several years of life, young birds have neatly defined white patches at the base of the tail and in the wings.

BEHAVIOR Found alone or in pairs, Golden Eagles soar with wings lifted into a slight V-shape, with wingtips spread. They capture prey on or near the ground, locating it by soaring, flying low over the ground, or hunting from a perch.

HABITAT Golden Eagles favor open country around mountains, hills, and cliffs. Their habitats range from the Arctic to deserts, including tundra, shrublands, grasslands, coniferous forests, farmland, and areas along rivers and streams.

Golden Eagle is one of the largest and nimblest raptors in North America. Look for them in the West, soaring in pursuit of small mammals. Sometimes seen attacking or fighting off coyotes or bears in defense of prey and young, the Golden Eagle inspires both reverence and fear. It is the national bird of Mexico.

ADULT MALE

ADULT FEMALE

JUVENILE MALE

JUVENILE FEMALE

SIZE & SHAPE Northern Harriers are slender, medium-sized raptors with long, broad wings and a long, rounded tail. They have a flat, owl-like face and a small, sharply hooked bill. They often fly with their wings held in a V-shape.

COLOR PATTERN Males are gray above and whitish below with black wingtips, a dark edge to the wing, and a black-banded tail. Females and immatures are brown, with black bands on the tail. For both sexes, a white rump patch is obvious in flight.

BEHAVIOR Northern Harriers fly low over the ground when hunting, weaving back and forth over fields and marshes as they watch and listen for small animals. They eat on the ground, and they perch on low posts or trees. On the breeding grounds, males perform elaborate flying barrel rolls to court females.

HABITAT Northern Harriers are found in open areas such as grasslands, marshes, and fields. They like undisturbed tracts with low, thick vegetation.

RANGE MAP

■ Breeding
■ Migration
■ Nonbreeding
■ Year-round

The **Northern Harrier** is distinctive from a distance: a slim, long-tailed hawk gliding low over a marsh grassland, wings held in a V-shape. Its owlish face helps it hear mice and voles beneath the vegetation Each male may mate with several females. These unusual raptors are found across much of North Ame

ADULT

ADULT

JUVENILE

JUVENILE

RANGE MAP

Breeding
Nonbreeding
Year-round

SIZE & SHAPE This is a medium-sized hawk with a slender body, vertical stance, rounded wingtips, and very long tail. In Cooper's Hawks, the head often appears large and square-shaped, the shoulders are broad, and the tail tip rounded. Females are significantly larger than males.

COLOR PATTERN Adults are steely blue-gray above with warm reddish bars on the breast, a pale nape that contrasts with the dark cap, and thick, dark bands on the otherwise pale gray tail. Juveniles are brown above and crisply streaked with brown on the upper breast, giving them a somewhat hooded look compared with young Sharp-shinned Hawks' more diffuse streaking.

BEHAVIOR Cooper's Hawks fly with a flap-flap-glide pattern typical of the genus *Accipiter*. Even when crossing large open areas, they rarely flap continuously. They can also thread their way through tree branches at top speed.

HABITAT Cooper's Hawks are forest and woodland birds, but leafy suburbs are nearly as good. They are a regular sight in parks, quiet neighborhoods, over fields, and at backyard feeders.

oper's Hawks are common woodland hawks and skillful fliers that tear through cluttered tree canopies rsuit of other birds. Similar to their smaller lookalike, the Sharp-shinned Hawk, Cooper's Hawks can be nted guests at bird feeders, looking for an easy meal (but not one of sunflower seeds).

ADULT

IMMATURE

JUVENILE

JUVENILE

SIZE & SHAPE The Bald Eagle dwarfs most other raptors. It has a heavy body, large head, and long, hooked bill. In flight, a Bald Eagle holds its broad wings flat like a board.

COLOR PATTERN Adults have white heads and tails with dark brown bodies and wings. Legs and bills are bright yellow. Immature birds have dark heads and tails and are mottled in white in varying amounts before they reach maturity at five years of age.

BEHAVIOR You'll find Bald Eagles soaring high in the sky, flapping low over treetops with slow wingbeats, perched in trees, or on the ground. They scavenge many meals by harassing other birds or by eating carrion or garbage. They eat mainly fish but also hunt mammals, gulls, and waterfowl.

HABITAT Look for Bald Eagles near lakes, reservoirs, rivers, marshes, and coasts. To see large Bald Eagle congregations, check out wildlife refuges or large bodies of water in winter over much of the continent, or fish processing plants and dumpsters year-round in the Pacific Northwest.

RANGE MAP

- Breeding
- Migration
- Nonbreeding
- Year-round

The **Bald Eagle** has been the U.S. national emblem since 1782 and a spiritual symbol for native people far longer. Look for these regal birds soaring in solitude, chasing other birds for their food, or gathering droves in winter. Once endangered by hunting and pesticides, Bald Eagles now thrive under protection

ADULT

ADULT

JUVENILE

JUVENILE

RANGE MAP

Breeding
Nonbreeding
Year-round

SIZE & SHAPE Red-shouldered Hawks are medium sized, with broad, rounded wings and medium-length tails that they fan when soaring. They glide or soar with their wingtips pushed slightly forward, giving them a distinctive "reaching" posture.

COLOR PATTERN Adults are colorful hawks with dark-and-white checkered wings and warm reddish barring on the breast. The tail is black with narrow white bands. Immatures are brown above and white, streaked with brown, below. All ages show narrow, pale crescents near the wingtips in flight.

BEHAVIOR Red-shouldered Hawks soar over forests or perch on tree branches or utility wires. Their whistled *kee-rah* is a distinctive sound of the forest. They hunt small mammals, amphibians, and reptiles from perches or in flight.

HABITAT Look for Red-shouldered Hawks in broadleaf woodlands, often near rivers and swamps. During migration, they often move high overhead along ridges or coastlines. They may be abundant at some hawk-watching overlooks.

her wheeling over a swamp forest or whistling from a riverine park, a **Red-shouldered Hawk** is a sign woods and water. It's one of our most distinctively marked common hawks, with barred, reddish underparts and a strongly banded tail. They hunt prey ranging from mice to frogs and snakes.

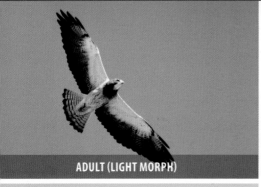

ADULT (LIGHT MORPH)

ADULT (DARK MORPH)

JUVENILE (LIGHT MORPH)

JUVENILE (DARK MORPH)

SIZE & SHAPE Swainson's Hawks are large with fairly narrow wings and short tails. However, they are less hefty than many other *Buteo* hawks. They are slimmer, have longer wings, and hold their wings in a shallow V when soaring.

COLOR PATTERN Though quite variable, most Swainson's Hawks are light-bellied birds with a dark or reddish brown chest and brown or gray upperparts. Underwings have distinct white wing linings that contrast strongly with blackish flight feathers. Most males have gray heads; females tend to have brown heads. Dark morphs are dark brown and rusty below.

BEHAVIOR Swainson's Hawks are social raptors, nearly always found in groups outside the breeding season. Look for them soaring with other migrating birds, foraging for grasshoppers, or chasing swarms of dragonflies on winter grounds.

HABITAT These hawks summer in open areas of the Great Plains and further west. They nest in grasslands, but also use sage flats and even swaths of agriculture intermixed with native habitat. Nests are placed in trees, often in the only tree visible for miles.

RANGE MAP

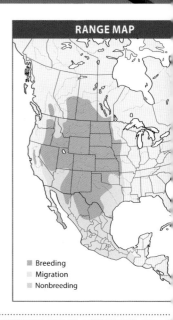

■ Breeding
■ Migration
■ Nonbreeding

Swainson's Hawks soar on narrow wings or perch on fence posts and irrigation spouts. They hunt rod in flight or run after insects on the ground. In fall, they take off for Argentine wintering grounds—one the longest migrations of any American raptor—forming flocks of hundreds or thousands as they trav

ADULT (LIGHT MORPH)

ADULT (INTERMEDIATE MORPH)

JUVENILE (LIGHT MORPH)

JUVENILE (LIGHT MORPH)

RANGE MAP

reeding
ear-round

SIZE & SHAPE Red-tailed Hawks are fairly large and have proportions typical of the genus *Buteo*: very broad, rounded wings and a short, wide tail. Females seen from a distance might fool you into thinking you're seeing an eagle—until an actual eagle comes along.

COLOR PATTERN Red-tailed Hawks have extremely variable plumage, and some of this variation is regional. Most are rich brown above and pale below with a streaked belly. The tail is usually pale below and cinnamon red above, though in young birds it's brown and banded. Dark-morph and intermediate-morph birds are variably dark brown and rusty below.

BEHAVIOR Red-tailed Hawks soar in wide circles high over a field. In high winds, they may hover without flapping, eyes fixed on the ground. Unlike a falcon's stoop, they attack in a slow, controlled dive with legs outstretched.

HABITAT The Red-tailed Hawk is a bird of open country. Look for it along fields and perched on telephone poles, fenceposts, or trees standing alone or along edges of fields.

bly the most common hawk in North America, the **Red-tailed Hawk** soars above open fields, turning s on its broad, rounded wings. Find it atop telephone poles, eyes fixed on the ground to catch prey ments, or simply waiting out cold weather before climbing a thermal updraft into the sky.

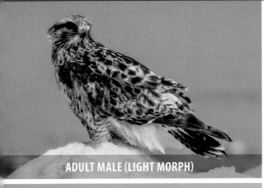

ADULT MALE (LIGHT MORPH)

ADULT FEMALE (LIGHT MORPH)

IMMATURE (LIGHT MORPH)

ADULT FEMALE (DARK MORPH)

SIZE & SHAPE Rough-legged Hawks are fairly large with broad wings. Proportionately, their wings are longer and narrower and their tails longer than in most members of the genus *Buteo*. Wingtips are swept back slightly from the wrist, giving a hint of an M-shape to wings in flight. Bill is fairly small.

COLOR PATTERN The Rough-legged Hawk is boldly patterned in brown and white. The tail is dark at the tip and pale at the base. Light morphs have pale underwings with dark patches at the bend of the wing. Dark morphs are mostly dark brown with pale trailing edges to the underwing.

BEHAVIOR When hunting, these hawks often face into the wind and hover, scanning the ground below for small mammal prey. They perch on fence posts and utility poles, and sometimes on slender branches at the very tops of trees.

HABITAT Rough-legged Hawks breed in the Arctic. In winter, they migrate to open habitats such as fields, prairies, deserts, and airports in the U.S. and southern Canada.

RANGE MAP

■ Breeding
■ Migration
■ Nonbreeding

The **Rough-legged Hawk** spends the summer capturing lemmings on the Arctic tundra, tending a cli[...] nest under a sun that never sets. In winter, look for this large, open-country hawk in southern Canada [...] the U.S. perched on a pole or hovering over a marsh or pasture while it hunts small rodents.

ADULT

ADULT

ADULT

JUVENILE

RANGE MAP

Year-round

SIZE & SHAPE Western Screech-Owls are small owls with stocky bodies. They have somewhat square heads, almost no neck, and conspicuous ear tufts. The tail is short.

COLOR PATTERN Western Screech-Owls are superbly camouflaged with a base color that can be grayish, brownish, or reddish brown. The upperparts are flecked with white; the breast and belly are pale with dark, spidery streaks. The face is pale, outlined with dark arcs. The eyes are yellow.

BEHAVIOR As nocturnal hunters, Western Screech-Owls are far more often heard than seen. They spend days either in a roost hole or looking out from the entrance, where they are sometimes found by noisy groups of mobbing songbirds.

HABITAT Western Screech-Owls live in forests, particularly among broadleaf trees, at elevations up to about 6,000 feet. They are fairly tolerant of people and may be found in suburbs or parks, or attracted to wooded backyards with a nest box.

n for the **Western Screech-Owl's** series of high toots accelerating through the night. These compact hunt in woods and deserts of western North America, where their diet includes everything from s and crayfish to rats and bats. They nest in tree cavities and will readily take to backyard nest boxes.

ADULT

ADULT

JUVENILES

ADULT

SIZE & SHAPE Great Horned Owls are large and thick-bodied with two prominent feathered tufts on the head. The wings are broad and rounded. In flight, the rounded face and short bill combine to create a blunt-headed appearance.

COLOR PATTERN Great Horned Owls are mottled grayish brown, with reddish brown faces and a neat white patch on the throat. Their overall color tone varies regionally from sooty to pale. The color of the facial disc also varies regionally from grayish to cinnamon.

BEHAVIOR You may see Great Horned Owls at dusk on fence posts or tree limbs at the edge of open areas, or flying across roads or fields with stiff, deep beats of their rounded wings. Their call is a stuttering series of mellow hoots.

HABITAT Look for this widespread owl in young woods interspersed with fields or other open areas. The broad range of habitats they use includes forests, swamps, desert, and tundra edges, as well as cities, suburbs, and parks.

RANGE MAP

■ Year-round
■ Year-round (scarce)

With long earlike tufts, yellow eyes, and deep hooting voice, the **Great Horned Owl** is the quintessential of storybooks. This powerful predator can take down birds and mammals larger than itself, but it also din daintier fare such as scorpions, mice, and frogs. It's one of the most common owls in North America.

ADULT

ADULT

JUVENILE

ADULTS

RANGE MAP

Breeding
Nonbreeding
Year-round

SIZE & SHAPE Burrowing Owls are small with long legs and short tails. The head is rounded and does not have ear tufts. It is about the same length/height as an American Robin but much bulkier.

COLOR PATTERN Adult Burrowing Owls are brown birds mottled with sand-colored pale spots on the upperparts. The breast is spotted, grading to dark brown bars on the belly. They have a bold white throat and eyebrows, and yellow eyes. Juveniles are unpatterned buffy below with a brown chest.

BEHAVIOR Burrowing Owls spend most of their time on the ground or low perches. They hunt close to the ground catching insects and small animals. When alarmed, they jerk their bodies quickly up and down. They are active during the day.

HABITAT Burrowing Owls live in open habitats with sparse vegetation such as prairies, pastures, desert or shrub-steppe, and airports. In parts of their range, they nest in the burrows of prairie dogs and ground squirrels.

are unmistakable, and that goes double for a long-legged owl that hunts on the ground during the Petite **Burrowing Owls** live underground in burrows they've dug themselves or taken over from a e dog or ground squirrel. Their numbers have declined sharply with human alteration of their habitat.

ADULT

ADULT

ADULT

JUVENILE

SIZE & SHAPE Barred Owls are large, stocky owls with rounded heads, no ear tufts, and medium-length, rounded tails.

COLOR PATTERN Barred Owls are mottled brown and white overall, with dark brown, almost black, eyes. The underparts are mostly marked with vertical brown bars on a white background, while the upper breast is crossed with horizontal brown bars. The wings and tail are barred brown and white.

BEHAVIOR Barred Owls are mostly nocturnal and roost quietly in forest trees during the day. At night they hunt small animals, especially rodents, and give an instantly recognizable *Who cooks for you?* call.

HABITAT Barred Owls live in large, mature forests made up of both broadleaf trees and conifers, often near water. They nest in tree cavities. In the Northwest, Barred Owls have moved into old-growth coniferous forest, where they compete with the threatened Spotted Owl.

RANGE MAP

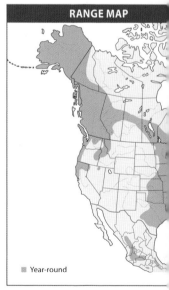

■ Year-round

The **Barred Owl's** hooting call, *Who cooks for you? Who cooks for you-all?*, is a classic sound of old forests and swamps. But this attractive owl, with soulful brown eyes and brown-and-white striped plumage, can pass completely unnoticed as it flies noiselessly through the dense canopy or snoozes on a tree limb.

ADULT

ADULT

ADULT

ADULT

RANGE MAP

Year-round
Nonbreeding (scarce)

SIZE & SHAPE Great Grays are one of our tallest owls; they have broad wings and a long tail. They are huge, big-headed owls with a large facial disk. They dwarf most other owls in size but not by weight; their bulk is mostly made of feathers. Females are larger than males.

COLOR PATTERN Great Gray Owls are silvery gray overall—patterned with white, gray, and brown streaking. Their yellow eyes shine through the gray-and-brown concentric circles of the facial disk. Two pale arcs form an "X" between the eyes. Their bill is yellow.

BEHAVIOR These owls generally do not call attention to themselves and avoid areas with people. They hunt at night and during the hours before dawn and dusk. They quietly fly low over meadows, watching and listening for small mammals.

HABITAT Great Gray Owls spend their time in dense coniferous pine and fir forests with small openings or meadows nearby. They also live in subarctic swampy coniferous forest dotted with bogs or other openings.

ine what it would be like if you could hear even the slightest noise and know exactly where the noise
coming from. Well, that is exactly what **Great Gray Owls** can do. Like the Barn Owl and Long-eared
they have asymmetrical ear openings that help them find prey by sound alone.

ADULT MALE

ADULT

ADULT FEMALE

ADULT FEMALE

SIZE & SHAPE Belted Kingfishers are stocky, large-headed birds with a shaggy crest on the top and back of the head and a straight, thick, pointed bill. Their legs are short and their tails are medium length and square-tipped.

COLOR PATTERN These ragged-crested birds are a powdery blue gray with white spotting on the wings and tail. Males have one blue band across the white breast, while females also have a broad rusty band on their bellies. Juveniles show irregular rusty spotting in the breast band.

BEHAVIOR Belted Kingfishers often perch alone along the edges of streams, lakes, and estuaries, searching for small fish. They fly quickly up and down rivers and shorelines giving loud rattling calls. They hunt by plunging directly from a perch, or by hovering over the water, bill downward, before diving after a fish they've spotted.

HABITAT Kingfishers live near streams, rivers, ponds, lakes, and estuaries. They spend winters in areas where the water doesn't freeze so they have continual access to their aquatic foods.

RANGE MAP

- Breeding
- Nonbreeding
- Year-round

With its top-heavy physique, energetic flight, and piercing, rattled call, the **Belted Kingfisher** seems to have an air of self-importance as it patrols up and down rivers and shorelines. The Belted Kingfisher is o of the few bird species in which the female is more brightly colored than the male.

ADULT MALE

ADULT MALE

ADULT FEMALE

JUVENILE

RANGE MAP

Breeding
Migration
Winter
Year-round

SIZE & SHAPE This fairly small woodpecker has a stout, straight bill, a smallish head, and a long, stiff tail. The wings are long. It may hold its crown feathers up to form a peak at the back of the head.

COLOR PATTERN Red-naped Sapsuckers are black and white overall with a red cap, nape, and throat, and a long white bar on the folded wing. A black stripe through the eye is bordered by white stripes. Female Red-naped Sapsuckers have a white patch on the chin; males have entirely red chins. Juveniles are duller and washed with dusky gray.

BEHAVIOR Sapsuckers often sit still for extended periods as they tend sap wells, clinging to a tree trunk and leaning against their tails. They drum on trees with a stuttering rhythm.

HABITAT Red-naped Sapsuckers breed in mountain forests, using willow, aspen, and conifers for sap wells. In winter, they use woodlands along streams, oak or pine-oak woodlands, and orchards.

naped Sapsuckers are industrious woodpeckers with a taste for sugar. They drill neat little rows of in aspen, birch, and willow to lap up the sugary sap that flows out. The presence of sap wells is a indication that they are around, but so are their harsh wailing cries and stuttered drumming.

ADULT

ADULT

JUVENILE

ADULT

SIZE & SHAPE The Red-breasted Sapsucker is a medium-sized woodpecker.

COLOR PATTERN Adult Red-breasted Sapsuckers have a vivid red head and breast and a white spot in front of the eye. A large vertical white patch is usually visible on the folded wing. Both sexes look alike. Juveniles are washed in brown with a darker back and a vertical white wing patch.

BEHAVIOR The Red-breasted Sapsucker forages for insects by gleaning, probing, prying, tapping, and flycatching. It drills a series of shallow holes in tree bark, then licks up the revealed sap.

HABITAT Red-breasted Sapsuckers breed primarily in coniferous forests of the northern Pacific Coast, but they also use broadleaf and riparian habitat, as well as orchards and power line cuts. They winter in a variety of forested habitats.

RANGE MAP

■ Breeding
■ Winter
■ Year-round

Red-breasted Sapsuckers seem to be generous forest neighbors. Hummingbirds of several species re on the Red-breasted Sapsucker for food by making use of their sap wells. In addition, their nest cavities provide nesting or roosting sites for Western Bluebirds and northern flying squirrels.

ADULT MALE

ADULT FEMALE

ADULT FEMALE

IMMATURE MALE

RANGE MAP

Year-round

SIZE & SHAPE Acorn Woodpeckers are medium-sized woodpeckers with straight, spikelike bills and stiff, wedge-shaped tails used for support as the birds cling to tree trunks.

COLOR PATTERN A clown-faced woodpecker with a black back, red cap, creamy white face, and black patch around the bill. Females have less red on the crown than males. In flight, they show three patches of white: one on each wing and one on the rump. Immature birds often have darker eyes.

BEHAVIOR Acorn Woodpeckers are unusual woodpeckers that live in large groups, hoard acorns, and breed cooperatively. Group members gather acorns by the hundreds and wedge them into holes they've made in a tree trunk or telephone pole. They give raucous, scratchy *waka-waka* calls frequently.

HABITAT These woodpeckers live in oak and mixed oak-conifer forests on slopes and mountains. Telephone poles and wood siding in urban areas also make for good granaries.

n Woodpeckers live in large groups, and their social lives are endlessly fascinating. Every year they store sands of acorns in specially made holes in trees, and a group member guards the hoard from thieves. y males and females also combine efforts to raise young in a single nest.

ADULT MALE (PACIFIC SLOPE)

ADULT MALE (INTERIOR WEST)

ADULT FEMALE (PACIFIC SLOPE)

JUVENILE (PACIFIC SLOPE)

SIZE & SHAPE The tiny, sparrow-sized Downy Woodpecker has a straight, chisel-like bill, blocky head, wide shoulders, and straight-backed posture as it leans away from tree limbs braced by its tail feathers. The bill is short for a woodpecker.

COLOR PATTERN Downy Woodpeckers have black upperparts checked with white on the wings, the head is boldly striped, and the back has a broad white stripe down the center. The white outer tail feathers are barred with black. Males have a small red patch on the head; it's on the nape in adults and on the crown in juveniles. Birds near the Pacific Coast are dingy brownish gray below and have little white in the wing. In the interior West, they are whiter below and have more white spotting in the wing.

BEHAVIOR Downy Woodpeckers hitch around tree trunks and even small weed stalks, moving more acrobatically than larger woodpeckers. In spring and summer, they are noisy, making shrill whinnying calls and drumming on trees.

HABITAT You'll find Downy Woodpeckers in open woodlands, particularly among broadleaf trees, and brushy or weedy edges. They're also at home in orchards, city parks, backyards, and vacant lots.

RANGE MAP

■ Year-round

This active little black-and-white woodpecker, the **Downy Woodpecker**, is a familiar sight. An acrobati[c] forager, it's at home on tiny branches or balancing on seed balls and suet feeders. Downies and their la[rge] lookalike, the Hairy Woodpecker, are one of the first ID challenges for beginner birdwatchers.

ADULT MALE (INTERIOR WEST)

ADULT FEMALE (INTERIOR WEST)

ADULT MALE (PACIFIC SLOPE)

ADULT FEMALE (PACIFIC SLOPE)

RANGE MAP

ear-round

SIZE & SHAPE The Hairy Woodpecker is a medium-sized woodpecker with a fairly square head, a long, straight, chisel-like bill, and stiff, long tail feathers it braces against tree trunks. The bill is nearly the same length as the head.

COLOR PATTERN Hairy Woodpeckers have mostly black wings. The white outer tail feathers lack black barring. The head has two white stripes, and in males, a red spot, which is on the nape in adults and on the crown in juveniles. The back and underparts range from gleaming white in interior Western birds to dingy brownish gray in birds near the Pacific Coast.

BEHAVIOR Hairy Woodpeckers hitch up tree trunks and along main branches. They sometimes feed at the bases of trees, along fallen logs, and, rarely, on the ground. They have the slowly undulating flight pattern of woodpeckers.

HABITAT You can find Hairy Woodpeckers in mature forests, woodlots, suburbs, parks, and cemeteries, as well as forest edges, open woodlands of oak and pine, recently burned forests, and stands infested by bark beetles.

rger of two lookalikes, **Hairy Woodpeckers** are powerful, medium-sized birds that forage along trunks ranches of large trees. They have a much longer bill than the Downy Woodpecker's smaller thornlike bill, ave a soldierly look, with an erect, straight-backed posture on tree trunks and cleanly striped heads.

ADULT MALE

ADULT MALE

ADULT FEMALE

JUVENILE

SIZE & SHAPE The White-headed Woodpecker is a medium-sized woodpecker with a trim body, a short, sharp bill, rather long wings, and long tail.

COLOR PATTERN White-headed Woodpeckers are black with a mostly white head and white bases to the outer primary flight feathers. Adult males have a bright red patch on the back of the head. Juveniles have a red patch on the middle of the crown.

BEHAVIOR White-headed Woodpeckers forage by clinging to pine cones and prying out or hammering out seeds, and by flaking bark and probing pine needle clusters for insects, especially during the breeding season. They will also dig rows of shallow holes in trees ("sapwells") in order to eat sap.

HABITAT White-headed Woodpeckers are found in montane forests dominated by pines and are most associated with old-growth ponderosa pine and sugar pine forests. They also often use recently burned areas.

RANGE MAP

■ Year-round

The **White-headed Woodpecker** is an unusual woodpecker of the montane pine forests of the far We is the only North American bird that has a white head and a black body. Both male and female incubat eggs, with the male doing all the nighttime work.

ADULT MALE (L) AND IMMATURES

ADULT FEMALE

ADULT

ADULT MALE

RANGE MAP

ear-round
ear-round (scarce)

SIZE & SHAPE The Pileated Woodpecker is a very large woodpecker with a long neck and a triangular crest that sweeps off the back of the head. The bill is long and chisel-like and is about the length of the head. In flight, wings are broad.

COLOR PATTERN Pileated Woodpeckers are mostly black with white stripes on the face and neck and a flaming red crest. Males have a red stripe on the cheek. In flight, the bird reveals extensive white underwings and small white crescents on the upper side at the base of the primary feathers.

BEHAVIOR Pileated Woodpeckers drill distinctive rectangular-shaped holes in rotten wood to get at carpenter ants and other insects. They are loud birds with strident calls.

HABITAT Pileated Woodpeckers require forests with large, standing dead trees and downed wood. Such forests are often old, particularly in the West. In the East, they live in young forests as well and may be seen in wooded suburbs.

with a flaming red crest, the **Pileated Woodpecker** is one of the biggest, most striking forest birds
e continent. Look for them whacking at dead trees and fallen logs in search of carpenter ants, leaving
e rectangular holes in the wood. These holes are crucial shelters for birds and other animals of the forest.

ADULT MALE (YELLOW-SHAFTED)

ADULT FEMALE (RED-SHAFTED)

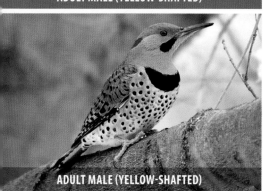
ADULT MALE (YELLOW-SHAFTED)

ADULT MALE (RED-SHAFTED)

SIZE & SHAPE Flickers are fairly large woodpeckers with a slim, rounded head, long, slightly curved bill, and long, flared tail that tapers to a point.

COLOR PATTERN Flickers in this region can be either yellow-shafted or red-shafted, or have a mixture of plumage markings. The undersides of the wing and tail feathers may be bright yellow or red. Up close, the brown or gray-brown plumage is richly patterned with black spots, bars, and crescents. Males may have a black or red whisker and may have a red patch on the nape. Female flickers do not have a mustache.

BEHAVIOR Unlike most woodpeckers, Northern Flickers spend lots of time on the ground. Ants and beetles are its main food, and the flicker often digs in the dirt to find them. When in trees, they usually perch upright on horizontal branches instead of leaning against their tails on a trunk.

HABITAT Look for Northern Flickers in woodlands, forest edges, and open fields with scattered trees, as well as city parks and suburbs. You can also find them in wet areas such as flooded swamps and marsh edges.

RANGE MAP

■ Breeding
■ Winter
■ Year-round

Northern Flickers are large, brown woodpeckers with a gentle expression and handsome black-scallo[...] plumage. On walks, don't be surprised if you scare one up from the ground. It's not where you'd expec[...] find a woodpecker, but flickers eat ants and beetles, digging for them with their slightly curved bill.

ADULT MALE

ADULT MALE

ADULT FEMALE

ADULT FEMALE

RANGE MAP

Breeding
Nonbreeding
Year-round

SIZE & SHAPE The slender American Kestrel is roughly the size and shape of a Mourning Dove, although it has a larger head; longer, narrow wings; and a long, square-tipped tail. In flight, the wings are often bent and the wingtips swept back.

COLOR PATTERN American Kestrels are pale when seen from below and a warm, rusty brown, spotted with black, above. The tail has a black band near the tip. Males have slate-blue wings; females' wings are reddish brown. Both sexes have pairs of black vertical slashes on the sides of their pale faces—sometimes called "mustaches" or "sideburns."

BEHAVIOR American Kestrels snatch their victims from the ground, though some catch quarry on the wing. They are gracefully buoyant in flight and small enough to get tossed around in the wind. When perched, kestrels often pump their tails as if they are trying to balance.

HABITAT You'll find kestrels in habitats ranging from deserts and grasslands to alpine meadows. You're most likely to see them perching on telephone wires along roadsides in open country with short vegetation and few trees.

American Kestrel, North America's smallest falcon, packs a predator's fierce intensity into its small body. hunt for insects and small prey in open territory, perch on wires, or hover in the wind, flapping and ting their long tails to stay in place. Kestrels are declining; you can help them by putting up nest boxes.

ADULT

ADULT

JUVENILE

JUVENILE

SIZE & SHAPE The largest falcon over most of the continent, the Peregrine Falcon has long, pointed wings and a long tail. The bill is strongly hooked. Males are smaller than females, so size can overlap with large female Merlins or small male Gyrfalcons.

COLOR PATTERN Adults are dark gray above with a blackish helmet and yellow eyering. The cere (a fleshy covering at the base of the upper bill) is also vivid yellow. Pale whitish underparts have fine, dark barring. Juveniles are heavily marked, with vertical streaks on the breast, and a gray bill. They lack the yellow eyering and cere.

BEHAVIOR Peregrine Falcons catch medium-sized birds in the air with swift, spectacular dives, called stoops. In cities, they are masterful at catching pigeons. Elsewhere, they feed especially on shorebirds and ducks. They often sit on high perches, waiting for the right opportunity to make their aerial assault.

HABITAT If a mudflat full of shorebirds suddenly erupts, scan the skies for a Peregrine Falcon. Also, look on skyscrapers, cliffs, and other tall structures. They are seen all over North America but are more common along coasts.

RANGE MAP

 Breeding
 Migration
 Nonbreeding
 Year-round

Powerful and fast flying, the **Peregrine Falcon** drops down on prey from high above in a spectacular s
Virtually eradicated from eastern North America by pesticide poisoning in the middle 20th century, th
are now thriving in many large cities and coastal areas thanks to recovery efforts.

ADULT

ADULT

JUVENILE

ADULT

RANGE MAP

Breeding
Migration

SIZE & SHAPE The Western Wood-Pewee is a medium-sized flycatcher with a long tail and wings, short legs, an upright posture, and a peaked crown that tends to give the head a triangular shape. The long wings help separate it from many other flycatchers.

COLOR PATTERN Western Wood-Pewees are grayish brown overall, with two pale wingbars. The underparts are whitish with smudgy gray on the breast and sides that can make them look like they are wearing a partially buttoned vest. The face is dark grayish brown with little to no eyering. The bill is mostly dark with yellow at the base of the lower mandible. Juveniles are similar to adults but have buffy wingbars.

BEHAVIOR Pewees sit on exposed perches and fly out to grab flying insects, repeatedly returning to the same or a nearby perch. The song, a harsh, burry *pee-eer*, is quite unlike that of the Eastern Wood-Pewee and the best way to tell the two apart.

HABITAT Western Wood-Pewees breed in open forests up to 10,000 feet. Look for them in cottonwoods and sycamores along rivers, or in stands of pine, oak, or aspen. They spend winters in mature tropical forests of South America.

mmer, open woodlands throughout the West come alive with returning **Western Wood-Pewees**. e flycatchers use exposed branches as their stage, flying to and fro to nab flying insects with stunning sion. They sit tall when perched, singing a burry and nasal version of their name all summer long.

SIZE & SHAPE Least Flycatchers are the smallest *Empidonax* flycatchers in the East. They tend to perch upright, but they appear a little more compact than most. The head is proportionately large and is round to square in shape. Note their short wings.

COLOR PATTERN Least Flycatchers are grayish olive above with a dusky breast. Their head is grayish olive as well, with a bold, white eyering. They have a very faint yellow wash to the belly and two white wingbars. Adult and immature birds look similar.

BEHAVIOR Least Flycatchers congregate in clusters in broadleaf forests during the breeding season. They sing incessantly in summer, tossing their head back with each *chebec*. They flit from perch to perch on dead branches in the middle to upper level of the forest canopy.

HABITAT These birds breed in broadleaf and mixed forests of all ages, including second-growth and mature forests. These forests tend to have a few shrubs or small saplings in the understory and a well-developed canopy.

RANGE MAP

■ Breeding
■ Migration
■ Nonbreeding

Least Flycatchers are fairly easy to identify due to their small size, white eyering, and *chebec* song. In summer, look for them singing in broadleaf forests. These little birds don't let others push them aroun may chase species as large as Blue Jays. Over half of their population has been lost since 1970.

ADULT

ADULT

ADULT

JUVENILE

RANGE MAP

reeding
onbreeding
ear-round

SIZE & SHAPE Black Phoebes are small, plump songbirds with large heads and medium-long, squared tails. They often show a slight peak at the rear of the crown. The bill is straight and thin.

COLOR PATTERN Black Phoebes are mostly sooty gray on the upperparts and chest, with a slightly darker black head. The belly is clean white, and the wing feathers are edged with pale gray. Juveniles are similar to adults but have buffy wingbars.

BEHAVIOR Black Phoebes sit upright on low perches near water and make short flights to catch insects. Although they mostly eat insects, they may snatch minnows from the surface of ponds. They pump their tails up and down incessantly when perched. They often keep up a string of sharp *chip* calls.

HABITAT Black Phoebes live along streams, rivers, lakes, and the Pacific Ocean. As long as there is water present and some kind of ledge, Black Phoebes could be around.

lack Phoebe is a dapper flycatcher of the western U.S. They sit in the open on low perches to scan for ts, giving a series of shrill chirps. They use mud to build cup-shaped nests against walls, overhangs, rts, and bridges. Look for them near any water source, from small streams to the Pacific Ocean.

SIZE & SHAPE This slender, long-tailed flycatcher appears large-headed for a bird of its size. The head often looks flat on top, but they sometimes raise their head feathers into a small peak at the back.

COLOR PATTERN Say's Phoebes are pale brownish gray above with a cinnamon belly, blackish tail, and gray breast. The immature bird is similar to the adult but browner and may have a buffy wingbar. Juveniles have a pink gape and cinnamon wingbars.

BEHAVIOR Like other phoebes, the Say's Phoebe wags or pumps its tail when perched. When foraging, they often perch around eye level on exposed twigs, jumping up to snatch a flying insect and returning to the same or a nearby perch.

HABITAT Say's Phoebes live in open country, sagebrush, badlands, dry barren foothills, canyons, and desert borders; they avoid forests. They often gravitate to buildings and aren't closely tied to watercourses like other phoebes.

RANGE MAP

■ Breeding
■ Migration
■ Nonbreeding
■ Year-round

Like other phoebes, the **Say's Phoebe** is seemingly undaunted by people and often nests on building They breed farther north than any other flycatcher and are seemingly limited only by the lack of nest s Its breeding range extends from central Mexico all the way to the Arctic tundra.

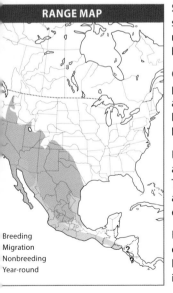

RANGE MAP

Breeding
Migration
Nonbreeding
Year-round

SIZE & SHAPE This medium-sized flycatcher is long and slender with a long tail. Its head is slightly peaked at the back, making it look large-headed for its size. It has a medium-sized bill that is fairly thick.

COLOR PATTERN Both sexes are grayish brown overall with a pale yellow belly and two whitish wingbars. The head and face are ashy gray, and the throat is whitish. The underside of the tail has a broad cinnamon stripe down the center. Immature birds look like adults.

BEHAVIOR These flycatchers tend to lean forward on perches and move their heads up and down, especially when agitated. They also tip their heads side to side while looking around from a perch. Ash-throated Flycatchers spend most of their time at eye level, flying out from low perches to nab an insect or two.

HABITAT The Ash-throated Flycatcher occupies dry scrub, open woodlands, and deserts in the West. They usually avoid humid forested areas, but do occur in woodlands along streams in dry regions.

Ash-throated Flycatcher's subtle hues are reminiscent of a desert just before sunset. This genteel flycatcher tips its head side to side with seeming curiosity while perched among low oaks and mesquite. A bird of dry places, it gets all the water it needs from the insects and spiders it eats.

ADULT

ADULT

ADULT

ADULT

SIZE & SHAPE Western Kingbirds are fairly large flycatchers with large heads and broad shoulders. They have heavy, straight bills, long wings, and medium-length, square-tipped tails.

COLOR PATTERN Western Kingbirds are gray-headed birds with a yellow belly, pale gray chest, and a whitish throat. The tail is black with white outer edges that are especially conspicuous in flight. Juvenile birds are not as brightly colored.

BEHAVIOR Easily found perched upright on fences and utility lines, Western Kingbirds hawk insects from the air or fly out to pick prey from the ground. They ferociously defend their territories with wing-fluttering, highly vocal attacks. Vocalizations include a long series of squeaky, bubbling calls as well as single, accented *kip* notes.

HABITAT Western Kingbirds live in open valleys and lowlands up to about 7,000 feet elevation. They perch on utility lines, fences, and trees in cities, grasslands, deserts, sagebrush, agricultural fields, and open woodlands.

RANGE MAP

- Breeding
- Breeding (scarce)
- Migration
- Nonbreeding

An eye-catching bird, the **Western Kingbird** is a familiar summertime sight in open habitats across muc western North America. They are aggressive and will scold and chase intruders (including Red-tailed Haw and American Kestrels) with a snapping bill and flared crimson crown feathers that are normally hidden.

ADULT

ADULT

JUVENILE

ADULT

RANGE MAP

Breeding
Migration

SIZE & SHAPE The Eastern Kingbird is a sturdy, large flycatcher with a large head, upright posture, square-tipped tail, and a relatively short, wide, straight bill.

COLOR PATTERN Eastern Kingbirds are blackish above and white below, with a darker head than the wings and back. The black tail has a white tip. Look for red feathers on the crown of an agitated male, though he usually keeps these hidden.

BEHAVIOR Eastern Kingbirds often perch in the open atop trees or along utility lines or fences. They fly with very shallow, rowing wingbeats and a raised head, usually accompanied by metallic, sputtering calls. Eastern Kingbirds are visual hunters, flying out from perches to snatch flying insects.

HABITAT Eastern Kingbirds breed in open habitats such as yards, fields, pastures, grasslands, or wetlands, and are especially abundant in open places along forest edges or water. They spend winters in forests of South America.

dark-gray upperparts and a neat white tip to the tail, the **Eastern Kingbird** looks like it's wearing a
ess suit. And this big-headed, broad-shouldered bird does mean business—just watch one harassing
s, Red-tailed Hawks, Great Blue Herons, and other birds that pass over its territory.

SIZE & SHAPE Warbling Vireos are small, chunky songbirds with thick, straight, slightly hooked bills. They are medium-sized for vireos, with a fairly round head and medium-length bill and tail.

COLOR PATTERN These birds are grayish olive above and whitish below, washed on the sides and vent with yellow. They have a dark line through the eye and a white line over the eye. The space between the eye and the bill is usually white. Adult and immature birds look similar.

BEHAVIOR Warbling Vireos forage sluggishly, intently peering at leaf surfaces from a single perch before pouncing or moving on. They eat mostly caterpillars. They give their loud, rollicking, finchlike song frequently on summer territories.

HABITAT Open, broadleaf woodlands, forest edges, and riverside woodlands are the preferred habitats of Warbling Vireos throughout the year, though they also use some mixed coniferous-broadleaf habitats. Even on migration, they typically occur in areas with taller trees.

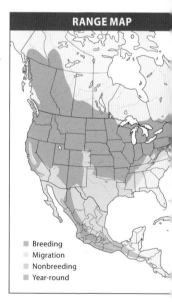

RANGE MAP

- Breeding
- Migration
- Nonbreeding
- Year-round

The rich, rollicking song of the **Warbling Vireo** is a common sound in many parts of central and northe North America during summer, making it a great bird to learn by ear. Warbling Vireos are otherwise fair plain birds that stay high in broadleaf treetops, hunting methodically among the leaves for caterpillars

ADULT

ADULT

IMMATURE

ADULT

RANGE MAP

reeding
reeding (scarce)
Migration

SIZE & SHAPE Red-eyed Vireos are chunky songbirds, a bit bigger than most warblers, with a long, angular head, thick neck, and a strong, long bill with a small but noticeable hook at the tip. The body is stocky and the tail fairly short.

COLOR PATTERN Red-eyed Vireos are olive green above and clean white below with a gray crown and white eyebrow stripe bordered above and below by blackish lines. Flanks and under the tail have a green-yellow wash. Adults have red eyes, immature birds have dark eyes.

BEHAVIOR These vireos forage in broadleaf canopies, moving slowly and methodically, carefully scanning leaves for caterpillars and other prey. They sing incessantly in summer, even in the afternoon heat.

HABITAT Red-eyed Vireos breed in broadleaf and mixed forests with shrubby understories. They are also found in neighborhoods with large trees. During migration, look for them in more varied habitats.

ess songster, the **Red-eyed Vireo's** brief but incessant songs—sometimes more than 20,000 per day by le male—contribute to the characteristic sound of summer in in eastern and northern forests. When fall s, they head for the Amazon basin, fueled by a summer of plucking caterpillars from leaves in the treetops.

ADULT

ADULT

ADULT

ADULT

SIZE & SHAPE The Loggerhead Shrike is a thick-bodied songbird with a large, blocky head. The thick bill has a small hook. The tail is fairly long and rounded.

COLOR PATTERN The Loggerhead Shrike is a gray bird with a wide black mask contrasting a white throat. Unlike the Northern Shrike, the black mask goes across the top of the bill. The tail is black with white corners; the wings are black with white at the base of the primaries that form a small "handkerchief" spot when the wing is closed and larger white patches in flight. Juveniles have darker barring above and below.

BEHAVIOR Loggerhead Shrikes sit on low, exposed perches and scan for rodents, lizards, birds, and insects. They eat smaller prey right away, but they are famous for impaling larger items on thorns or barbed wire to be eaten later.

HABITAT Open country with scattered shrubs and trees is the typical habitat of Loggerhead Shrike, but the species can also be found in more heavily wooded habitats with large openings, and in very short habitats with few or no trees.

RANGE MAP

- Breeding
- Breeding (scarce)
- Nonbreeding
- Year-round

The **Loggerhead Shrike** is a songbird with a raptor's habits, hunting small prey from conspicuous per
These masked predators lack a raptor's talons, so they skewer their kills on thorns or barbed wire or w
them into tight places for easy eating. Their numbers have dropped sharply in the last half-century.

ADULT

ADULT

IMMATURE

IMMATURE

RANGE MAP

Breeding
Migration
Nonbreeding
Nonbreeding (scarce)
Year-round

SIZE & SHAPE The Northern Shrike is a chunky, big-headed songbird with a thick, hooked bill and a medium-long tail. It is larger than the Loggerhead Shrike.

COLOR PATTERN Northern Shrikes are gray birds with black masks and black in the wings and tail. They are paler below, often with faint, fine gray barring. The black mask does not go across the top of the bill. The tail is edged in white, and the wings have a white flash, especially noticeable in flight. Juveniles and immatures are brownish with a faint mask, and show more distinct barring below than adults. The bill often has a pink base.

BEHAVIOR This bird waits for prey on an exposed perch, then seizes it near the ground with its feet or bill. It often impales prey on thorns or barbed wire. Otherwise, it kills vertebrates by biting through the neck and removes wings, spines, and stingers from insects.

HABITAT The Northern Shrike breeds in open parts of the boreal forest (taiga) and along the northern edge where boreal forest gives way to tundra. It winters in and migrates through similar habitats with a patchwork of small trees and bushes.

urly, bull-headed **Northern Shrike** is a pint-sized predator of birds, small mammals, and insects. A black mask and stout, hooked bill heighten the impression of danger in these fierce predators. They save food for later by impaling it on thorns or barbed wire.

ADULT (PACIFIC SLOPE)

ADULT (NORTHERN ROCKIES)

ADULT (CENTRAL AND SOUTHERN ROCKIES)

JUVENILE

SIZE & SHAPE Canada Jays are stocky, fairly large songbirds with short, stout bills. They have round heads and long tails, with broad, rounded wings.

COLOR PATTERN Canada Jays are dark gray above and light gray below, with black on the back of the head forming a partial hood. The amount of gray on the head varies from region to region. Juveniles are grayish black overall with a pale whisker mark, and they often show a pale gape at the base of the bill.

BEHAVIOR Canada Jays are typically found in small groups. They fly in quiet swoops, generally holding their wings below the horizontal. They have a large variety of vocalizations including hoots and chatters, but are less noisy overall than other jays. Canada Jays have very broad diets, eating anything from berries to carrion to handouts from hikers.

HABITAT Canada Jays live in coniferous (especially spruce) and mixed conifer-broadleaf forest across the northern United States and Canada, as well as in high mountain ranges of the West.

RANGE MAP

■ Year-round

The deceptively cute **Canada Jay** is one of the most intrepid birds in North America. They live in north forests all year and rear chicks in the dark of winter. Highly curious and always on the lookout for food, may even land on your hand to grab a peanut. In summer, they hoard food for winter sustenance.

ADULT

ADULTS

JUVENILE

ADULTS

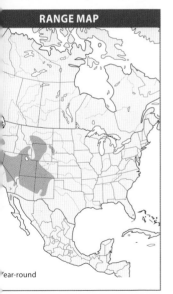

RANGE MAP

year-round

SIZE & SHAPE The Pinyon Jay is a medium-sized crestless jay that kind of looks like a miniature crow. It has a shorter, square-tipped tail, and a longer, more daggerlike bill than other jays.

COLOR PATTERN Males and females are dusky blue overall with a paler, often dingy, blue-gray belly. Note the white-streaked throat. Juveniles are duller and duskier.

BEHAVIOR Pinyon Jays scour pinyon-juniper patches for seeds in large groups that forage in trees and on the ground. They extract seeds from green pinyon-pine cones, which can be a messy affair. To get the sticky sap off their bill, they frequently wipe it side to side on a branch. They also eat plants and insects and occasionally visit feeders. They move across the landscape in tightly packed flocks, flying with quick and strong wingbeats. Their flight is direct and crowlike, unlike that of most jays.

HABITAT Look for Pinyon Jays in pinyon-juniper woodland, sagebrush, scrub oak, chaparral, and sometimes in pine forests.

inyon Jay travels in large, noisy flocks throughout the West, giving a laughing *caw* to stay in touch he group. They breed and forage together year-round and will hide tens of thousands of pinyon pine , a favorite food, only to unearth them later using their excellent spatial memory.

ADULT

ADULT

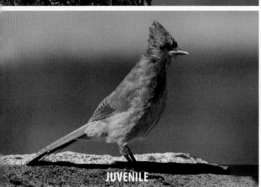

JUVENILE

ADULT

SIZE & SHAPE Steller's Jays are hefty, crested birds with an attitude. They have rounded wings, and a long, rounded tail. The bill is long, straight, and powerful, with a slight hook. The prominent triangular crest often stands nearly straight up from their head.

COLOR PATTERN Steller's Jays are a real standout, with a charcoal black head and a blue body that is lightest, almost sparkling, on the wings. Birds along the Pacific Coast are darker and have small blue streaks above the eye.

BEHAVIOR Like other jays, Steller's Jays are bold, inquisitive, intelligent, and noisy. Steller's Jays spend much of their time exploring the forest canopy, flying with patient wingbeats. They come to the forest floor to investigate visitors and look for food, moving with decisive hops of their long legs.

HABITAT Look for Steller's Jays in coniferous forests of western North America, at elevations of 3,000–10,000 feet (lower along the Pacific Coast).

RANGE MAP

■ Year-round

A large, dark jay of coniferous forests in the mountainous West, **Steller's Jays** are common in the wilderness but are also fixtures of campgrounds, parklands, and backyards, where they are quick to sp bird feeder or an unattended picnic. You'll hear their harsh, scolding calls if they are nearby.

ADULT

ADULT

ADULT

ADULT

RANGE MAP

Nonbreeding (scarce)
Year-round

SIZE & SHAPE Blue Jays are large crested songbirds with broad, rounded tails. They are smaller than crows, but larger than robins.

COLOR PATTERN Blue Jays are a brilliant blue above and white or light gray below, with a prominent crest and a bold black necklace. The wings and tail are barred with black, and the wings are spangled with white. Large white tail corners are prominent in flight.

BEHAVIOR Blue Jays make a large variety of calls that carry long distances. Most calls are produced while the jay is perched in a tree. It flies across open areas silently, especially during migration. Blue Jays stuff food items in a throat pouch to cache elsewhere. When eating, it will hold a seed or nut securely in its feet and peck it open.

HABITAT Blue Jays are birds of forest edges. A favorite food is acorns, and they are often found near oaks, in forests, woodlots, towns, cities, and parks.

ommon, large **Blue Jay** is familiar to many people, with its perky crest; blue, white, and black age; and noisy calls. This songbird is known for its intelligence and complex social systems with tight bonds. Its fondness for acorns is credited with helping spread oak trees after the last glacial period.

SIZE & SHAPE The California Scrub-Jay is fairly large with lanky dimensions. It has a long and floppy tail, and a straight and stout bill with a hook at the tip. The bird often adopts a hunched-over posture.

COLOR PATTERN These birds are rich cobalt blue and gray above with a thin white stripe over the eye. They have a clean, pale underside broken up by a partial blue necklace. In birds, the color blue depends on lighting, so California Scrub-Jays can also look simply dark. Juveniles are duller and duskier.

BEHAVIOR California Scrub-Jays are assertive, vocal, and inquisitive. You'll often notice them silhouetted high in trees, on wires, or on posts, where they act as lookouts. Their flight is slow, with bouts of fluttering alternating with glides.

HABITAT Look for these scrub-jays in open habitats, oak woodlands, and chaparral along the West Coast, as well as in backyards, pastures, and orchards. They are typically found in lower and drier habitats than Steller's Jay.

RANGE MAP

■ Year-round
■ Year-round (scarce)

Look closely for an intriguing difference between the **California Scrub-Jay** and its close relative, Woodhe Scrub-Jay. The bill of a California Scrub-Jay is stout and hooked, giving it extra power and grip as the bird hammer open acorns in their oak woodland habitats. Woodhouse's have thinner, more pointed bills.

RANGE MAP

Nonbreeding (scarce)
Year-round

SIZE & SHAPE Black-billed Magpies are slightly larger than jays, and they have much longer, diamond-shaped tails and heavier bills. In flight, their wings seem to be too short to support their graceful flight.

COLOR PATTERN Black-billed Magpies are elegant looking birds that are black and white overall with blue-green iridescent flashes in the wing and tail. They have a white patch in the outer wing and two white stripes on the back. Adult and immature birds look similar.

BEHAVIOR Black-billed Magpies are social, inquisitive birds that eat fruits, grains, insects, small animals, and frequently gather in large flocks at carrion. They move in groups and give a variety of trill, cackle, and whistle calls. In flight, they flap steadily, alternating deep and shallow wingbeats, and use their very long tails to negotiate abrupt turns.

HABITAT Black-billed Magpies are widespread in towns, fields, and stream corridors of the West. They also concentrate in flocks at feedlots and other areas where food is easy to find.

k-billed Magpies are familiar and entertaining birds of western North America. They sit on fenceposts oad signs or flap across rangelands, white wing patches flashing and very long tails trailing behind . Large, flashy relatives of jays and crows, they gather in numbers to feed on carrion.

SIZE & SHAPE Clark's Nutcracker is the size of a large jay but the shape of a crow, with a short tail and rounded, crestless head. The bill is long and straight with a sharp tip.

COLOR PATTERN Clark's Nutcrackers are pale gray birds with black wings. In flight, the wings show large white patches along the trailing edges (secondaries). The tail is black in the center with white along either side. They have black bills, legs, and feet. Adult and immature birds look similar.

BEHAVIOR Clark's Nutcrackers travel in flocks and use their spikelike bills to pick seeds out of pine cones. They eat some of the seeds and bury thousands of others for the winter. Nutcrackers fly on broad, floppy wings and make rolling, gravelly calls, audible from far away.

HABITAT Clark's Nutcrackers are mountain birds. They are closely associated with whitebark and limber pines that produce large seeds, but are also found in other montane coniferous forests from about 3,000 to more than 11,000 feet elevation in the West.

RANGE MAP

■ Year-round

High in the mountains of the West, **Clark's Nutcrackers** use their daggerlike bills to pull seeds from pine c which are stashed in a pouch under the tongue for later burial. They bury tens of thousands of seeds e summer, and while locations of many are remembered, forgotten seeds play a crucial role in growing new fo

RANGE MAP

Breeding
Nonbreeding
Year-round

SIZE & SHAPE American Crows are long-legged, thick-necked, oversized songbirds with a heavy, straight bill. In flight, the wings are fairly broad and rounded with the wingtip feathers spread like fingers. The short tail is rounded or squared off at the end.

COLOR PATTERN American Crows are all black, including the legs and bill and eyes. As they molt, old feathers can appear brownish or scaly compared to glossy new feathers. Adult and immature birds look similar.

BEHAVIOR American Crows are very social, sometimes forming flocks in the thousands. Inquisitive and sometimes mischievous, crows are good learners and problem solvers, often raiding garbage cans and picking over discarded food containers. They're also aggressive and chase away larger birds including hawks, owls, and herons.

HABITAT American Crows are common birds of fields, open woodlands, and forests. They thrive around people, and you'll often find them in farm fields, lawns, parking lots, athletic fields, roadsides, towns, and garbage dumps.

rican Crows are familiar over much of the continent: large, intelligent, all-black birds with hoarse, cawing s. They are a common sight in treetops, fields, and on roadsides, and in habitats ranging from open ds and empty beaches to town centers. They usually feed on the ground and eat almost anything.

SIZE & SHAPE The Common Raven is not just large but massive, with a thick neck, shaggy throat feathers, and a Bowie knife of a beak. In flight, ravens have long, wedge-shaped tails. They're more slender than crows, with longer, narrower wings, and longer, thinner "fingers" at the wingtips.

COLOR PATTERN Common Ravens are entirely black, right down to the legs, eyes, and beak. Adult and immature birds look similar.

BEHAVIOR Common Ravens aren't as social as crows and tend to be alone or in pairs, except at food sources like landfills. They're confident, inquisitive birds that strut around or bound forward with light, two-footed hops. In flight, they are buoyant and graceful, interspersing soaring, gliding, and slow flaps.

HABITAT Look for the Common Raven in open and forest habitats across western and northern North America, as well as high desert, seacoast, and grasslands. It also does well in rural settlements, towns, and cities.

RANGE MAP

■ Year-round

The **Common Raven** has accompanied people around the Northern Hemisphere for centuries, followi them in hopes of a quick meal. Ravens are among the smartest of all birds, gaining a reputation for sol ever more complicated problems invented by ever more creative scientists.

ADULT

ADULT

ADULT

ADULT

RANGE MAP

Year-round

SIZE & SHAPE The Black-capped Chickadee is small and compact with a thin, short bill. The short neck and large head accentuate the spherical body shape. It has a long, narrow tail and a short bill, a bit thicker than a warbler's but thinner than a finch's.

COLOR PATTERN The Black-capped Chickadee's cap and bib are black, the cheeks white, the back soft gray, and the wing feathers gray edged with white. Underparts are a soft buff color on the sides grading to white beneath.

BEHAVIOR Black-capped Chickadees seldom remain at feeders except to grab a seed to eat elsewhere. They are acrobatic and associate in flocks; the sudden activity when a flock arrives is distinctive. They often fly across roads and open areas one at a time with a bouncy flight.

HABITAT Chickadees may be found in any habitat that has trees or woody shrubs, from forests and woodlots to residential neighborhoods and parks. They frequently nest in birch or alder trees.

Black-capped Chickadee is almost universally considered "cute" thanks to its oversized round head, body, and curiosity about everything, including humans. Most birds that associate with chickadee s respond to chickadee alarm calls, even when their own species doesn't make a similar sound.

ADULT

ADULT

ADULT

ADULT

SIZE & SHAPE Mountain Chickadees are tiny, large-headed but small-bodied songbirds, with a long, narrow tail, small bill, and full, rounded wings.

COLOR PATTERN Like most chickadees, this species is strikingly black and white on the head, and gray elsewhere. The white stripe over the eye distinguishes Mountain Chickadees from all other chickadees.

BEHAVIOR Active and acrobatic, this chickadee clings to small limbs and twigs or hangs upside down from pine cones. In winter, Mountain Chickadees flock with kinglets and nuthatches, with birds following each other one by one from tree to tree.

HABITAT Mountain Chickadees are common across most coniferous forests of the mountains of the West, particularly pine, mixed conifer, spruce-fir, and pinyon-juniper forests on higher slopes.

RANGE MAP

▨ Year-round

The tiny **Mountain Chickadee** is a busy presence overhead in the dry coniferous forests of the mounta West. Often found in mixed flocks of small birds, they flit through high branches, hang upside down to insects or seeds from cones, and give a scolding *chick-a-dee* call to anyone who will listen.

RANGE MAP

Year-round

SIZE & SHAPE The Chestnut-backed Chickadee is a tiny, large-headed but small-billed bird, with a rather long, narrow tail and short, rounded wings.

COLOR PATTERN The Chestnut-backed Chickadee's head is patterned like that of most other chickadees, but the crown is dark brown instead of black. In addition, the back is a rich chestnut instead of the more typical slaty gray. North of San Francisco, the flanks are rich brown. Adult and immature birds look similar.

BEHAVIOR These active and acrobatic birds cling to small limbs and twigs or hang upside down from cones. In winter, they flock with kinglets and nuthatches. Flock members set out to cross openings one at a time.

HABITAT Chestnut-backed Chickadees are found in dense coniferous and mixed forests of the Pacific Coast and also the inland Northwest. You can also find them in shrubs, trees, and parks within cities, towns, and suburbs.

ndsome chickadee that matches the rich brown bark of the coastal trees it lives among, the
tnut-backed Chickadee is the species to look for up and down the West Coast. Though they're at home
rk, wet woods, they've also readily taken to suburbs and ornamental shrubs of cities like San Francisco.

ADULT

ADULT

ADULT

ADULT

SIZE & SHAPE About the size of a Black-capped Chickadee, the Boreal Chickadee is a small songbird with a husky body and head, and a slim, rather long tail.

COLOR PATTERN Overall a brownish gray chickadee, the Boreal Chickadee is distinguished by its brown cap, gray collar, small white cheek patch, and cinnamon flanks.

BEHAVIOR Boreal Chickadees forage agilely and restlessly among limbs and branches, with frequent acrobatic turns while perched. Sometimes they hover as they glean prey from tips of branches. They eat mostly seeds and insects, which they take while foraging in the middle and higher parts of the forest canopy.

HABITAT Boreal Chickadees inhabit mostly mature spruce-fir forests in Canada and some adjacent states, often near water. In western Canada, mixed and broadleaf forests also host this species.

RANGE MAP

■ Year-round
▪ ▪ ▪ Year-round (scarce)

A chickadee with a brown cap, the **Boreal Chickadee** lives in coniferous forests of the far north year-rou
When it's not nesting season, they travel and forage in small groups, sometimes with other songbirds su
kinglets. In summer and fall, they cache seeds and insects to help them get through the long, brutal win

RANGE MAP

Breeding

Year-round (scarce)

SIZE & SHAPE The Oak Titmouse is a small songbird with a short, stubby bill and a short crest on the head that can be raised or lowered. It has a medium-long tail.

COLOR PATTERN These are plain gray-brown birds. They are slightly darker above than below, and may show a slight buffy wash on the flanks. Beady black eyes stand out on a plain face. Adult and immature birds look similar.

BEHAVIOR Active and constantly moving, the Oak Titmouse flits between branches and trees, flying with a shallow, undulating motion. They tend to feed among the woody twigs in the lower part of the oak canopy where they eat seeds and insects that they glean from bark and leaves. Listen for their rapid, harsh calls from the tops of oaks year-round.

HABITAT The Oak Titmouse is strongly tied to oak trees, although it also lives in areas of open pine or mixed oak-pine forest. The species is almost entirely restricted to dry slopes in California, but its full range is north to Oregon and south to Baja California.

Nondescript save for its crest, the **Oak Titmouse** might not wow many bird watchers at first sight. But these vocal, active birds characterize the warm, dry oak woods from southern Oregon to Baja California—they are "the voice and soul of the oaks," according to one early naturalist.

SIZE & SHAPE The Juniper Titmouse is small, but the long body, short neck, and medium-long tail make it appear bigger than it is. A short crest gives the fairly large head a pointed silhouette. The short bill is fairly thick and round.

COLOR PATTERN The Juniper Titmouse is gray overall with a slightly paler gray belly. The dark eye stands out on an otherwise plain gray bird. The bill is also dark. Adult and immature birds look similar.

BEHAVIOR The Juniper Titmouse is the acrobat of the pinyon-juniper forest. Their strong feet allow them to hang upside down from branches while they forage for seeds and insects. They hop and fly in an undulating motion between trees and shrubs.

HABITAT The Juniper Titmouse occurs in pinyon pine and juniper woodlands from about 2,250-8,000 feet elevation. They tend to nest in mature woodlands, where older pinyon and juniper trees offer a ready supply of cavities for nesting.

RANGE MAP

■ Year-round
■ Year-round (scarce)

The **Juniper Titmouse** is a plain bird with attitude. Its scratchy chatter can be heard all year in the pinyon juniper woodlands of the interior West. Look for them flitting through trees or acrobatically dangling ups down from thin branches. They are very similar to the Oak Titmouse, but they live in different habitats.

BREEDING MALE

NONBREEDING MALE

JUVENILE

ADULT FEMALE

RANGE MAP

eeding
igration
onbreeding
onbreeding (scarce)
ar-round

SIZE & SHAPE Horned Larks are small, long-bodied songbirds that usually adopt a horizontal posture. They have short, thin bills, short necks, and rounded heads that sometimes show two small "horns" of feathers sticking up toward the back.

COLOR PATTERN Males are sandy brown above and white beneath, with a black chest band, mask, and head stripes, which are sometimes raised like tiny "horns." The face and throat are yellow or white. Females have less defined markings. Juveniles are brown overall with white-edged feathers and a brown breast band.

BEHAVIOR Horned Larks are usually found in flocks except during the breeding season. They creep along bare ground, searching for small seeds and insects. They often join in winter flocks with other open-country species.

HABITAT Horned Larks favor starkly open habitats with bare earth: deserts, tundra, beaches, dunes, grazed pastures, plowed fields, roadsides, and feedlots. They are drawn to fields spread with waste grain and manure. In winter, they mostly feed in areas free of snow.

arefully at a bare field, especially in winter, and you may see it crawling with little **Horned Larks**. songbirds are widespread in fields, deserts, and tundra, where they forage for seeds and insects, ng a high, tinkling song. Though still common, they have declined sharply in the last half-century.

ADULT MALE

ADULT MALE

ADULT FEMALE / IMMATURE (L) AND ADULT MALE (R)

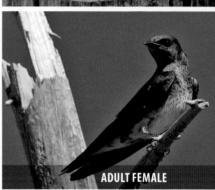

ADULT FEMALE

SIZE & SHAPE Purple Martins are very large, broad-chested swallows. They have stout, slightly hooked bills, short, forked tails, and long, tapered wings.

COLOR PATTERN Adult males are an iridescent, dark bluish purple overall with brown-black wings and tail. Females and immatures are duller, with variable amounts of gray on the head and chest and a whitish lower belly.

BEHAVIOR Purple Martins fly rapidly with a mix of flapping and gliding. They feed in midair, catching large, aerial insects such as dragonflies. Martins feed and roost in flocks, often mixed with other species of swallows. They often feed higher in the air than other swallows, which can make them tough to spot.

HABITAT Purple Martins are colonial, with dozens nesting in the same spot. They feed in open areas, especially near water. In the East, they nest almost exclusively in nest boxes and martin houses; in the West, they nest in natural cavities.

RANGE MAP

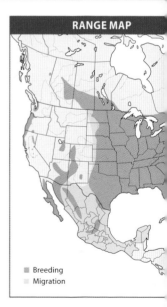

■ Breeding
■ Migration

Putting up a **Purple Martin** house is like installing a miniature neighborhood in your backyard. In the they will peer from the entrances and chirp from the rooftops all summer. In the West, martins mainly r woodpecker holes. North America's largest swallow, it performs aerial acrobatics to snap up flying ins

ADULT MALE

ADULT MALE

JUVENILES

ADULT FEMALE

RANGE MAP

Breeding
Migration
Winter
Year-round

SIZE & SHAPE Tree Swallows are small streamlined songbirds with long, pointed wings and a short, squared or slightly notched tail. Their bills are very short and flat.

COLOR PATTERN Adult males are blue green above and white below with blackish flight feathers and a thin black eye mask. Females are duller with more brown in their upperparts, and juveniles are completely brown above. Juveniles and some females can show a weak, blurry gray-brown breast band.

BEHAVIOR Tree Swallows feed on small, aerial insects that they catch during acrobatic flight. After breeding, they will gather in large flocks to molt and migrate. In the nonbreeding season, they form huge communal roosts.

HABITAT Tree Swallows feed on small, aerial insects that they catch in their mouths during acrobatic flight. After breeding, Tree Swallows gather in large flocks to molt and migrate. In the nonbreeding season, they form huge communal roosts.

some aerialists with deep, iridescent blue backs and clean white fronts, **Tree Swallows** are a familiar in summer fields and wetlands across northern North America. They chase after flying insects with atic twists and turns, their steely blue-green feathers flashing in the sunlight.

ADULT MALE

ADULT MALE

JUVENILE

ADULT FEMALE

SIZE & SHAPE Violet-green Swallows are small, sleek songbirds with long, pointed wings and a short, slightly forked tail. Swallows have short necks and streamlined bodies for acrobatic flight.

COLOR PATTERN This swallow may look dark above and crisp white below, but in good light the greenish bronze back and iridescent violet rump come to life. Males have white cheek patches while females and juveniles have dusky cheeks. They can be distinguished from other swallows by the white patches on the sides of their rump and their pale cheeks.

BEHAVIOR When not foraging for insects, Violet-green Swallows perch on wires or exposed tree branches. They are social songbirds and often occur in groups with other swallows and swifts.

HABITAT Violet-green Swallows breed in a variety of open woodlands, including broadleaf, coniferous, and mixed woodlands as well as areas near human habitation. They like open water, where they forage for flying insects.

RANGE MAP

▨ Breeding
▨ Nonbreeding
▨ Year-round

Violet-green Swallows perform acrobatic stunts over lakes and streams in search of flying insects. Thei colors come to life when sunlight illuminates their metallic green backs and iridescent purple rumps. Comn in the western U.S. and Canada in spring and summer, they vanish to Mexico and Central America in w

ADULT MALE

ADULT MALE

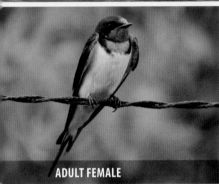

ADULT FEMALE

JUVENILES

RANGE MAP

reeding
Migration
Nonbreeding
ear-round

SIZE & SHAPE When perched, the sparrow-sized Barn Swallow appears cone shaped, with a slightly flattened head, no visible neck, and broad shoulders that taper to long, pointed wings. The tail extends well beyond the wingtips and the long outer feathers give the tail a deep fork.

COLOR PATTERN Barn Swallows have a steely blue back, wings, and tail, and rufous to tawny underparts. The blue crown and face contrast with the cinnamon-colored forehead and throat. White spots under the tail can be difficult to see except in flight. Males are more boldly colored than females. Juveniles are dark above and pale cinnamon below with a rich rusty throat and forehead.

BEHAVIOR Watch for the Barn Swallow's smooth, fluid wingbeats. They often follow farm implements, cattle herds, and humans to snag flushed insects.

HABITAT You can find the adaptable Barn Swallow feeding in open habitats from fields, parks, and roadway edges to marshes, meadows, ponds, and coastal waters.

ning cobalt blue above and tawny below, **Barn Swallows** dart gracefully over fields, barnyards, and water in search of flying insects. They often cruise low, flying just a few inches above the ground or . The Barn Swallow is the most abundant and widely distributed swallow species in the world.

ADULT

ADULT

JUVENILE

ADULTS

SIZE & SHAPE These compact swallows have rounded, broad-based wings, a small head, and a medium-length, squared tail. They are sparrow-sized.

COLOR PATTERN In poor light, Cliff Swallows look brown with dark throats and white underparts. In good light, you'll see their metallic, dark blue backs and pale, buff-colored rumps. They have rich, brick-red faces and a bright buff-white forehead patch like a headlamp. Some juveniles show whitish throats in summer and fall.

BEHAVIOR Cliff Swallows zoom around in intricate aerial patterns catching insects on the wing. When feeding with other species of swallows, they often stay higher in the air.

HABITAT Cliff Swallows traditionally built their nests on cliff faces but now have adopted bridges, overpasses, and culverts as colonial nesting sites. They feed near and over water, frequently mixing with other species of swallows.

RANGE MAP

■ Breeding
■ Migration

In summer, flocks of **Cliff Swallows** swarm around bridges and overpasses, where clusters of their intr mud nests cling to vertical walls. These sociable swallows are nearly always found in large groups, cha insects high above the ground, preening on perches, or dipping into a river for a bath.

ADULT MALE (PACIFIC SLOPE)

ADULT FEMALE (PACIFIC SLOPE)

ADULT MALE (INTERIOR WEST)

ADULT FEMALE (INTERIOR WEST)

RANGE MAP

ear-round

SIZE & SHAPE Bushtits are tiny, plump, and large-headed, with long tails and short, stubby bills. They are slightly smaller than a chickadee; about the size of a kinglet.

COLOR PATTERN Bushtits are fairly plain brown and gray. Slightly darker above than below, they have brown-gray heads, gray wings, and tan-gray underparts. Females have light eyes, males have dark eyes.

BEHAVIOR Bushtits move quickly through vegetation, almost always in flocks, and continuously make soft chips and twitters. They forage much as chickadees do, frequently hanging upside down to grab small insects and spiders from leaves.

HABITAT Bushtits live in oak forest, coniferous woodlands, dry scrublands, streamsides, and suburbs. You can find them at elevations from sea level to over 10,000 feet.

tits are sprightly, social songbirds that twitter as they fly between shrubs and thickets. Found in lively , they move constantly, often hanging upside down to pick at insects underneath leaves. Bushtits e an unusual hanging nest, shaped like a pouch or sock, from moss, spiderwebs, and grasses.

SIZE & SHAPE Wrentits are small birds with fairly large, round heads and short rounded wings, giving them an overall plump appearance. They have long legs and long tails, which they often hold up and away from their body at different angles. Their bills are short and slightly curved.

COLOR PATTERN Wrentits are plain brownish gray with paler, slightly streaked, pinkish bellies. They have a distinctive pale eye. Adult and immature birds look similar.

BEHAVIOR Males and females sing from deep inside shrubs, where they are difficult to find. Occasionally males perch on top of a low shrub to sing with their tails cocked up. Wrentits move slowly, often pausing to look around before hopping to the next spot. When they fly between shrubs, they fly slowly and pump their tails slightly to maintain elevation.

HABITAT The Wrentit lives in coastal scrub and chaparral along the West Coast, including suburban yards and parks with shrubs. Inland, they live in thickets along creeks, oak woodlands, mixed coniferous forests, and dense shrublands.

RANGE MAP

■ Year-round

The **Wrentit's** bouncing-ball song is a classic sound of scrub and chaparral areas along the West Coast. Seeing one is difficult, as they skulk among the shrubs, rarely making an appearance. Patience may be rewarded by the sight of this brownish gray bird with a piercing white eye popping out of the shrubs.

ADULT

ADULT MALE

JUVENILE

ADULT FEMALE

RANGE MAP

Breeding
Migration
Nonbreeding
Year-round

SIZE & SHAPE Golden-crowned Kinglets are tiny songbirds with a rounded body, short wings, and skinny tail. They have relatively large heads, and their bills are short and thin—perfect for gleaning small insects.

COLOR PATTERN Golden-crowned Kinglets are pale olive above and gray below, with a black-and-white striped face and a bright yellow crown patch. In males, the crown patch is accented with a red-orange stripe down the middle. Both sexes have a thin white wingbar and yellow edges to their black flight feathers.

BEHAVIOR Golden-crowned Kinglets stay concealed high in dense trees, giving thin, very high-pitched calls. They pluck small insects from conifer needles, hovering to reach them. In migration and winter, they join other insectivorous songbirds in mixed flocks.

HABITAT These birds live mainly in coniferous forests, breeding in boreal or montane forests, and conifer plantations. In winter, look for them in broadleaf forests, suburbs, swamps, bottomlands, and scrubby habitat.

ugh the **Golden-crowned Kinglet** is barely larger than a hummingbird, this frenetically active bird urvive –40° nights, sometimes huddling together for warmth. A good look can require some patience, y spend much of their time high up in dense spruce or fir foliage.

ADULT MALE

ADULT MALE

ADULT / IMMATURE

ADULT / IMMATURE

SIZE & SHAPE Ruby-crowned Kinglets are tiny songbirds with relatively large heads, almost no neck, and thin tails. They have very small, thin, straight bills.

COLOR PATTERN Ruby-crowned Kinglets are olive green with a prominent broken white eyering and white wingbar. This wingbar contrasts with an adjacent blackish bar in the wing. The brilliant ruby crown of the male is only occasionally visible, usually in spring and summer.

BEHAVIOR These are restless, acrobatic birds that move quickly through foliage, typically at lower and middle levels. They flick their wings almost constantly as they go.

HABITAT Ruby-crowned Kinglets breed in tall, dense conifer forests such as spruce, fir, and tamarack. In winter and during migration, also look for them in shrubby habitats, broadleaf forests, parks, and suburbs.

RANGE MAP

- Breeding
- Migration
- Nonbreeding
- Year-round

A tiny bird overflowing with energy, the **Ruby-crowned Kinglet** forages frantically through the lower branches of shrubs and trees. Its habit of constantly flicking its wings is a key identification clue. This bird a large clutch of eggs—up to 12 in a single nest. The entire clutch may weigh as much as the female hers

MALE

MALE

FEMALE

FEMALE

RANGE MAP

Nonbreeding
Year-round

SIZE & SHAPE Red-breasted Nuthatches are small, compact songbirds with slightly upturned, pointed bills, extremely short tails, and almost no neck. The body is plump or barrel-chested, and the short wings are very broad. It is slightly smaller than a sparrow.

COLOR PATTERN Both sexes are blue gray above. Males have cinnamon underparts, while the females' are a peach color. The male has a black cap, white stripe above the eye, and black stripe through the eye. The female's dark head markings are gray. Immature and adult birds look similar.

BEHAVIOR Red-breasted Nuthatches creep up, down, and sideways over trunks and branches, probing for food in crevices and under flakes of bark. They don't lean against their tail as woodpeckers do. Their flight is short and bouncy.

HABITAT Red-breasted Nuthatches live mainly in coniferous forests. Eastern populations use some broadleaf woods. During some winters, they may "irrupt" or move far south of their normal range.

Red-breasted Nuthatch is a tiny, active songbird of northern woods and western mountains. It travels through the canopy with chickadees, kinglets, and woodpeckers but sticks to tree trunks and branches, searching for hidden food. Its excitable *yank-yank* call sounds like a tiny horn honking in the treetops.

ADULT MALE (EASTERN)

ADULT MALE (INTERIOR WEST)

ADULT MALE (PACIFIC SLOPE)

ADULT FEMALE (PACIFIC SLOPE)

SIZE & SHAPE The White-breasted Nuthatch is small, with a large head and almost no apparent neck. The tail is very short, and the long, narrow, sharp bill is straight or slightly upturned. It is sparrow-sized.

COLOR PATTERN White-breasted Nuthatches are gray blue on the back, with a frosty white face and underparts. The lower belly and under the tail are often chestnut. The black or gray cap (male or female, respectively) and nape make it look like this bird is hooded. Size of the hood varies by region.

BEHAVIOR Like other nuthatches, they creep along trunks, probing into furrows with their bills and often turning sideways or upside down as they forage. Unlike woodpeckers, they don't use their tails to brace against a vertical trunk.

HABITAT Look for White-breasted Nuthatches in mature broadleaf woods, woodland edges, parks, wooded suburbs, and backyards. They're rarely found in coniferous woods, where Red-breasted Nuthatches are more likely.

RANGE MAP

Nonbreeding
Year-round

A common feeder bird, the **White-breasted Nuthatch** is an active, agile little bird with an appetite for insects and large, meaty seeds. It gets its common name from its habit of jamming large nuts and acor into tree bark, then whacking them with its sharp bill to "hatch" out the seed from the inside.

RANGE MAP

Year-round

SIZE & SHAPE Pygmy Nuthatches are tiny songbirds with a relatively large, rounded head, no discernible neck, and a straight, sharp bill. The legs are short, the wings are short and broad, and the tail is short and square.

COLOR PATTERN Pygmy Nuthatches have a slate-gray back and wings, with a dull brown cap that ends in a sharp line through the eye. The throat is white, and the underside creamy buff. Some subspecies show a blackish line through the eye. Adult and immature birds look similar.

BEHAVIOR Pygmy Nuthatches move constantly and give short, squeaky calls, often mixing with chickadees, kinglets, and other songbirds. They are highly social, breed cooperatively, and pile into cavities in groups to stay warm.

HABITAT Pygmy Nuthatches live almost exclusively in pine forests, particularly ponderosa pine. They occur in open, parklike stands of older, large trees as well as forests with a mix of oak, aspen, and fir trees.

l even by nuthatch standards, **Pygmy Nuthatches** are tiny bundles of energy that climb up and n ponderosa pines across the West, giving rubber-ducky calls to their flockmates. They breed in large nded-family groups, which is one reason why you'll often see a half-dozen at a time.

SIZE & SHAPE The Brown Creeper is a tiny and delicate songbird with a long, spine-tipped tail, slim body, and a slender, decurved bill.

COLOR PATTERN Streaked brown and buff above, with their white underparts usually hidden against a tree trunk, Brown Creepers blend easily into bark. Their brownish heads show a broad, buffy stripe over the eye. Adult and immature birds look similar.

BEHAVIOR Brown Creepers search for small insects and spiders by hitching upward in a spiral around tree trunks and limbs. They move with short, jerky motions using their stiff tails for support. To move to a new tree, they fly weakly to its base and resume climbing up. Brown Creepers sing a high, warbling song.

HABITAT Look for these birds in broadleaf or coniferous forests with large, live trees. In summer, they're often among hemlock, pine, fir, and cypress. In winter, they use a wider variety of wooded habitats, parks, and yards.

RANGE MAP

■ Breeding
■ Nonbreeding
■ Year-round

Listen for the piercing call of the **Brown Creeper**, a tiny woodland bird with an affinity for the biggest t it can find. They spiral up stout trunks and main branches, probing crevices and picking at loose bark w their slender, downcurved bills. They build hammock-shaped nests behind peeling bark.

BREEDING MALE

BREEDING MALE

JUVENILE

ADULT FEMALE / NONBREEDING MALE

RANGE MAP

Breeding
Migration
Nonbreeding
Year-round

SIZE & SHAPE Blue-gray Gnatcatchers are tiny, slim songbirds with long legs, a long tail, and a thin, straight bill.

COLOR PATTERN These blue-gray birds have pale gray underparts and a mostly black tail with white edges. The face is highlighted by white eyerings. In summer, males sport a black 'V' on their foreheads. Young birds tend to be brownish gray.

BEHAVIOR The energetic Blue-gray Gnatcatcher rarely slows down, fluttering after small insects among shrubs and trees with its tail cocked at a jaunty angle. Blue-gray Gnatcatchers often take food from spiderwebs and also abscond with strands of webbing for their tiny nests, which are shaped like tree knots.

HABITAT In the East, gnatcatchers breed in broadleaf forests and near forest edges. In the West, look for them in shorter woodlands and shrublands including pinyon-juniper and oak woodlands.

ny **Blue-gray Gnatcatcher** makes itself known in broadleaf forests by its soft but insistent calls and ant motion. It forages in dense outer foliage for insects and spiders, flicking its tail from side to side re up prey. Pairs use spiderweb and lichens to build small, neat nests, which sit on top of branches.

ADULT

ADULT

JUVENILE

ADULT

SIZE & SHAPE The Rock Wren is a medium-sized wren with a long tail and a long, thin bill. It is sparrow-sized.

COLOR PATTERN The Rock Wren is pale brown above and whitish below with a slightly buffy or peachy wash on the lower belly. The long tail is barred, and the back and wings are finely speckled. Note the pale eyebrow stripe. Juveniles look like adults, but are a little more ragged and have a cleaner white belly.

BEHAVIOR Rock Wrens glean prey from rocks or remove prey from spiderwebs. They have a habit of bobbing quickly up and down while standing. They also repeatedly hop vertically from the ground to capture flying insects.

HABITAT Rock Wrens inhabit arid or semiarid areas with exposed rock, anywhere from desert to alpine habitats.

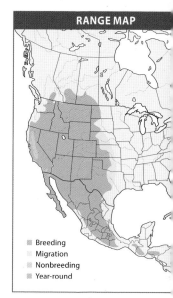

RANGE MAP

Breeding
Migration
Nonbreeding
Year-round

A pale gray bird of rocky areas, the **Rock Wren** is found throughout arid western North America. The m Rock Wren is a truly remarkable singer and can have a large song repertoire of 100 or more song types many of which seem to be learned from neighbors.

RANGE MAP

year-round

SIZE & SHAPE The Canyon Wren is a distinctive, pot-bellied, sparrow-sized wren with a long, slender, slightly curved bill, a fairly long tail, and strong, short legs. The wings are short and rounded.

COLOR PATTERN Canyon Wrens are rusty brown birds with a neat white throat. The crown is a grayer brown than the body and speckled with white, while the tail is a brighter rusty brown than the back. The wings and tail are barred with black. Juveniles are similar, but their upperparts are more textured and less spotted, and their flanks lack barring. Adult and immature birds look otherwise similar.

BEHAVIOR Canyon Wrens cling to rock walls like nuthatches, scaling even vertical surfaces with ease. They move deliberately and deftly, looking into crevices that might hold prey, which they extract with quick jabs of the fine bill. Males sing from favored rocky song perches in spring and summer and sometimes in winter. Females sing on occasion.

HABITAT Look for Canyon Wrens on cliffs, rocky outcrops, and boulder piles, and in canyons.

bird with a big voice, the **Canyon Wren** sings a gorgeous series of sweet, cascading whistles that echo rocky walls of its canyon habitat. They are incredibly agile birds that hunt for insects mostly among scaling cliff faces and using their long, slender bills to probe into crevices with surgical precision.

ADULT

ADULT

ADULT / IMMATURE

ADULT

SIZE & SHAPE The House Wren is small and compact, with a flat head and fairly long, thin, curved bill. It has short wings and a longish tail that it keeps either cocked above the line of the body or slightly drooped. Juveniles and late-summer molting adult birds may have little or no tail.

COLOR PATTERN The House Wren is subdued brown overall with darker barring on the wings and tail. The pale eyebrow that is characteristic of so many wren species is much fainter or completely lacking in House Wrens.

BEHAVIOR Bubbly and energetic, House Wrens hop or flit quickly through tangles and low branches. They call attention to themselves year-round with harsh scolding chatter and, in spring and summer, frequent singing.

HABITAT House Wrens live in habitats featuring trees, shrubs, and tangles interspersed with clearings. They thrive around humans, often exploring the nooks and crannies in houses, garages, and play spaces.

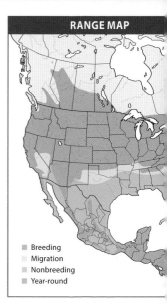

RANGE MAP

Breeding
Migration
Nonbreeding
Year-round

A plain brown bird with an effervescent voice, the **House Wren** is a common backyard bird. Listen for rush-and-jumble song in summer to find it zipping through foliage, snatching at insects. House Wrens use nestboxes, but you may also find their twig-filled nests in old cans, boots, or boxes in your garage.

ADULT / IMMATURE

ADULT / IMMATURE

JUVENILE

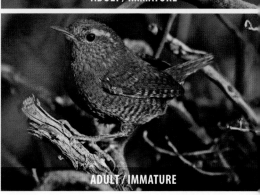

ADULT / IMMATURE

RANGE MAP

reeding
Ionbreeding
ear-round

SIZE & SHAPE One of the smallest wrens in the United States, the Pacific Wren has a short, stubby tail, usually held upright. Its small size and short tail give it a round appearance. It has short wings and a thin bill.

COLOR PATTERN The Pacific Wren is brown overall, with darker brownish-black barring on the wings, tail, and belly. The face is also brown, with a subtle pale eyebrow.

BEHAVIOR Pacific Wrens hop through the understory, investigating upturned roots and decaying logs for food. They often bob their heads or entire bodies when standing still. In flight, they rapidly beat their tiny wings to move between cover.

HABITAT Pacific Wrens are most common in old-growth coniferous forests but also live in broadleaf forests, treeless islands in Alaska, and in mixed-species forests near streams. They forage and nest near fallen logs, upturned tree roots, dead trees, and thick understory cover.

c Wrens are tiny brown wrens with a vocal repertoire much larger than themselves. One researcher ed them a "pinnacle of song complexity." This tinkling, bubbly songster hides in the dark understory -growth coniferous forests or darts between patches of cover like a mouse.

SIZE & SHAPE Bewick's Wrens are medium-sized wrens with a slender body and a strikingly long tail often held upright. They have long, slender bills that are slightly downcurved.

COLOR PATTERN Bewick's Wrens are subdued brown-and-gray wrens with a long, white stripe over the eye. The back and wings are plain brown, underparts are grayish white, and the long tail is barred with black and tipped with white spots. Males, females, and immature birds look the same.

BEHAVIOR Bewick's Wrens cock their long tails up over their backs, often flicking their tails from side to side or fanning them as they skulk through tangles of branches and leaves searching for insects. During breeding season, males sing vigorously from prominent perches.

HABITAT Bewick's Wrens favor dry brushy areas, chaparral, scrub, thickets in open country, and open woodlands near rivers and streams. They are at home in gardens, residential areas, and parks in cities and suburbs.

RANGE MAP

■ Breeding
■ Nonbreeding
■ Year-round

Look for the hyperactive **Bewick's Wren** flicking its long tail as it hops between branches in much of west North America. These master vocalists belt out a string of whistles, warbles, burrs, and trills to attract ma and defend their territory. Unfortunately, these birds have virtually disappeared from the East.

ADULT

ADULT

ADULT

JUVENILE

RANGE MAP

Year-round

SIZE & SHAPE American Dippers are chunky, round-bodied birds with a large head, short neck, long legs, and a short tail. The bill is thin and dark. They are larger than sparrows but smaller than robins.

COLOR PATTERN Adult American Dippers are slaty gray with dark brown heads and white eyelids, which are obvious when they blink. Immature dippers are similar to adults but are paler with subtly barred underparts and a yellowish bill.

BEHAVIOR American Dippers are often seen perched on rocks in the middle of a rushing stream, where they frequently bob up and down. They wade, swim, and dive either from the water or the air, and can move rocks on the stream-bottom to get at aquatic insects. They build nests on cliff ledges, behind waterfalls, on boulders, on dirt banks, or under bridges, always above or close to fast moving streams.

HABITAT American Dippers live on rushing, unpolluted waters with rocky bottoms in mountain, coastal, or even desert streams of the West. They use overhanging banks for cover and nesting sites.

merican Dipper is North America's only exclusively aquatic songbird. It catches all of its food water in swiftly flowing streams by swimming and walking on the stream bottom. To survive in cold s, it has a low metabolic rate, extra oxygen-carrying capacity in its blood, and a thick coat of feathers.

BREEDING ADULT

NONBREEDING ADULT

ADULT

JUVENILE

SIZE & SHAPE Starlings are chunky and blackbird-sized, with short tails and long, slender bills. In flight, their wings are short and pointed. They are larger than sparrows but smaller than robins.

COLOR PATTERN At a distance, starlings look black. In summer, they are iridescent purplish green with yellow beaks, and in fresh winter plumage, they are brown and covered in brilliant white spots that look like stars in a night sky (giving them their name). Juveniles are pale brown overall.

BEHAVIOR Boisterous starlings travel in large groups, often with blackbirds and grackles. They race across fields, beak down and probing the grass for food; or sit high on wires or trees. They make a bewildering variety of sounds, from thin whistles, to rattles, to imitations of birds, including Red-tailed Hawks, American Robins, and others.

HABITAT Starlings are common in towns, suburbs, farms, and countryside near human settlements. They feed on lawns, fields, sidewalks, and in parking lots. They perch and roost high on wires, trees, and buildings.

RANGE MAP

Year-round

All **European Starlings** in North America descended from 100 birds released in New York's Central Pa the early 1890s by a group who wanted America to have all the birds mentioned by Shakespeare. Too more than 200 million starlings range from Alaska to Mexico and are largely considered pests.

ADULT / IMMATURE

ADULT / IMMATURE

JUVENILE

ADULT / IMMATURE

RANGE MAP

Breeding
Migration
Nonbreeding
Year-round

SIZE & SHAPE The Gray Catbird is a medium-sized, slender songbird with a long, round-tipped tail and a narrow, straight bill. Catbirds are fairly long-legged and have broad, rounded wings.

COLOR PATTERN Catbirds give the impression of being entirely slate gray. Looking closer, you may see the small black cap, blackish tail, and rich rufous-brown patch under the tail. Adult and immature birds look similar.

BEHAVIOR Catbirds are secretive but energetic, hopping and fluttering from branch to branch through tangles of vegetation. Singing males sit atop shrubs and small trees. Catbirds are reluctant to fly across open areas, preferring quick, low flights over vegetation.

HABITAT Look for Gray Catbirds in dense tangles of shrubs, small trees, and vines, along forest edges, streamside thickets, old fields, and fence rows. They are often found in backyards that have shrubs or thickets.

...learning bird calls by listening in thickets and vine tangles for the **Gray Catbird**, whose catty *mew* is unforgettable. They are relatives of mockingbirds and thrashers, and they share that group's vocal abilities, mimicking the sounds of other species and stringing them together to make their own song.

ADULT MALE

ADULT MALE (L) ADULT FEMALE (R)

ADULT FEMALE

JUVENILE

SIZE & SHAPE Western Bluebirds are small thrushes that usually perch upright. They are stocky with thin, straight bills and fairly short tails.

COLOR PATTERN Male Western Bluebirds are shiny blue above with rusty orange extending from a vest on the breast onto the upper back. They have a blue throat. Females are gray buff with a pale orange wash on the breast and blue tints to the wings and tail. They have a gray-buff throat, and the lower belly is whitish. Juveniles are spotted.

BEHAVIOR Highly social, Western Bluebirds feed in flocks during the nonbreeding season. They hunt for insects by dropping to the ground from a low perch, and eat berries in trees. They use trees, fences, and utility lines as perches.

HABITAT Look for Western Bluebirds in open woodland, both coniferous and broadleaf. They also live in backyards, burned areas, and farmland, from sea level far up into the mountains.

RANGE MAP

- Breeding
- Migration
- Nonbreeding
- Nonbreeding (scarce)
- Year-round

Western Bluebirds may look gentle, but territorial battles can get heated. Rival males may grab each other's legs, tumble to the ground and pin their opponent, then stand over the rival and jab with their Interestingly, studies show that many nests include young that were not fathered by the resident ma

ADULT MALE

ADULT FEMALE

JUVENILE

ADULT FEMALE

RANGE MAP

Breeding
Nonbreeding
Year-round

SIZE & SHAPE Mountain Bluebirds are fairly small thrushes with round heads and straight, thin bills. Compared with other bluebirds, they are lanky and long-winged, with a long tail.

COLOR PATTERN Male Mountain Bluebirds are sky blue, a bit darker on wings and tail and paler below, with white under the tail. Females are mostly gray brown with tinges of pale blue in the wings and tail. They occasionally show a suffusion of orange brown on the breast. Mountain Bluebirds' bills are black. Juveniles have fewer spots than the young of other bluebirds and lack spotting on the back.

BEHAVIOR Unlike other bluebirds, they often hover while foraging and pounce on insect prey from elevated perches. In winter, they occur in large flocks, wandering the landscape and feasting on berries.

HABITAT Mountain Bluebirds are common in the West's wide open spaces, particularly at middle and higher elevations.

Mountain Bluebirds lend a bit of cerulean sparkle to open habitats across much of western North ʳica. These cavity nesters flit between perches in mountain meadows, in burned or cut-over areas, or e prairie meets forest—especially in places where people have provided nest boxes.

ADULT

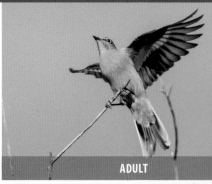
ADULT

JUVENILE

ADULT

SIZE & SHAPE This thrush is a medium-sized songbird with a long tail, a short bill, and a small rounded head relative to its body size. Its upright posture and long tail give it a long and slender appearance.

COLOR PATTERN Townsend's Solitaires are gray with prominent white eyerings, buffy wing patches, and white outer tail feathers. Juveniles are dark gray overall and heavily spotted with buff and white, giving them a scaly look.

BEHAVIOR The elegant Townsend's Solitaire perches upright and sings from prominent perches at all times of the year. Birds fly out and back to nab flying insects or pounce on insects on the ground. In the winter, they move south or to lower elevations to feed on juniper berries, which they aggressively defend.

HABITAT Townsend's Solitaires inhabit open pine, fir, and spruce forests in mountainous regions from about 1,100–11,500 feet. During the nonbreeding season, some birds migrate short distances to lower elevations, especially where juniper berries are abundant.

RANGE MAP

- Breeding
- Migration
- Nonbreeding
- Nonbreeding (scarce)
- Year-round

The **Townsend's Solitaire** is a wide-eyed songbird of mountain forests of the West. Though they're thru
they perch upright atop trees and shrubs to advertise their territories all year long, and can be mistaken
flycatchers. In winter, they switch from eating primarily insects to fruit, particularly juniper berries.

ADULT MALE

ADULT MALE

ADULT FEMALE / IMMATURE

ADULT FEMALE

RANGE MAP

Breeding
Nonbreeding
Nonbreeding (scarce)
Year-round

SIZE & SHAPE Varied Thrushes are stocky robinlike songbirds with large, rounded heads, straight bills, and long legs. Usually seen standing horizontally on the ground or in a tree, they often look plump-bellied with a relatively short tail.

COLOR PATTERN Male Varied Thrushes are dark blue gray on the back and rich burnt orange below with a sooty-black breastband and orange line over the eye. The wings are blackish with a complex pattern of orange. Females have the same patterns, but are a paler gray brown. Juveniles resemble females but are duller and smudged with dusky below.

BEHAVIOR Varied Thrushes hop on the ground or low in shrubs and trees. They eat mainly insects in summer and switch to nuts and fruit in fall and winter. On breeding territories, male Varied Thrushes sit on exposed perches to sing their haunting, trilling songs.

HABITAT Varied Thrushes breed in the dark understories of humid coniferous and mixed forests along the Pacific Coast. In the winter, many move into dense parks, gardens, and backyards.

Varied Thrush's simple, ringing song gives a voice to the quiet forests of the Pacific Northwest, with towering conifers and wet understories of ferns, shrubs, and mosses. Catch a glimpse of this shy bird Cascades, in the Northern Rockies, and along the Pacific Coast.

ADULT

ADULT

ADULT

ADULT

SIZE & SHAPE Swainson's Thrushes are medium-sized, slim songbirds with round heads and short, straight bills. Their fairly long wings and medium-length tail can make the back half of the bird appear long.

COLOR PATTERN Swainson's Thrushes are brownish above with buffy spectacles and dark spotting on the whitish underparts. The brownish tail is not contrastingly rusty. The white throat is bordered by a dark brown stripe. Immature birds have pale wingbars that are lacking in adults.

BEHAVIOR Swainson's Thrushes are shy but vocal birds that skulk in the shadows of their dark forest-interior habitat. They forage for insects and other arthropods on or near the ground. On migration, particularly in fall, they also eat small fruits such as wild cherries and Virginia creeper.

HABITAT This bird is rarely found far from closed-canopy forest. Breeding habitat is usually a mix of broadleaf and coniferous forest. In the West, look for them in dense alder thickets along streams running through coniferous forest.

RANGE MAP

- Breeding
- Migration
- Nonbreeding

More likely heard than seen, **Swainson's Thrushes** enliven summer mornings and evenings with their upward-spiraling, flutelike songs. When flying overhead at night during spring and fall migration, they soft, bell-like *peep* calls which may be mistaken for frogs.

ADULT

ADULT

IMMATURE

ADULT

RANGE MAP

Breeding
Migration
Nonbreeding
Year-round

SIZE & SHAPE Hermit Thrushes have a chunky shape similar to an American Robin, but they are smaller. They stand upright, often with the slender, straight bill slightly raised. Like other thrushes, the head is round and the tail fairly long.

COLOR PATTERN The Hermit Thrush is soft brown on the head and back, with a distinctly warm, reddish tail. The underparts are pale with distinct spots on the throat and smudged spots on the breast. Look closely for a thin, pale eyering. Immature birds have pale wingbars that are lacking in adults.

BEHAVIOR Hermit Thrushes hop and scrape in leaf litter while foraging. They perch low to the ground and often wander into open areas such as forest clearings. They have a habit of raising the tail and then lowering it slowly.

HABITAT Hermit Thrushes breed in open areas inside boreal forests, broadleaf woods, and mountain forests. In winter, they often occupy lower elevation forests with dense understory and berry bushes.

nassuming bird with a lovely, melancholy song, the **Hermit Thrush** lurks in the understories of far hern forests in summer and is a frequent winter companion across much of the U.S. and Mexico. It ges on the forest floor by rummaging through leaf litter or seizing insects with its bill.

ADULT MALE (SPRING / SUMMER)

ADULT FEMALE / IMMATURE MALE (FALL / WI

JUVENILE

ADULT FEMALE (SPRING / SUMMER)

SIZE & SHAPE American Robins are among the largest songbirds with a round body, long legs, and fairly long tail. Robins are the largest of the North American thrushes and are a good reference point for comparing the size and shape of other birds, too.

COLOR PATTERN American Robins are gray-brown birds with warm orange underparts and dark heads. Compared with males, females sometimes have paler heads that contrast less with the gray back. In fall and winter, birds are covered with pale feather edges. Juveniles are spotted.

BEHAVIOR American Robins are industrious birds that bound across lawns or stand erect, beak tilted upward, to survey their environs. When alighting, they habitually flick their tails downward several times. In fall and winter, they form large flocks and gather in trees to roost or eat berries.

HABITAT You'll find American Robins on lawns, fields, and in city parks, as well as more wild places like forests and mountains up to near treeline, recently burned forests, and tundra.

RANGE MAP

- Breeding
- Year-round
- Winter

Quintessential early birds, **American Robins** are common across temperate North America, where they often seen tugging earthworms from lawns. Robins are popular for their cheery song, and appearance a the end of winter. They are also at home in wild areas, like mountain forests and the Alaskan wilderness

ADULT

ADULT

ADULT

IMMATURE (FIRST YEAR)

RANGE MAP

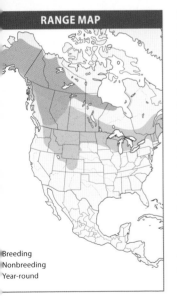

Breeding
Nonbreeding
Year-round

SIZE & SHAPE Bohemian Waxwings are full-bellied, thick-necked birds with a shaggy crest atop a small head. The wings are broad and pointed, like a starling's. The tail is fairly short and square-tipped.

COLOR PATTERN Bohemian Waxwings are grayish brown overall with a rusty wash around a black mask. The wings of adults have white and yellow markings, as well as red waxlike tips on the secondaries. Rusty undertail coverts can be hard to see. The tail is yellow-tipped. Immature birds lack the red tips on their wings. Juveniles are grayer overall and streaked below.

BEHAVIOR In the nonbreeding season, these social birds form large, noisy groups—sometimes in the thousands—as they scour the landscape for fruit. They dangle on flimsy branches to reach fruit or perch side by side in fruiting trees.

HABITAT Bohemian Waxwings breed in open coniferous forests and spend the nonbreeding season in open areas that have plentiful fruit, from city parks to forest patches near streams.

to their name, **Bohemian Waxwings** wander like bands of vagabonds across the northern United es and Canada in search of fruit during the nonbreeding season. High-pitched trills emanate from the as large groups descend on fruiting trees and shrubs at unpredictable places and times.

ADULT

IMMATURE (FIRST YEAR)

JUVENILE

IMMATURE (FIRST YEAR)

SIZE & SHAPE The Cedar Waxwing is a medium-sized, sleek bird with a large head, short neck, and short, wide bill. Its crest often lies flat, and its wings are broad and pointed, like a starling's. The tail is fairly short and square-tipped.

COLOR PATTERN Cedar Waxwings have a pale brown head and chest fading to gray wings with red, waxy tips that are not always easy to see. The belly is pale yellow, and the gray tail has a bright yellow tip, which may be orange due to diet. The face has a narrow black mask outlined in white. Immature birds lack the red tips on their wings. Juveniles are streaky below.

BEHAVIOR These social birds live in flocks when not nesting. They sit in fruiting trees, swallowing berries whole or plucking them with a brief, fluttering hover. They also course over water for insects, flying like tubby, slightly clumsy swallows.

HABITAT Cedar Waxwings live in broadleaf or coniferous forests, old fields, and sagebrush, especially near water. They're increasingly common in towns and suburbs, where ornamental fruit trees flourish.

RANGE MAP

- Breeding
- Nonbreeding
- Year-round

In fall, **Cedar Waxwings** gather by the hundreds to eat berries, filling the air with their high, thin whistles. summer, you'll find them flitting about over rivers in pursuit of flying insects, where they show off dazzlin aeronautics for a forest bird. To attract them to your yard, plant native trees and shrubs that bear small fru

BREEDING MALE

NONBREEDING MALE

JUVENILE

ADULT FEMALE

RANGE MAP

ear-round
ear-round (scarce)

SIZE & SHAPE Introduced from Europe, House Sparrows aren't related to North American sparrows. They're chunkier and fuller in the chest, with a larger, rounded head, shorter tail, and stouter bill than most American sparrows.

COLOR PATTERN Males have a gray forehead, white cheeks, a black bib, and a rufous neck, although urban birds can be dull and grubby. Females are a buffy brown with dingy underparts. The backs of both are striped with buff, black, and brown.

BEHAVIOR House Sparrows flutter from eaves or hidden nests and hang around parking lots and outdoor cafés, waiting for crumbs. Their noisy, sociable *cheep cheep* calls are familiar wherever they are found.

HABITAT Look for House Sparrows on city streets, taking handouts in parks and zoos, or cheeping from a perch on trees in your yard. They are absent from undisturbed forests and grasslands, but common around farmsteads.

ouse Sparrow was introduced into Brooklyn, New York, in 1851. By 1900, it had spread to the Rocky tains. Today they are some of our most common birds. They aggressively defend their nest holes and imes evict native birds from them. These include Eastern Bluebirds, Purple Martins, and Tree Swallows.

ADULT MALE

ADULT MALE

ADULT FEMALE / IMMATURE

ADULT FEMALE / IMMATURE

SIZE & SHAPE Evening Grosbeaks are large, heavyset finches with very thick, powerful, conical bills. They have a thick neck, full chest, and relatively short tail.

COLOR PATTERN Adult male Evening Grosbeaks are yellow and black birds with a prominent white wing patch. They have dark heads with a bright yellow stripe over the eye. Females and immatures are mostly gray, with white-and-black wings and a greenish yellow tinge to the neck and flanks. The massive bill varies from ivory to greenish yellow.

BEHAVIOR Evening Grosbeaks forage in flocks in winter and break off into small groups or pairs during the breeding season. They forage in treetops for insect larvae during the summer, buds in spring, and seeds, berries, and small fruits in winter.

HABITAT Evening Grosbeaks breed in mature and second-growth coniferous forests of northern North America and the Rocky Mountains. In winter, they live in coniferous and broadleaf forests as well as in urban and suburban areas. When wintering in urban environments, they are most abundant in small woodlots near bird feeders.

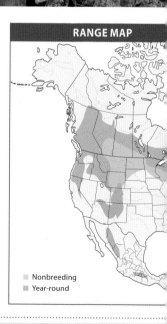

RANGE MAP

■ Nonbreeding
■ Year-round

The **Evening Grosbeak** adds a splash of color to winter bird feeders every few years, when large flocks depart their northern breeding grounds en masse to seek food to the south. This declining species is becoming uncommon, particularly in the eastern United States.

ADULT MALE

ADULT MALE

ADULT FEMALE / IMMATURE MALE

ADULT FEMALE / IMMATURE FEMALE

RANGE MAP

onbreeding (scarce)
ear-round

SIZE & SHAPE The Pine Grosbeak is a large, plump, heavy-chested finch with a round head. Its bill is thick and conical, but much stubbier than in other finch species. The tail is long and slightly notched.

COLOR PATTERN Adult male Pine Grosbeaks are reddish pink and gray. Females and immatures are grayish with tints of reddish orange or yellow on the head and rump. They all have dark gray wings marked by two white wingbars. The amount of reddish pink on the bellies of males and the head and rump color on females is variable.

BEHAVIOR Pine Grosbeaks hop among branches to nip off fresh buds and needles or hop on the ground to grab fallen seeds. Males sing a warbling song from treetops during the breeding season. In winter, they form small groups that travel in search of food, often showing up at feeders.

HABITAT Pine Grosbeaks inhabit open spruce, fir, and pine forests as well as subalpine forests. In winter, they tend to use mountain ash, maple, and ash forests with abundant seeds.

Pine Grosbeaks easily crush seeds and nip off tree buds and needles with their thick and stubby ey breed in open spruce, fir, and pine forests, but drop in on feeders in winter, especially in the East. r flocks may stay near a tree with abundant fruit until all of it is consumed.

ADULT MALE

ADULT MALE

ADULT MALE (YELLOW VARIANT)

ADULT FEMALE

SIZE & SHAPE House Finches are small with fairly large bills and somewhat long, flat heads. Wings are short, making the tail seem long. Tails have a relatively shallow notch when compared to other finches.

COLOR PATTERN Adult males are rosy red around the face and upper breast, with a streaky brown back, belly, and tail. In flight, the red rump is conspicuous. Adult females aren't red; they are plain grayish brown with thick, blurry streaks. Some adult males are decidedly more yellow than red. This is due to diet and can be temporary.

BEHAVIOR House Finches are gregarious birds that collect at feeders or perch high in nearby trees. They move fairly slowly and sit still as they crush seeds with rapid bites. Their flight is bouncy, like that of many finches.

HABITAT House Finches frequent city parks, backyards, urban centers, farms, and forest edges across the continent. In the West, you'll also find them in their native habitats of deserts, grassland, chaparral, and open woods.

RANGE MAP

■ Year-round

The **House Finch** is a recent introduction from western into eastern North America (and Hawaii), but i has received a warmer reception than other arrivals like the European Starling and House Sparrow. Th partly due to the cheerful, long, twittering song, which can now be heard across much of the continer

ADULT MALE

ADULT MALE

ADULT FEMALE / IMMATURE

ADULT FEMALE / IMMATURE

RANGE MAP

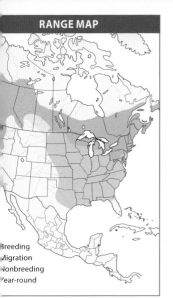

Breeding
Migration
Nonbreeding
Year-round

SIZE & SHAPE Among small forest birds like chickadees, kinglets, and nuthatches, Purple Finches are large and chunky. Their powerful, conical beaks are larger than any sparrow's. The tail seems short and is notched at the tip.

COLOR PATTERN Adult male Purple Finches are pinkish red on the head and breast, mixing with brown on the back and white on the belly. Females and immature birds have no red and are coarsely streaked below, with strong facial markings, including a whitish eyestripe.

BEHAVIOR Purple Finches readily come to feeders for black oil sunflower seeds. You'll also see them in forests, foraging high up in trees. In winter, they'll eat seeds from plants and stalks in weedy fields. Their flight is undulating.

HABITAT In winter, look for Purple Finches in old fields, forest edges, and backyards. In summer, they prefer moist, cool coniferous forests. You'll also find them in mixed forests, along wooded streams, and in tree-lined suburbs.

Tory Peterson famously described the **Purple Finch** as a "sparrow dipped in raspberry juice." Separating from House Finches requires a careful look, but the reward is a delicately colored, cleaner version of the Finch. In forests, you're likely to hear their warbling song from the highest parts of trees.

ADULT MALE

ADULT MALE

IMMATURE MALE

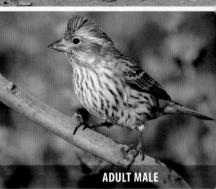

ADULT MALE

SIZE & SHAPE Cassin's Finches are small songbirds with peaked heads and short-medium tails. Their heavy bills are fairly long and straight-sided, and their tails are obviously notched. Their wings are long and, when perched, the tips project farther down the tail than in other finches.

COLOR PATTERN Adult males are rosy pink overall with a brighter red crown. Females and immature birds are brown and white with crisp, dark streaks on the chest and underparts. Both sexes have fine streaks under the tail. Some immature males have a golden wash on the face and rump.

BEHAVIOR Cassin's Finches fly with an undulating pattern, rising when they flap and dipping when they glide. After breeding, they join foraging groups of Red Crossbills, Evening Grosbeaks, Pine Siskins, and other finches.

HABITAT Cassin's Finches often live in mature coniferous and quaking aspen forests, as well as sagebrush shrublands. They breed mostly between 3,000 and 10,000 feet elevation and winter at lower elevations.

RANGE MAP

■ Breeding
■ Nonbreeding
■ Year-round

Slightly less well known than the House Finch and Purple Finch, **Cassin's Finch** is a rosy-tinged finch c mountains of western North America. Small flocks twitter and forage in the tall coniferous forests and groves of quaking aspen. Males sing a rollicking song that includes mimicked calls of other birds.

ADULT MALE

ADULT MALE

ADULT FEMALE / IMMATURE

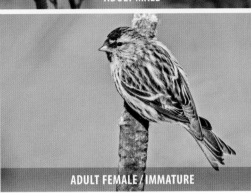

ADULT FEMALE / IMMATURE

RANGE MAP

Breeding
Winter
Winter (scarce)
Year-round
Irruptive

SIZE & SHAPE Common Redpolls are small songbirds with small heads and small, pointed bills, perfect for eating seeds. The tail is short with a small notch at the tip.

COLOR PATTERN Common Redpolls are brown-and-white finches with heavily streaked sides and white wingbars. The small red forehead patch and black around the yellow bill distinguish them from Pine Siskins. Males have a pale red vest on the chest and upper flanks. Female and immature birds are brown and streaky with a tiny red patch on the crown.

BEHAVIOR Redpolls travel in flocks of up to several hundred individuals. They move frenetically, foraging on seeds in fields or small trees one minute, and swirling away in a mass of chattering birds the next.

HABITAT Common Redpolls frequent tundra and associated habitats such as willow flats, open conifer forest, and open weedy fields. They visit backyard bird feeders as well, especially during winter and early spring.

ergetic as their electric zapping call notes would suggest, **Common Redpolls** are active foragers that in busy flocks. Look for them in birch trees or visiting feeders in winter. These small finches of the ra and boreal forest migrate erratically, and may show up in large numbers as far south as Kansas.

ADULT MALE

IMMATURE MALE

ADULT FEMALE

JUVENILE

SIZE & SHAPE The Red Crossbill is a stocky, medium-sized songbird with a short, notched tail and an unusual, twisted bill that crosses when closed.

COLOR PATTERN Adult males are brick red overall, with darker wings and tail. Females are yellowish with dark, unmarked wings. Immatures males are a patchy mix of red and orangish yellow feathers as they molt into adult plumage. Juveniles are streaked overall with thin buffy wingbars which can be hard to see.

BEHAVIOR Red Crossbills eat conifer seeds, forage in flocks, and may gather grit on the ground in the morning. Adult males perch atop conifers to sing and watch for predators. They sometimes attend feeders that offer sunflower seed, especially in the West.

HABITAT Red Crossbills are found in mature coniferous forests in mountains and the boreal forest, but during "irruptions," single birds and flocks may appear in forests, towns, and backyards far to the south and east of their typical range.

RANGE MAP

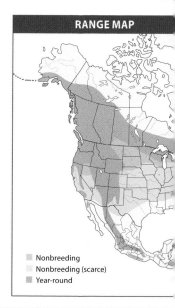

Nonbreeding
Nonbreeding (scarce)
Year-round

A fascinating finch of coniferous woodlands, the **Red Crossbill** forages on nutritious seeds in pine, hemlock, Douglas fir, and spruce cones. Their specialized bills allow them to break into unopened cone giving them an advantage over other finch species.

ADULT MALE (GREEN-MORPH)

ADULT / IMMATURE

ADULT / IMMATURE

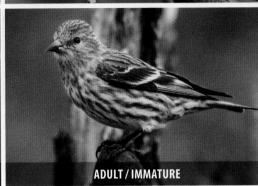

ADULT / IMMATURE

RANGE MAP

Breeding
Nonbreeding
Nonbreeding (scarce)
Year-round

SIZE & SHAPE Pine Siskins are very small songbirds with sharp, pointed bills and short, notched tails. Their uniquely shaped bill is more slender than that of most finches. In flight, look for their forked tails and pointed wingtips.

COLOR PATTERN Pine Siskins are brown and very streaky birds with subtle yellow edgings on wings and tails. Flashes of yellow can erupt as they take flight, flutter at branch tips, or display during mating. The occasional adult male is washed with green, but this is rare. Adults and immatures look mostly similar.

BEHAVIOR Pine Siskins often visit feeders in winter or cling to branch tips of pines and other conifers, sometimes hanging upside down to pick at seeds. They forage in tight flocks and twitter incessantly to each other, even in flight.

HABITAT Pine Siskins prefer coniferous or mixed coniferous-broadleaf forests with open canopies, but they'll forage in weedy fields, scrubby thickets, or yards and gardens. They flock at feeders in woodlands and suburbs.

s of tiny **Pine Siskins** may monopolize your thistle feeder one winter and be absent the next. This adic finch ranges widely and erratically across the continent each winter in response to seed crops. e brown-streaked acrobats flash yellow wing markings as they flutter while feeding or explode into flight.

ADULT MALE

IMMATURE MALE

ADULT FEMALE / IMMATURE

ADULT FEMALE / IMMATURE

SIZE & SHAPE Lesser Goldfinches are tiny, stub-billed songbirds with long, pointed wings, and short, notched tails.

COLOR PATTERN Males are bright yellow below with a glossy black cap and white patches in the wings; their backs are dull green with varying amounts of black mixed in. Females and immatures have olive backs, dull yellow underparts, and black wings marked by two whitish wingbars.

BEHAVIOR Lesser Goldfinches feed in busy flocks of up to several hundred at a time. They cling to dried flower heads or hang upside down to reach seeds. On the wing, they have the same dipping, bouncy flight as the American Goldfinch.

HABITAT Lesser Goldfinches feed in weedy fields, budding treetops, and in brush of open areas and edges. Depending on food availability, they may concentrate in mountain canyons and desert oases, but are also fairly common in suburbs.

RANGE MAP

Breeding
Winter
Year-round

Jabbering clouds of yellow, green, and black, **Lesser Goldfinches** gather in scrubby oak, cottonwood, willow habitats of the western U.S. They also visit suburban yards for seeds and water. Listen closely to wheezy songs, which often include snippets from the songs of other birds.

BREEDING MALE

NONBREEDING MALE

BREEDING FEMALE

NONBREEDING FEMALE / IMMATURE

RANGE MAP

Breeding
Year-round
Nonbreeding

SIZE & SHAPE The American Goldfinch is a small finch with a short, conical bill and small head, long wings, and short, notched tail.

COLOR PATTERN Adult males in spring and early summer are bright yellow with a black forehead, black wings with white markings, and white patches both above and beneath the tail. Adult females in spring and summer are duller yellow beneath, olive above. Nonbreeding winter birds are drab, unstreaked brown, with blackish wings and two pale wingbars. Immature birds have buffy wingbars on dark wings.

BEHAVIOR Active and acrobatic little finches that cling to weeds and seed socks, American Goldfinches sometimes mill about in large numbers at feeders or on the ground beneath them. They fly with a bouncy, undulating pattern and often call in flight, drawing attention to themselves.

HABITAT Their main natural habitats are weedy fields and floodplains, where plants such as thistles and asters are common. They're also found in cultivated areas, roadsides, orchards, and backyards. They show up at feeders any time of year, but most abundantly during winter.

American Goldfinch is our only finch that molts its body feathers twice a year, once in late winter again, in late summer. The brightening yellow of male goldfinches is a welcome mark of approaching g. Among the strictest vegans in the bird world, they select an entirely plant-based diet.

ADULT

ADULT

JUVENILE

ADULT

SIZE & SHAPE The Grasshopper Sparrow is small with a distinctive compact shape. The head is large and has a flat crown with a conspicuous bill, and the tail is very short. It is among the smallest birds in its habitat.

COLOR PATTERN The Grasshopper Sparrow is a brown and tan bird with light streaking. The belly is white, but the entire breast is buffy. The back is mottled tan, black, and chestnut and isn't as streaky as other sparrows. The face is relatively plain with a conspicuous white eyering. They often show a yellow spot between the eye and bill (the lore) and on the bend of the wing. Juveniles have a band of streaks across the breast.

BEHAVIOR Grasshopper Sparrows stay close to the ground, preferring to run or walk rather than fly. During the breeding season, males sing from exposed perches near the tops of grass stalks or along barbed wire fences.

HABITAT This species breeds in open grasslands, prairies, hayfields, and pastures, typically with some bare ground. They usually avoid breeding in grasslands with shrub cover, but may inhabit them on migration and in winter.

RANGE MAP

- Breeding
- Breeding (scarce)
- Nonbreeding
- Nonbreeding (scarce)
- Year-round

When not singing a quiet, insectlike song from atop a stalk in a weedy pasture, the **Grasshopper Spar** disappears into grasses, running along the ground rather than flying. Appropriately, grasshoppers are primary prey. Adults prepare them for chicks by vigorously shaking the legs off the insects.

ADULT

ADULT

JUVENILE

ADULT

RANGE MAP

reeding
ear-round

SIZE & SHAPE The Black-throated Sparrow is a medium-sized sparrow with a large, round head, a conical bill which is perfect for eating seeds, and a medium-length tail.

COLOR PATTERN Black-throated Sparrows have a neat gray face bordered by two white stripes and a black triangular throat patch. The upperparts are grayish brown, and the underparts are a mix of cream and white. The tail is dark with white spots on the corners. Juveniles look like adults but lack the black throat patch and have faint streaks above and below.

BEHAVIOR Black-throated Sparrows hop along the ground, pecking for insects and seeds. They make short flights, low to the ground, across desert scrub areas. They often perch in trees and shrubs, giving quiet calls.

HABITAT These sparrows frequent semiopen areas with shrubs and small trees. They are common in canyons, desert washes, and desert scrub. In some parts of their range, they occur as high as 7,000 feet elevation in pinyon-juniper forests.

esident of open, shrubby deserts is one of the sharpest looking of all sparrows. **Black-throated** ows have neat gray faces with two bold white stripes and a black triangular patch on the throat. intently for little tinkling calls as these quiet birds forage on the ground for seeds and insects.

ADULT

ADULT

IMMATURE

ADULT

SIZE & SHAPE The Lark Sparrow is large and long-tailed (for a sparrow). When perched, it often looks long-bodied with a thin neck and a round head.

COLOR PATTERN Adults have a very striking head pattern with a chestnut crown and cheek patch, a pale stripe over the eye, and a strong black malar or mustache stripe. Note the black spot in the center of the white breast. Immature Lark Sparrows have similar face patterns but lack the chestnut coloration in the crown and cheek.

BEHAVIOR Lark Sparrows usually feed on the ground for seeds and insects and will fly into trees and shrubs when disturbed. During the breeding season, males sing from elevated perches.

HABITAT Lark Sparrows breed in open grassy habitats like orchards, fallow fields, woodlands, mesquite grasslands, savanna, and sagebrush steppe. In migration and winter, look for them in pine-oak forest, thorn scrub, and agricultural areas.

RANGE MAP

- Breeding
- Breeding (scarce)
- Migration
- Nonbreeding
- Irruptive
- Year-round

This large, brown sparrow's harlequin facial pattern and white tail spots make it a standout among spar Male **Lark Sparrows** sing a melodious jumble of churrs, buzzes, and trills. Their unusual courtship invol hopping and crouching display, unlike other sparrows.

BREEDING MALE

ADULT MALE (EARLY SPRING)

ADULT FEMALE / IMMATURE

ADULT FEMALE / IMMATURE

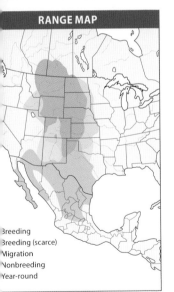

RANGE MAP

Breeding
Breeding (scarce)
Migration
Nonbreeding
Year-round

SIZE & SHAPE The Lark Bunting is heavyset with a very large, conical bill, and a compact, robust body; larger than a House Sparrow's. The bill and overall shape are reminiscent of a grosbeak or bunting.

COLOR PATTERN Breeding males are an unmistakable black with white wing patches. Nonbreeding males, as well as females and immatures, are brownish above, pale with brown streaking below, with extensive white in the upperwing coverts and small white tips to the tail feathers. The bill is a distinctive pale blue gray.

BEHAVIOR Lark Buntings forage on or near open ground and may employ a gallop when pursuing fast insects, with one foot coming down just before the next. On migration and in winter, they form flocks of up to several hundred birds.

HABITAT Lark Buntings breed in open grasslands, usually with some element of sagebrush, but they may also forage and nest in hayfields and other agricultural fields. Wintering flocks are found in many similar habitats.

Buntings breed in beautiful, windswept habitats such as the grasslands and shrub-steppe of the : Plains, where they prefer large expanses of native grasslands with sagebrush. Watch and listen for ding males as they deliver their flight song, rising up and then gliding down to earth as they sing.

BREEDING ADULT

NONBREEDING ADULT

JUVENILE

NONBREEDING ADULT

SIZE & SHAPE The Chipping Sparrow is a tiny, slender, fairly long-tailed sparrow with a bill that is a bit small compared to those of some other sparrows.

COLOR PATTERN Summer Chipping Sparrows look clean and crisp, with frosty underparts, pale faces, a black line through the eyes, and a bright rusty crown to top them off. In winter, Chipping Sparrows are a subdued buff brown with darkly streaked upperparts. The black line through the eye is still visible, and the cap is a warm but more subdued reddish brown. Juveniles have streaked underparts and a streaked brown crown.

BEHAVIOR Chipping Sparrows feed on the ground, take cover in shrubs, and sing from the tops of small trees. You'll often see loose groups of them flitting up from open ground. When singing, they cling to high outer limbs.

HABITAT Look for Chipping Sparrows in open woodlands and forests with grassy clearings across North America, all the way up to the highest elevations. You'll also see them in parks, along roadsides, and in your backyard.

RANGE MAP

■ Breeding
■ Migration
■ Nonbreeding
■ Year-round

A crisp, pretty sparrow whose bright rufous cap provides a splash of color and makes adults fairly easy identify. **Chipping Sparrows** are common across much of North America wherever trees are intersper with grassy openings. Their loud, trilling songs are one of the most common sounds of spring.

BREEDING ADULT

BREEDING ADULT

JUVENILE

NONBREEDING ADULT

RANGE MAP

Breeding
Migration
Nonbreeding

SIZE & SHAPE The Brewer's Sparrow is typical of the Spizella group of sparrows: dainty and slim, with a long, notched tail, short, rounded wings, and a small, sharply conical bill. Though its size varies, it is on average North America's smallest sparrow.

COLOR PATTERN Brewer's Sparrows are dusky gray brown, with grayish underparts and a thin white eyering. The back and nape are streaked. A faint gray stripe over the eye contrasts with a darker eyeline. The throat is grayish white. Juveniles are streaked below.

BEHAVIOR In spring and early summer, breeding males sing long, trilled songs from atop sagebrush. They forage in dense shrubs to glean insects and tend to stay out of open areas. In fall and winter, they often convene in large flocks with other *Spizella* sparrows.

HABITAT These birds live in the arid sagebrush steppe of the interior West—the region's most abundant bird. In some northwestern mountains, the "Timberline Sparrow" form lives in subalpine trees and dwarf shrubs.

er's Sparrows** are at first glance so subtly marked that they've been called the "bird without a field ." These streaky, gray-brown sparrows are notable for their reliance on sagebrush breeding habitat, heir plumage is elegantly tuned to their muted, gray-green home.

ADULT (SOOTY)

ADULT (SLATE-COLORED)

ADULT (RED)

ADULT (THICK-BILLED)

SIZE & SHAPE Fox Sparrows are large, round-bodied sparrows with stout bills and medium-length tails.

COLOR PATTERN Fox Sparrows vary greatly across their range. "Red" Fox Sparrows are rusty above with some pale gray on the head and rufous splotches on the underparts. The "Slate-colored" form is small-billed and dull gray above with brownish splotches below and rusty wings and tail. The "Sooty" form along the Pacific Coast is very dark brown above, and the "Thick-billed" form is a much larger-billed version of the "Slate-colored" form.

BEHAVIOR Fox Sparrows spend a lot of time on the ground, using their legs to kick away leaf litter in search of insects and seeds. They rarely venture far from cover. In spring and summer, listen for their sweet, whistled song from scrub or forest; also, pay attention for a sharp *smack* call.

HABITAT Fox Sparrows breed in coniferous forest and dense mountain scrub. They spend winters in scrubby habitat and forest, when they are most likely to be seen kicking around under backyard bird feeders.

RANGE MAP

■ Breeding
  Migration
  Nonbreeding
  Nonbreeding (scarce)
■ Year-round

Typically seen sending up a spray of leaf litter as they kick around in search of food, **Fox Sparrows** are splotchy sparrows of dense thickets. Named for the rich red hues that many Fox Sparrows wear, this sp is nevertheless one of our most variable birds; they range from foxy red to gray to dark brown.

ADULT

ADULT

ADULT

ADULT

RANGE MAP

Breeding
Migration
Nonbreeding

SIZE & SHAPE American Tree Sparrows are small, round-headed birds that fluff out their feathers, making their plump bodies look even chubbier. Among sparrows, they have fairly small bills and long, thin tails.

COLOR PATTERN A rusty cap and rusty (not black) eyeline on a gray head, a streaked brown back, and a smooth gray to buff breast in both male and female American Tree Sparrows give an overall impression of reddish brown and gray. A dark smudge in the center of the unstreaked breast is common.

BEHAVIOR Small flocks of American Tree Sparrows hop about on the ground, scrabbling for grass and weed seeds, calling back and forth with a soft, musical twitter. Individuals may perch in the open atop goldenrod stalks or shrubs, or on low tree branches.

HABITAT In winter, look for American Tree Sparrows in fields with hedgerows, along forest edges, or near marshes. They readily visit backyards, especially if there's a seed feeder. In summer, they are rarely seen south of northern Canada.

American Tree Sparrows are busy visitors in winter backyards and weedy, snow-covered fields across northern Canada and the northern U.S. They scratch and peck the ground in small flocks, trading soft, musical ters. Come snowmelt, these sparrows begin their long migration to breeding grounds of the far north.

ADULT MALE (SLATE-COLORED)

ADULT MALE (PINK-SIDED)

ADULT FEMALE (OREGON)

ADULT MALE (OREGON)

SIZE & SHAPE The Dark-eyed Junco has a rounded head, short, stout bill, and a fairly long tail.

COLOR PATTERN All juncos have pale bills and white outer tail feathers that they flash in flight. The male "Slate-colored" form is mostly gray with a white belly. "Pink-sided" birds have a slate-gray head, brown back, and pinkish brown sides. The "Oregon" form has a dark brown to black hood (male and female, respectively), light brown back with buffy sides, and a white belly. Female and immature birds are duller and browner in all forms. Juveniles are streaky.

BEHAVIOR Dark-eyed Juncos hop around the bases of trees and shrubs in forests or venture onto lawns looking for seeds. They give high *chip* notes while foraging or as they take short, low flights through cover.

HABITAT Dark-eyed Juncos breed in coniferous or mixed-coniferous forests across the United States. During winter, you'll find them in open woodlands, fields, parks, roadsides, and backyards.

RANGE MAP

- Breeding
- Nonbreeding
- Year-round

Dark-eyed Juncos are neat, even flashy little sparrows that flit about forest floors of the western moun, and Canada, then flood the rest of temperate North America for winter. They're easy to recognize by th crisp (though extremely variable) markings and the bright white tail feathers they habitually flash in flig

ADULT (GAMBEL'S)

IMMATURE (DARK-LORED)

ADULT (PACIFIC SLOPE)

JUVENILE (PACIFIC SLOPE)

RANGE MAP

Breeding
Migration
Nonbreeding
Nonbreeding (scarce)
Year-round

SIZE & SHAPE The White-crowned Sparrow is a large sparrow with a small bill and a long tail. The head can look either distinctly peaked or smooth and flat, depending on the bird's posture and activity.

COLOR PATTERN White-crowned Sparrows are gray-and-brown birds with large, bold, black-and-white stripes on the head. Dark-lored forms have pink bills and black between the bill and the eye. The Gambel's form has an orange bill and is pale between the bill and the eye. Pacific slope forms have yellow bills, are pale between the bill and the eye, and are duller and browner overall. Young birds have rusty brown stripes on a gray head. Juveniles are streaky.

BEHAVIOR White-crowned Sparrows stay low near brushy habitat, hopping on the ground or on branches, usually below waist height. They're also found on open ground but will quickly retreat to nearby shrubs or trees to hide.

HABITAT White-crowned Sparrows live where safe tangles of brush mix with open or grassy ground for foraging. In much of the United States, they're most common in winter; they're found year-round in parts of the West.

e-crowned Sparrows** appear in droves each winter over much of North America, gracing gardens rails. Flocks scurry through brushy borders, overgrown fields, and backyards. As spring approaches, start singing their sweet but buzzy song before and during migration.

BREEDING ADULT

NONBREEDING ADULT

IMMATURE

NONBREEDING ADULT

SIZE & SHAPE Golden-crowned Sparrows are large, plump, long-tailed sparrows with small heads, thick necks, and short but stout bills, perfect for eating seeds.

COLOR PATTERN Golden-crowned Sparrows are streaked brown above and smooth gray to brown below, with a black crown and bright yellow forehead. Winter and immature birds are duller, with brown replacing black on the head and less obvious yellow on the crown.

BEHAVIOR Golden-crowned Sparrows feed on the ground and in low vegetation. They whistle slow, mournful songs from high perches. In migration and winter, they gather in loose flocks and mix with other sparrows.

HABITAT Golden-crowned Sparrows are most often seen in fall and winter, in forest edges, shrubs, and backyards of the West Coast. They nest much farther north, in low, shrubby areas of tundra and at boreal forest edges.

RANGE MAP

- Breeding
- Migration
- Nonbreeding

The large, handsome **Golden-crowned Sparrow** is a common bird of weedy or shrubby lowlands and edges in winter along the Pacific Coast. It seems to vanish for the summer into tundra and shrublands British Columbia to Alaska, where little is known of its breeding habits.

ADULT (WHITE-STRIPED)

ADULT (WHITE-STRIPED)

ADULT (TAN-STRIPED)

ADULT (TAN-STRIPED)

RANGE MAP

Breeding
Migration
Nonbreeding
Year-round

SIZE & SHAPE The White-throated Sparrow is a large, full-bodied sparrow with a fairly prominent bill, rounded head, long legs, and long, narrow tail.

COLOR PATTERN White-throated Sparrows are brown above and gray below. The "white-striped" form has a black-and-white-striped crown, bright white throat, and yellow between the eye and the gray bill. A second "tan-striped" form has a buff-on-brown face. The two forms persist because they almost always mate with a bird of the opposite morph.

BEHAVIOR White-throated Sparrows stay near the ground, scratching through leaves in search of food, often in flocks. In spring, look for them in bushes eating fresh buds. They sing their distinctive songs frequently, even in winter.

HABITAT Look for these sparrows in woods and forest edges, in regrowth following logging or fires, and at pond and bog edges. In winter, you can find them in thickets, overgrown fields, parks, and woodsy suburbs.

facial markings make the **White-throated Sparrow** an attractive bird as well as a hopping, flying anatomy ... There's the black eyestripe, the white crown and eyebrow stripe, the yellow lores, and the white throat ...red by a black whisker, or malar stripe. Listen for their pretty, wavering whistle of *Oh-sweet-Canada*.

ADULT

ADULT

ADULT

ADULT

SIZE & SHAPE Savannah Sparrows are small sparrows with short, notched tails. The head appears small for the plump body, and the crown feathers often flare up to give the bird's head a small peak. The thick-based bill, perfectly shaped for eating seeds, is small for a sparrow.

COLOR PATTERN Savannah Sparrows are generally brown above with dark streaks. They are white below with thin brown or black streaks on the breast and flanks. They usually show a small yellow mark above and in front of the eye. The shade of brown varies regionally.

BEHAVIOR Savannah Sparrows forage on or near the ground. When flushed, they usually fly up, flare their short tails, and circle before landing a few yards away. Males sing from exposed, low perches such as fence posts.

HABITAT Savannah Sparrows breed on tundra, grasslands, marshes, and farmland. On their winter range, they stick to the ground or in low vegetation in open areas; look for them along the edges of roads adjacent to farms.

RANGE MAP

■ Breeding
■ Migration
■ Nonbreeding
■ Year-round

Savannah Sparrows are understated but distinctive, with a short tail, small head, and a telltale yellow spot before the eye. They're one of the most abundant songbirds in North American grasslands and fields, and in summer, their soft but distinctive insectlike song drifts lazily over farm fields and grassl

RANGE MAP

Breeding
Nonbreeding
Year-round

SIZE & SHAPE Song Sparrows are medium-sized and fairly bulky sparrows. For a sparrow, the bill is short and stout and the head fairly rounded. The tail is long and rounded, and the wings are broad.

COLOR PATTERN Song Sparrows are brown with thick streaks on a white chest and flanks. The head is an attractive mix of warm red brown and slate gray, though these shades, and the amount of streaking, vary across its range. Adult and older, immature birds look similar.

BEHAVIOR Song Sparrows flit through dense vegetation, occasionally moving onto open ground after food. Flights are short, with a characteristic downward pumping tail. Males sing from exposed perches.

HABITAT Look for Song Sparrows in nearly any open habitat, including marsh edges, overgrown fields, backyards, desert washes, and forest edges. Song Sparrows commonly visit bird feeders and build nests in residential areas.

Song Sparrow is one of the most familiar North American sparrows. Don't let its bewildering variety of regional plumage differences deter you: if you see a streaky sparrow in an open, shrubby or wet area, perched on a low shrub and leaning back to sing a stuttering, clattering song, this is probably your bird.

ADULT

ADULT

ADULT

JUVENILE

SIZE & SHAPE The Lincoln's Sparrow is a medium-sized sparrow with a round belly and head, but the back of its head often looks pointed when it raises its crown feathers. Its tail is fairly short, and its conical bill is thinner than those of other sparrows.

COLOR PATTERN This bird is a streaky brown, buff, and gray with rusty wing and tail edges. Its chest and sides are buff with black streaking that fades to a white belly. A buffy mustache is outlined in brown, and it has a thin eyering. Its crown is striped brown and black.

BEHAVIOR Lincoln's Sparrows are secretive little birds that forage on or near the ground, rarely straying far from dense cover. During the breeding season, males sing either from exposed perches or tucked inside a shrub.

HABITAT Lincoln's Sparrows breed in wet meadows, patches of aspens, cottonwoods, and willows, and shrubby areas near streams. In winter, they use tropical and pine-oak forests, tropical scrub, weedy pastures, and shrubby fields.

RANGE MAP

■ Breeding
■ Migration
■ Nonbreeding
■ Year-round

The dainty **Lincoln's Sparrow** has a talent for concealing itself. It sneaks around the ground amid w thickets in wet meadows, rarely straying from cover. When it decides to pop up and sing from a will twig, its sweet, jumbling song may seem more fitting of a House Wren than a sparrow.

ADULT

ADULT

JUVENILE

IMMATURE

RANGE MAP

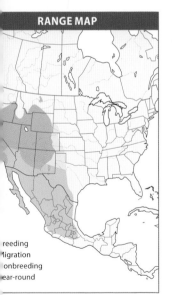

reeding
Migration
onbreeding
ear-round

SIZE & SHAPE Green-tailed Towhees are large, chunky sparrows with a big head, stocky body, and longish tail. The bill is thick and sparrowlike. They are larger than most sparrows and have shorter tails than most other towhees.

COLOR PATTERN Green-tailed Towhees are grayish birds with olive-yellow wings, back, and tail. The head is strongly marked with a bright rufous crown, white throat, and a dark "mustache" stripe.

BEHAVIOR Green-tailed Towhees forage on the ground or in dense shrubby foliage. They can be hard to see except when males sing from the top of a shrub. Their call, a quiet, catlike *mew*, can help you find them.

HABITAT Look for Green-tailed Towhees in shrubby habitats of the West, particularly disturbed areas of montane forest and open slopes in the Great Basin, sagebrush steppes, and high desert. In winter, they join mixed flocks in dense mesquite areas of desert washes.

's nothing quite like the color that gives the **Green-tailed Towhee** its name—from a deep olive to ∕-green on the edges of the wings and tail. Set off by a gray chest, white throat, and rufous crown, rge sparrow is a colorful resident of the West's shrubby mountainsides and sagebrush expanses.

ADULT MALE

ADULT FEMALE

ADULT FEMALE

JUVENILE

SIZE & SHAPE The Spotted Towhee is a large sparrow with a thick, pointed bill, short neck, chunky body, and long, rounded tail.

COLOR PATTERN Males have jet-black upperparts and throat; their wings and back are spotted bright white. The flanks are warm rufous, and the belly is white. Females have the same pattern but are grayish brown where males are black. In flight, look for white corners to the black tail. Juveniles are heavily streaked and brownish from the time they hatch into the fall.

BEHAVIOR Spotted Towhees hop over the ground beneath dense shrubs, scratching in leaf litter for food. They also climb into lower branches to search for insects and fruits, or to deliver their quick, buzzy song. Towhees can fly long distances, but more often make short, slow flights between patches of cover.

HABITAT Look for Spotted Towhees in open, shrubby habitat with thick undergrowth. Spotted Towhees are also at home in backyards, forest edges, and overgrown fields.

RANGE MAP

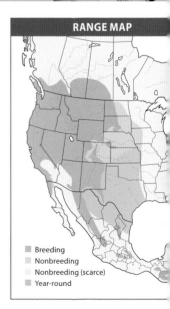

■ Breeding
■ Nonbreeding
■ Nonbreeding (scarce)
■ Year-round

The **Spotted Towhee** is a large, striking sparrow of sunbaked thickets of the West. When you catch sig of one, they're gleaming black above (females are grayish brown), and spotted and striped with brillia white. Their warm rufous flanks match the dry leaves where they hop and scratch for food.

ADULT

ADULT

ADULT

IMMATURE

RANGE MAP

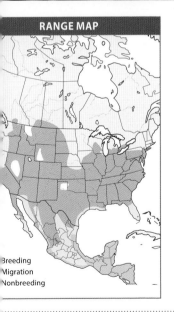

Breeding
Migration
Nonbreeding

SIZE & SHAPE The Yellow-breasted Chat is a small songbird about the size of a sparrow. It has a long tail, large head, and a relatively thick, heavy bill.

COLOR PATTERN Chats are olive green above with a bright yellow breast. The face is gray, with a white eyering that connects to the bill, forming "spectacles." They also have a white mustache stripe bordering the cheek. The lower belly is white. Immature birds are duller overall.

BEHAVIOR Yellow-breasted Chats are loud birds that tend to skulk in low, thick brush. In spring, males may sing from an exposed perch, but otherwise these birds will typically stay well hidden. Calls include a low, chattering scold.

HABITAT Yellow-breasted Chats live in thickets and other dense, regrowing areas such as bramble bushes, clearcuts, powerline corridors, and shrubs along streams.

Yellow-breasted Chat offers a cascade of song in the spring, when males deliver streams of whistles, es, chuckles, and gurgles with the fluidity of improvisational jazz. It's seldom seen or heard during the f the year, when both males and females skulk silently in the shadows of dense thickets.

ADULT MALE

ADULT MALE

ADULT FEMALE

JUVENILE

SIZE & SHAPE The Yellow-headed Blackbird is a fairly large blackbird with a stout body, large head, and long, conical bill.

COLOR PATTERN Adult male Yellow-headed Blackbirds are striking, with yellow heads and chests and black bodies with prominent white patches at the bend of the wing. Females and immatures are dark brown instead of black, with duller yellow heads. Juveniles are dark with a buffy head and a black ear patch.

BEHAVIOR Yellow-headed Blackbirds breed in loose colonies, and males mate with several females. During the breeding season, they eat insects and aquatic invertebrates. They form huge flocks in winter, often mixing with other blackbirds, and feed on seeds and grains in cultivated fields.

HABITAT Yellow-headed Blackbirds breed and roost in freshwater wetlands with dense, emergent vegetation such as cattails. They often forage in fields, typically wintering in large, open agricultural areas.

RANGE MAP

- ■ Breeding
- Migration
- Nonbreeding
- Nonbreeding (scarce)
- ■ Year-round

With a golden head, a white patch on black wings, and a call that sounds like a rusty farm gate opening the **Yellow-headed Blackbird** demands attention. Look for them in wetlands, where they nest in reed directly over the water. They're just as impressive in winter, when huge flocks seem to roll across farm f

BREEDING MALE (SUMMER)

BREEDING MALE (EARLY SPRING)

BREEDING FEMALE

NONBREEDING ADULT

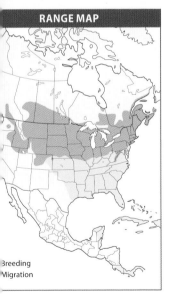

RANGE MAP

Breeding
Migration

SIZE & SHAPE Bobolinks are small songbirds with large, somewhat flat heads, short necks, and short tails. They are related to blackbirds and orioles, and they have a similar shaped, sharply pointed bill.

COLOR PATTERN Breeding male Bobolinks are mostly black with a white back and rump, and a rich buffy nape. Females and nonbreeding males are buffy brown, streaked with dark brown on the back and flanks. They have bold brown stripes on the crown but the nape is plain. The bill is pinkish.

BEHAVIOR In spring, males give display flights low over grasslands, fluttering their wings while singing. Otherwise, Bobolinks hide in tall grasses or brush, clinging to seed heads or foraging on the ground. They often migrate in large flocks.

HABITAT Bobolinks favor tall grasslands, uncut pastures, overgrown fields and meadows, and the continent's remaining prairies. While molting and on migration, look for them in marshes and in agricultural fields, particularly rice fields.

ed on a grass stem or displaying in flight over a field, breeding male **Bobolinks** are striking. No other American bird has a white back and black underparts (sometimes described as a backwards tuxedo). d to this are the male's straw-colored patch on the head and his bubbling, virtuosic song.

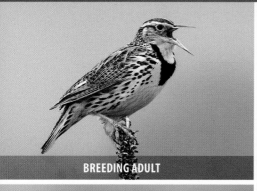

BREEDING ADULT

BREEDING ADULT

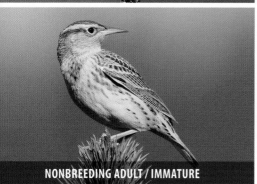

NONBREEDING ADULT / IMMATURE

NONBREEDING ADULT / IMMATURE

SIZE & SHAPE The Western Meadowlark is the size of a robin but chunkier and shorter-tailed, with a flat head, long, slender bill, and a round-shouldered posture that conceals its neck. The wings are triangular (like a starling's), and the tail is short, stiff, and spiky.

COLOR PATTERN Western Meadowlarks have yellow underparts with intricately patterned brown, black, and buff upperparts. A black V crosses the bright yellow breast and yellow creeps up the cheek toward the eye. The tail has a small amount of white along the outer edges. Nonbreeding and immature birds are duller and covered in buffy markings that obscure the summer pattern.

BEHAVIOR Western Meadowlarks fly in brief bursts, alternating rapid, stiff wingbeats with short glides. In spring, males perform a "jump flight," springing straight up into the air with fluttering wings and legs hanging limp below.

HABITAT Western Meadowlarks seek wide open native grasslands, prairies, meadows, and agricultural fields ranging from sea level to 10,000 feet. Look for them among low- to medium-height grasses more so than in tall fields.

RANGE MAP

- Breeding
- Nonbreeding
- Year-round

More easily seen than heard, the colorful **Western Meadowlark** sings a flutelike melody across grassla meadows, pastures, and along marsh edges throughout the West and Midwest. Look and listen for floc these stout ground feeders, strutting and feeding on seeds and insects.

ADULT MALE

ADULT MALE

IMMATURE MALE

ADULT FEMALE

RANGE MAP

Breeding
Migration
Nonbreeding
Year-round

SIZE & SHAPE Bullock's Orioles are medium-sized songbirds, slightly smaller than robins, with slim but sturdy bodies and medium-long tails. Orioles are related to blackbirds and share their long, thick-based, sharply pointed bills.

COLOR PATTERN Adult males are bright orange with a black back and throat, large white wing patch, orange face with a black line through the eye, and a black throat. Females and immatures are yellowish orange on the head and tail, with a grayish back and white-edged wing coverts. Immature males are similar to adult females, but show a black throat patch.

BEHAVIOR Bullock's Orioles feed in slender branches of trees and shrubs, catching caterpillars and also feeding on nectar or fruit. They are agile and active, often hanging upside down or stretching to reach prey.

HABITAT Look for Bullock's Orioles in open woodlands along streams, particularly among cottonwoods. They also favor orchards, parks, and oak or mesquite woodlands.

le canopy dwellers of open woodlands, **Bullock's Orioles** dangle upside down from branches to n insects, or while weaving their hanging nests. Listen for their whistling, chuckling song in tall trees g rivers and streams. Both male and female Bullock's Orioles sing.

ADULT MALE

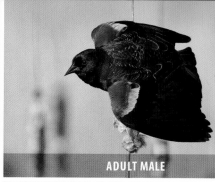
ADULT MALE

ADULT FEMALES

IMMATURE MALE

SIZE & SHAPE A stocky, broad-shouldered blackbird with a slender, conical bill and a medium-length tail. Red-winged Blackbirds often show a hump-backed silhouette while perched; males often sit with tail slightly flared.

COLOR PATTERN Male Red-winged Blackbirds are an even glossy black with red-and-yellow shoulder badges. The superficially sparrow-like females are crisply streaked and dark brownish overall, paler on the breast, and often show a whitish eyebrow. Immature and nonbreeding males have rufous feather edges.

BEHAVIOR Male birds sit on high perches and belt out a *conk-la-ree!* song all day long. Females skulk through vegetation for food and quietly weave their remarkable nests. In winter, they gather in huge mixed flocks to eat grains. Males display by holding their wings out to show off their red shoulder patches.

HABITAT Look for these birds in freshwater and saltwater marshes, along watercourses, and water hazards on golf courses, as well as drier meadows and old fields. In winter, you can find them at crop fields, feedlots, and pastures.

RANGE MAP

Breeding
Nonbreeding
Year-round

One of the most abundant birds in North America, the **Red-winged Blackbird** is a familiar sight atop cattails, along roadsides, and on telephone wires. Males have scarlet-and-gold shoulder patches they c puff up or hide. Their *conk-la-ree!* songs are happy indications of the return of spring.

ADULT MALE

ADULT MALE

JUVENILE

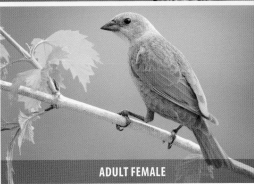
ADULT FEMALE

RANGE MAP

Breeding
Nonbreeding
Year-round

SIZE & SHAPE Brown-headed Cowbirds are smallish blackbirds, with a shorter tail and thicker head than most other blackbirds. The bill is much shorter and has a thicker base than other blackbirds. In flight, look for the shorter tail.

COLOR PATTERN Male Brown-headed Cowbirds have glossy black plumage and a rich brown head that looks black in low light or at distance. Females are gray-brown birds, lightest on the head and underparts, with fine streaking on the belly. Juveniles are brown overall with a scaly-looking back and streaked underparts.

BEHAVIOR Brown-headed Cowbirds feed on the ground in mixed flocks of blackbirds and starlings. Brown-headed Cowbirds are noisy, making a multitude of clicks, whistles, and chattering calls, in addition to a gurgling song.

HABITAT Brown-headed Cowbirds favor open habitats, such as fields, pastures, meadows, forest edges, and lawns. When not displaying or feeding on the ground, they often perch high on prominent tree branches.

le **Brown-headed Cowbirds** forgo building nests in favor of producing eggs, sometimes over three n a summer. Eggs are laid in the nests of other birds and young are raised by foster parents, often at xpense of the hosts' chicks. Their numbers and range have grown as forests are fragmented.

ADULT MALE

IMMATURE MALE

ADULT FEMALE

ADULT FEMALE

SIZE & SHAPE The Brewer's Blackbird is a long-legged, robin-sized songbird with a fairly long tail balanced by a full body, round head, and long, thick-based beak. In perched birds, the tail appears widened and rounded toward the tip.

COLOR PATTERN Males are glossy black all over with a staring yellow eye and a purple sheen on the head grading to greenish on the body. Females are plainer brown, darkest on the wings and tail, and they have dark eyes. Occasionally, females will have a pale eye. Immature birds look like washed-out, lighter brown versions of the females.

BEHAVIOR Brewer's Blackbirds feed on open ground in parks and busy streets. Their long legs give them a head-jerking, chickenlike walk. In flocks, they rise and fall as they fly. When landing, birds may circle slowly before settling.

HABITAT Look for Brewer's Blackbirds in open habitats of the West, such as coastal scrub, grasslands, riversides, meadows, as well as lawns, golf courses, parks, and city streets.

RANGE MAP

Breeding
Migration
Nonbreeding
Year-round

A bird to be seen in the full sun, the male **Brewer's Blackbird** is a glossy combination of black, midnig blue, and metallic green. Females are a staid brown. Common in much of the West, you'll see these ground-foraging birds on sidewalks, in city parks, and chuckling in flocks atop shrubs, trees, and reeds.

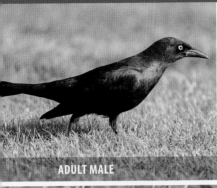

ADULT MALE

ADULT MALE

JUVENILE

ADULT FEMALE

RANGE MAP

Breeding
Nonbreeding
Year-round

SIZE & SHAPE Common Grackles are large, lanky blackbirds with long legs. The head is flat, and the bill is longer than in most blackbirds, with the hint of a downward curve. In flight, wings appear short in comparison to the tail, which is very long and hangs down in the middle.

COLOR PATTERN Common Grackles appear black from afar, but up close, glossy blue-green heads contrast with bronzy iridescent bodies and a golden eye. Females are less glossy and have shorter tails than males. Juveniles are all dark brown with dark eyes and shorter tails.

BEHAVIOR Common Grackles form large flocks, flying or foraging on lawns and in agricultural fields. They strut on their long legs, pecking for food rather than scratching. At feeders, they dominate smaller birds. Their flight is direct, with stiff wingbeats.

HABITAT Common Grackles thrive around agricultural fields, feedlots, city parks, and suburban lawns. They're also common in open habitats including woodland, forest edges, meadows, and marshes.

Common Grackles are blackbirds that look like they've been slightly stretched. They're taller and longer-tailed than a typical blackbird, with a longer, more tapered bill and glossy, iridescent bodies. Grackles walk around lawns and fields on their long legs or gather in noisy groups high in trees, typically conifers.

SIZE & SHAPE Orange-crowned Warblers are songbirds, smaller than a sparrow. Compared with other warblers, they have noticeably thin, sharply pointed bills. They have short wings and short, square tails.

COLOR PATTERN Orange-crowned Warblers are plain yellowish or olive, with a faint pale stripe over the eye, blackish line through the eye, and pale broken eyering. The undertail coverts are bright yellow. The orange crown may become visible if the bird is agitated, but is not often seen. Adult and immature birds look similar.

BEHAVIOR Orange-crowned Warblers forage in dense shrubbery and low trees. They tend to be unobtrusive, but their low foraging habits can help you spot them. They often give a high, faint contact call while foraging.

HABITAT Orange-crowned Warblers breed in dense broadleaf shrubs, usually within or adjacent to forest. During migration, you may find them in any habitat, though they still show a preference for dense, low vegetation.

RANGE MAP

- Breeding
- Migration
- Nonbreeding
- Year-round

Orange-crowned Warblers aren't the most dazzling warblers, but they're useful to learn. These grayish to green birds have few bold markings. There's rarely any sign of an orange crown, which is usually only visible when the bird is excited. They are one of the few warblers that are more common in the West than the East.

ADULT MALE

ADULT MALE

IMMATURE MALE

ADULT FEMALE

RANGE MAP

reeding
reeding (scarce)
ligration
onbreeding
ear-round

SIZE & SHAPE Common Yellowthroats are small songbirds with chunky, rounded heads and medium-length, slightly rounded tails. They are smaller than sparrows.

COLOR PATTERN Adult males are bright yellow below, with a sharp black face mask and olive upperparts. A whitish line sets off the black mask from the head and neck. Immature males show traces of the full mask of adult males. Females are a plain olive brown, usually with yellow brightening the throat and under the tail. They lack the black mask.

BEHAVIOR Common Yellowthroats spend much of their time skulking low to the ground in dense thickets and fields, searching for small insects and spiders. Males sing a distinctive, rolling *wichety-wichety-wichety* song. During migration, this is often the most common warbler found in fields and edges.

HABITAT Yellowthroats live in open areas with thick, low vegetation, ranging from marsh to grassland to open pine forest. During migration, they use an even broader suite of habitats, including backyards and forests.

ad black mask lends a touch of highwayman's mystique to the male **Common Yellowthroat**. Look for furtive warblers skulking through tangled vegetation, often at the edges of marshes and wetlands. vthroats are vocal, and their songs and distinctive call notes reveal their presence.

ADULT MALE

MALE

IMMATURE FEMALE (FIRST YEAR)

ADULT FEMALE

SIZE & SHAPE Yellow Warblers are small, evenly proportioned songbirds with medium-length tails and rounded heads. For a warbler, the straight, thin bill is relatively large.

COLOR PATTERN Yellow Warblers are uniformly yellow birds. Males are a bright, egg-yolk yellow with reddish streaks on the underparts. Females are yellow overall with a yellow-green back and mostly unstreaked yellow underparts. Both sexes flash yellow patches in the tail. The face is unmarked, accentuating the large black eye. Immatures are duller overall, and some can be almost entirely grayish.

BEHAVIOR Look for Yellow Warblers near the tops of tall shrubs and small trees. They forage with quick hops along small branches to glean caterpillars and other insects. Males sing a sweet, whistled song from high perches.

HABITAT Yellow Warblers breed in shrubby thickets and woods, particularly along watercourses and in wetlands. They are found in willows, alders, and cottonwoods across North America and up to 9,000 feet in the West. In winter, they mainly occur in mangrove forests of Mexico and Central and South America.

RANGE MAP

- Breeding
- Migration
- Nonbreeding
- Year-round

Few warblers combine brilliant color and easy viewing quite like the **Yellow Warbler**. In summer, the buttery yellow males sing their sweet, whistled song from willows, wet thickets, and roadsides across ▸ of North America. Yellow Warblers eat mostly insects, so they don't come to backyard feeders.

ADULT MALE (AUDUBON'S)

ADULT FEMALE (AUDUBON'S)

ADULT MALE (MYRTLE)

IMMATURE (MYRTLE)

RANGE MAP

reeding
Migration
Nonbreeding
ear-round

SIZE & SHAPE The Yellow-rumped Warbler is a small songbird, although fairly large and full-bodied for a warbler. It has a large head, sturdy but slender bill, and a fairly long, narrow tail.

COLOR PATTERN "Audubon's" adult males are charcoal gray and black with a yellow throat and rump, yellow patches on their sides, and a yellow crown. Adult male "Myrtle" birds are similarly marked but have bright white throats. Females are duller than males. Immature "Myrtle" birds are overall brown, with a pale throat patch that wraps up around the bottom of the ear, and brown streaks below. They may have some yellow patches like the adults, or none at all.

BEHAVIOR Yellow-rumped Warblers forage in outer branches at middle heights. They often fly out to catch insects in midair. In winter, they spend lots of time eating berries from shrubs, and often travel in large flocks.

HABITAT In summer, they live in open coniferous forests and edges, and to a lesser extent in broadleaf forests. In fall and winter, they move to open woods and shrubby habitats, including coastal areas, parks, and residential areas.

Yellow-rumped Warblers flood the continent, filling shrubs and trees with distinctive chirps. In spring, molt to reveal a mix of bright yellow, charcoal gray, black, and bold white. In the Northwest, both the y-throated "Audubon's" form and the white-throated "Myrtle" form are common.

ADULT MALE

ADULT MALE

ADULT FEMALE

IMMATURE

SIZE & SHAPE Townsend's Warblers are small songbirds with a standard warbler shape, including a medium-length tail and a thin, fairly straight bill.

COLOR PATTERN Adult males have a black ear patch surrounded by yellow, a black cap and throat, and a yellow crescent below the eye. Females are duller, and the throat is mostly yellow. Both sexes have white wingbars.

BEHAVIOR Townsend's Warblers pick insects from leaf surfaces and needles, usually in the upper third of a tree's canopy. They also catch flying insects and hover to take insects from the outermost leaves.

HABITAT Townsend's Warblers breed in tall coniferous and mixed forests. They winter in a variety of habitats, including chaparral, mature forest, suburban yards, and parks.

RANGE MAP

Breeding
Migration
Nonbreeding
Year-round

The ethereal, buzzy songs of **Townsend's Warblers** wafting through old-growth conifer forests provide a dreamlike soundtrack to an enchanting environment. Here, high in the treetops, they seem like tiny colorful ornaments as they forage high in dense foliage, hunting small insects and larvae.

ADULT MALE

ADULT FEMALE / IMMATURE

ADULT FEMALE/IMMATURE

ADULT FEMALE/IMMATURE

RANGE MAP

Breeding
Migration
Nonbreeding

SIZE & SHAPE Wilson's Warblers are one of the smallest warblers. They have long, thin tails and small, thin bills. They have a large head and a round body for their size.

COLOR PATTERN Wilson's Warblers in the West are golden yellow below and yellowish olive above. Black eyes stand out on plain cheeks. Adult males have a distinctive black cap. Females and immatures have an olive crown, but some females show a small dark cap.

BEHAVIOR Wilson's Warblers flit restlessly between perches and make direct flights with rapid wingbeats through the understory. Unlike many warblers, they spend much of their time in the understory.

HABITAT Wilson's Warblers breed in mountain meadows and thickets near streams, especially those with willows and alders. They also breed along the edges of lakes, bogs, and aspen stands. Pacific Coast populations breed in shrubby habitat and in young stands of conifers, alders, or maples. During migration they use woodlands, suburban areas, desert scrub, and shrubby areas near streams.

even by warbler standards, the **Wilson's Warbler** dances through wet thickets to the beat of its chattering They breed in the north and in the mountains of the West but are widespread across the U.S. and Mexico on tion. They rarely slow down, dashing between shrubs, grabbing insects or popping up onto low perches.

BREEDING MALE

NONBREEDING MALE

ADULT FEMALE/IMMATURE

ADULT FEMALE/IMMATURE

SIZE & SHAPE Western Tanagers are small- to medium-sized stocky songbirds; they are heavier-bodied than warblers. They have short, thick-based bills and medium-length tails. They are larger than sparrows but smaller than robins.

COLOR PATTERN Adult male Western Tanagers are yellow with a flaming orange-red head. A yellow shoulder and white wingbar contrasts with their black wings and tail. Females and immatures are yellowish overall with dark wings marked by two wingbars. Some females are duller than others.

BEHAVIOR Western Tanagers forage slowly and methodically along branches and among leaves or needles of trees. In spring and summer, males sing a song from the treetops that sounds like a hoarse American Robin.

HABITAT Western Tanagers breed in coniferous forests, but their winter habitat is generally woodlands and forest edges. During migration, they spend time in shrubby or wooded habitats.

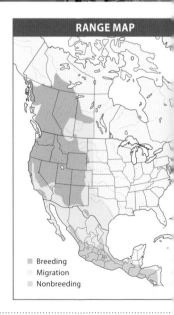
RANGE MAP

■ Breeding
■ Migration
■ Nonbreeding

Western Tanagers live in open woods all over the West, often hidden in coniferous canopies. Neverth they're a quintessential woodland denizen in summertime, where they fill the woods with their short, song and low, chuckling call notes.

ADULT MALE

ADULT MALE

ADULT FEMALE / IMMATURE FEMALE

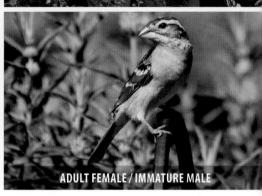

ADULT FEMALE / IMMATURE MALE

RANGE MAP

reeding
ligration
onbreeding
ear-round

SIZE & SHAPE Black-headed Grosbeaks are hefty songbirds with large, conical bills that are thick at the base. They have large heads and short, thick necks. A short tail imparts a compact, chunky look. They are slightly smaller than robins.

COLOR PATTERN Breeding males are rich orange-cinnamon with a black head and black-and-white wings. Females and immature males are brown above with warm orange or buff on the breast, and some have streaks on the sides of the breast. Immature males tend to be a deeper orange underneath. All have grayish bills. In flight, they flash bright yellow under the wings.

BEHAVIOR Often hidden as they hop about in dense foliage gleaning insects and seeds, Black-headed Grosbeaks feed readily on sunflower seeds at feeders. Males sing in a rich, whistled lilt from treetops in spring and summer. The short, squeaky *chip* note is distinctive and can be a good way to find these birds.

HABITAT Look for Black-headed Grosbeaks in mixed woodlands and forest edges, from mountain forests to thickets along desert streams, to backyards and gardens. Ideal habitat includes some large trees and a diverse understory.

ale **Black-headed Grosbeak** does not get its adult breeding plumage until it is two years old. ear males can vary from looking like a female to looking nearly like an adult male. Only yearling that most closely resemble adult males are able to defend a territory and attempt to breed.

BREEDING MALE

NONBREEDING MALE

BREEDING FEMALE

NONBREEDING FEMALE / IMMATURE MA

SIZE & SHAPE Lazuli Buntings are small, stocky, finchlike, sparrow-sized songbirds with conical bills and gently sloping foreheads. The tail is notched or slightly forked.

COLOR PATTERN Breeding males are brilliant sky blue above with a pumpkin-colored breast, a white belly, and a prominent white shoulder patch. Females are warm gray above, with a blue tinge to wings and tail, two buffy wingbars, and a tan breast.

BEHAVIOR Male Lazuli Buntings perch upright and sing from exposed perches in low trees and shrubs. They spend most of their time in the understory, hopping between branches and on the ground while reaching for insects or seeds.

HABITAT Lazuli Buntings breed in brushy hillsides, near streams, wooded valleys, thickets and hedges along agricultural fields, recently burned areas, and residential gardens of the West, up to about 9,500 feet elevation.

RANGE MAP

■ Breeding
  Migration
■ Winter

When young male **Lazuli Buntings** copy older, nearby males, they create a "song neighborhood" whe songs from a particular area all sound similar. Males from the same neighborhood learn to recognize a tolerate each other and respond more aggressively to unfamiliar songs from outside their neighborho

IMAGE CREDITS

Front matter photos: p. 11 Mallard ©Greg Gillson/Macaulay Library; p. 12 bird watcher ©Jill Leichter; p. 16 White-throated Sparrow ©Keenan Yakola/Macaulay Library; p. 18 Terns on a beach ©Jay McGowan/Macaulay Library; p. 19 Hairy Woodpecker ©Herb Elliott/Macaulay Library, Downy Woodpecker ©Evan Lipton/Macaulay Library; p. 20 Wilson's Warbler ©Ad Konings/Macaulay Library; p. 21 Lesser Scaup ©Brian L. Sullivan/Macaulay Library, Red-winged Blackbird ©Jonathan Eckerson/Macaulay Library; p. 22 Purple Finch ©Jay McGowan/Macaulay Library, House Finch ©Andrew Simon/Macaulay Library; p. 26 Herring Gulls ©Jay McGowan/Macaulay Library; p. 28 Ruby-throated Hummingbird ©Ian Davies/Macaulay Library; p. 31 binoculars ©Ivonne Wierink/Shutterstock; p. 32 birdfeeder ©Le Do/Shutterstock, scope ©Chokniti Khongchum/Shutterstock; p. 34 birders ©Jill Leichter; p. 35 Wood Thrush ©Ryan Schain/Macaulay Library; p. 36 camera ©EML/Shutterstock; p. 37 Sanderling ©Ryan Schain/Macaulay Library; p. 38 Rose-breasted Grosbeak ©Kevin J. McGowan/Macaulay Library; p. 39 American Goldfinch ©Kevin J. McGowan/Macaulay Library; p. 42 American Goldfinch ©Daniel Irons/Macaulay Library; p. 43 garden path ©Hannamariah/Shutterstock, bee ©Per-Boge/Shutterstock; p. 47 (top to bottom) ©NWStock/Shutterstock, ©spline_x/Shutterstock, ©Sarah Marchant/Shutterstock; p. 48 (top to bottom) ©motorolka/Shutterstock, ©ntstudio/Shutterstock, ©EML/Shutterstock; p. 49 (top to bottom) ©Tiger Images/Shutterstock, ©Jiang Zhongyan/Shutterstock, ©Roman Rubin/Shutterstock, ©Mirek Kijewski/Shutterstock; p. 50 (top to bottom) ©Egor Rodynchenko/Shutterstock, ©matin/Shutterstock; p. 51 Blackburnian Warbler ©Terence Zahner/Macaulay Library; p. 52 birdhouse ©Feng Yu/Shutterstock; p. 64 Northern Cardinal ©Linda Petersen; p. 65 child and binoculars ©Pigprox/Shutterstock; p. 66 Song Sparrow nest ©Bob Vuxinic; p. 67 parade ©Karen Purdell; p. 68 cat ©Claudia Paulussen /Shutterstock; p. 69 Orange-crowned Warbler ©Brian L. Sullivan/Macaulay Library, cup of coffee ©Alina Rosanova/Shutterstock. All other photos are ©Shutterstock.

Front matter illustrations: p. 17 House Finch and silhouette ©Liz Clayton Fuller, Bartels Science Illustrator; How Big is It? ©Bird Academy; p. 24, 25, 29, 30 illustrations ©Cornell Lab of Ornithology; pp. 44, 45 feeder illustrations ©Virginia L. Greene/Bartels Science Illustrator; pp. 52–55 birdhouse illustrations ©NestWatch.

Photos in the *Guide to Species* section were primarily sourced from the Macaulay Library, a collection of photos and sound recordings contributed by citizen scientists from all over the world. The diagram on the right shows placement for photos in the book. We are especially grateful to the following Macaulay Library photographers who each contributed over 25 photographs to this series: Sue Barth, Shawn Billerman, Darren Clark, Ian Davies, Matt Davis, Herb Elliott, Paul Fenwick, Greg Gillson, Daniel Irons, Ad Konings, Alex Lamoreaux, Evan Lipton, Scott Martin, Jay McGowan, Ollie Oliver, Arlene Ripley, Ryan Schain, Brian L. Sullivan, Christopher Wood, and Terence Zahner. All photos are ©the photographer/Macaulay Library, except those marked with an asterisk.

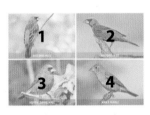

Snow Goose
1. Jay McGowan
2. Matt Brady
3. Marky Mutchler
4. Ryan Schain

Brant
1. Matt Brady
2. Matt Davis
3. John Puschock
4. Paul Fenwick

Canada Goose
1. Paul Fenwick
2. Matt Davis
3. Paul Fenwick
4. Louis Hoeniger

Trumpeter Swan
1. Caleb Strand
2. Jay McGowan
3. Jay McGowan
4. Marya Moosman

Wood Duck
1. Ryan Schain
2. Jay McGowan
3. Ollie Oliver
4. Paul Fenwick

Northern Shoveler
1. Arlene Ripley
2. Christopher Wood
3. Paul Fenwick
4. Ryan Schain

Gadwall
1. Brian L. Sullivan
2. Ryan Schain
3. Melissa James
4. Terence Zahner

American Wigeon
1. Greg Gillson
2. Greg Gillson
3. Greg Gillson
4. Matt Davis

Mallard
1. Brian L. Sullivan
2. Greg Gillson
3. Evan Lipton
4. Evan Lipton

Northern Pintail
1. Louis Hoeniger
2. Scott Martin
3. Ryan Schain
4. Amanda Guercio

Canvasback
1. Brian L. Sullivan
2. Alex Lamoreaux
3. Matt Davis
4. Ian Davies

Redhead
1. Matt Davis
2. Greg Gillson
3. Jay McGowan
4. Jay McGowan

Greater Scaup
1. Russ Morgan
2. Ian Davies
3. John D. Reynolds
4. Brian L. Sullivan

Lesser Scaup
1. Brian L. Sullivan
2. Dorian Anderson
3. Ryan Schain
4. Dorian Anderson

Harlequin Duck
1. Ian Davies
2. Alex Lamoreaux
3. Shawn Billerman
4. Jay McGowan

Ruddy Duck
1. Arlene Ripley
2. Ryan Schain
3. Liam Wolff
4. Louis Hoeniger

California Quail
1. Brian L. Sullivan
2. Matt Davis
3. Paul Fenwick
4. Paul Fenwick

Wild Turkey
1. Brian L. Sullivan
2. Louis Hoeniger
3. Matthew Pendleton
4. Doug Hitchcox

Ruffed Grouse
1. Doris Ratchford
2. Max Malmquist
3. Luke Seitz
4. Shawn Billerman

Spruce Grouse
1. Alex Lamoreaux
2. David Robichaud
3. Mark Ludwick
4. Fred Forssell

Greater Sage-Grouse
1. Jeff Bleam
2. Matthew Pendleton
3. Darren Clark
4. Bryan Calk

Dusky Grouse
1. Steve Calver
2. Jim Merritt
3. Alex Lamoreaux
4. Alex Lamoreaux

Sooty Grouse
1. Kent Leland
2. Steve Calver
3. Alex Lamoreaux
4. Alex Lamoreaux

Ring-necked Pheasant
1. Andrew Simon
2. Paul Poronto
3. Matt Davis
4. Tim Lenz

Chukar
1. Matthew Pendleton
2. Brian L. Sullivan
3. Eric VanderWerf
4. Eric VanderWerf

Pied-billed Grebe
1. Ryan Schain
2. Matt Davis
3. Matt Davis
4. Paul Fenwick

Red-necked Grebe
1. Brian L. Sullivan
2. Matt Davis
3. Paul Fenwick
4. John D. Reynolds

Eared Grebe
1. Matt Davis
2. Matt Davis
3. Luke Seitz
4. Matt Davis

Western Grebe
1. Marya Moosman
2. Matt Davis
3. Ad Konings
4. Ryan Schain

Rock Pigeon
1. Ryan Schain
2. Matt Davis
3. Sue Barth
4. Dan Vickers

Band-tailed Pigeon
1. Paul Fenwick
2. Jim Merritt
3. Paul Fenwick
4. Jim Merritt

Eurasian Collared-Dove
1. Jay McGowan
2. Steven G. Mlodinow
3. Ryan Schain
4. Louis Hoeniger

Mourning Dove
1. Ryan Schain
2. Terence Zahner
3. Arlene Ripley
4. Nick Pulcinella

Common Nighthawk
1. Jane Mann
2. Jay McGowan
3. Mark Ludwick
4. Betty Fenton

Chimney Swift
1. Janet Rathjen
2. Katherine Edison
3. Brian L. Sullivan
4. Steve Calver

White-throated Swift
1. Matt Davis
2. Jay McGowan
3. Brian L. Sullivan
4. Paul Fenwick

Black-chinned Hummingbird
1. Herb Elliott
2. Ad Konings
3. Kyle Blaney
4. Ad Konings

Anna's Hummingbird
1. Alan Versaw
2. Brian L. Sullivan
3. Matt Davis
4. Ryan Schain

Broad-tailed Hummingbird
1. Nicolas Forestell
2. Brian L. Sullivan
3. Terence Zahner
4. Bill Maynard

Calliope Hummingbird
1. Matthew Pendleton
2. Marya Moosman
3. Louis Hoeniger
4. Ad Konings

Rufous Hummingbird
1. Kent Leland
2. Matthew Pendleton
3. Matt Davis
4. Paul Fenwick

Allen's Hummingbird
1. Brian L. Sullivan
2. Robert A. Hamilton
3. Giovanni Pari
4. Nicolas Forestell

Sora
1. Marky Mutchler
2. Ad Konings
3. Brad Imhoff
4. Matt Davis

American Coot
1. Brad Imhoff
2. Melissa James
3. Ad Konings
4. August Davidson-Onsgard

Sandhill Crane
1. Paul Fenwick
2. Paul Fenwick
3. Matt Davis
4. Ad Konings

Black-necked Stilt
1. Sean Fitzgerald
2. Dorian Anderson
3. Shawn Billerman
4. Alex Lamoreaux

Black Oystercatcher
1. Dorian Anderson
2. William Higgins
3. Greg Gillson
4. Matt Davis

Black-bellied Plover
1. Matt Davis
2. Dorian Anderson
3. Sue Barth
4. Paul Fenwick

Killdeer
1. Jay McGowan
2. Brian L. Sullivan
3. Jay McGowan
4. Ollie Oliver

Upland Sandpiper
1. Alex Lamoreaux
2. Brian L. Sullivan
3. Jay McGowan
4. Liam Wolff

Long-billed Curlew
1. Brian L. Sullivan
2. Brian L. Sullivan
3. Brian L. Sullivan
4. Brian L. Sullivan

Marbled Godwit
1. Matt Davis
2. Dorian Anderson
3. Kent Leland
4. Brian L. Sullivan

Ruddy Turnstone
1. Jay McGowan
2. Jay McGowan
3. Ryan Schain
4. Shawn Billerman

Sanderling
1. Ryan Schain
2. Matt Davis
3. Paul Fenwick
4. David Wilson

Western Sandpiper
1. Ian Davies
2. Ian Davies
3. Matthew Pendleton
4. Brian L. Sullivan

Spotted Sandpiper
1. Matt Brady
2. Ian Davies
3. Jay McGowan
4. Ad Konings

Willet
1. Evan Lipton
2. Dorian Anderson
3. Ad Konings
4. Patrick Maurice

Common Murre
1. Michael Weaver
2. Brian L. Sullivan
3. Ollie Oliver
4. Shawn Billerman

Pigeon Guillemot
1. Brian L. Sulivan
2. Christopher Wood
3. Brian L. Sulivan
4. Ollie Oliver

Black-legged Kittiwake
1. Daniel Irons
2. Ian Davies
3. Evan Lipton
4. Matt Brady

Franklin's Gull
1. Brian L. Sullivan
2. Alan Versaw
3. Sue Barth
4. Brian L. Sullivan

Heermann's Gull
1. Brian L. Sullivan
2. Brian L. Sullivan
3. Brian L. Sullivan
4. Brian L. Sullivan

Mew Gull
1. Ian Davies
2. Ryan Schain
3. Brian L. Sullivan
4. Matt Davis

Ring-billed Gull
1. Paul Fenwick
2. Liam Wolff
3. Herb Elliott
4. Jay McGowan

Western Gull
1. Matt Davis
2. Brian L. Sullivan
3. Brian L. Sullivan
4. Matthew Pendleton

California Gull
1. Andrew Simon
2. Logan Southall
3. Steven G. Mlodinow
4. Matt Brady

Herring Gull
1. Darren Clark
2. Brian L. Sullivan
3. Evan Lipton
4. Christopher Wood

Glaucous-winged Gull
1. Shawn Billerman
2. Paul Fenwick
3. Brian L. Sullivan
4. Paul Fenwick

Glaucous Gull
1. Ian Davies
2. Steve Kelling
3. Steve Kelling
4. Brian L. Sullivan

Caspian Tern
1. Brian L. Sullivan
2. Jay McGowan
3. Paul Fenwick
4. Herb Elliott

Black Tern
1. Paul Fenwick
2. Melissa James
3. Daniel Irons
4. Ryan Schain

Forster's Tern
1. August Davidson-Onsgard
2. Steve Tucker
3. Ryan Schain
4. David Wilson

Red-throated Loon
1. Bryan Calk
2. Brian L. Sullivan
3. Ryan Schain
4. Dorian Anderson

Common Loon
1. Brad Imhoff
2. Matt Davis
3. Brian L. Sullivan
4. Patrick Maurice

Brandt's Cormorant
1. Matt Davis
2. Matt Davis
3. Brian L. Sullivan
4. Ollie Oliver

Double-crested Cormorant
1. Evan Lipton
2. Chris S. Wood
3. Steve Kolbe
4. Jane Mann

American White Pelican
1. Jerry Ting
2. Paul Fenwick
3. Herb Elliott
4. Gordon W. Dimmig

Brown Pelican
1. Greg Gillson
2. Paul Fenwick
3. Matt Davis
4. Matt Davis

Great Blue Heron
1. Herb Elliott
2. Daniel Irons
3. Shawn Billerman
4. Terence Zahner

Great Egret
1. Jonathan Eckerson
2. Melissa James
3. Alex Lamoreaux
4. Matt Davis

Green Heron
1. Evan Lipton
2. Brad Imhoff
3. Evan Lipton
4. Paul Fenwick

Black-crowned Night-Heron
1. Ad Konings
2. Matt Davis
3. Alex Lamoreaux
4. Evan Lipton

White-faced Ibis
1. Ad Konings
2. Paul Fenwick
3. Matt Davis
4. Matt Davis

Turkey Vulture
1. Louis Hoeniger
2. Paul Fenwick
3. Ryan Shaw
4. Brian L. Sullivan

Osprey
1. Matt Davis
2. Matt Davis
3. Jay McGowan
4. Melissa James

Golden Eagle
1. Jeff Bleam
2. Matt Davis
3. Brian L. Sullivan
4. Brian L. Sullivan

Northern Harrier
1. Brian L. Sullivan
2. Matt Davis
3. Brian L. Sullivan
4. Brian L. Sullivan

Cooper's Hawk
1. Evan Lipton
2. Ryan Schain
3. Sue Barth
4. Alan Versaw

Bald Eagle
1. Sue Barth
2. Chris S. Wood
3. Scott Martin
4. Jay McGowan

Red-shouldered Hawk
1. Paul Fenwick
2. Herb Elliott
3. August Davidson-Onsgard
4. Matt Davis

Swainson's Hawk
1. Steven G. Mlodinow
2. Matt Davis
3. Brian L. Sullivan
4. Brian L. Sullivan

Red-tailed Hawk
1. Arlene Ripley
2. Alan Versaw
3. Paul Fenwick
4. Herb Elliott

Rough-legged Hawk
1. Matthew Pendleton
2. Jay McGowan
3. Christopher Wood
4. Brian L. Sullivan

Western Screech-Owl
1. Louis Hoeniger
2. Arlene Ripley
3. Greg Gillson
4. Arlene Ripley

Great Horned Owl
1. Ollie Oliver
2. Ollie Oliver
3. Ollie Oliver
4. Dean LaTray

Burrowing Owl
1. Shawn Billerman
2. Darren Clark
3. Janine McCabe
4. Terence Zahner

Barred Owl
1. Luke Seitz
2. Alex Lamoreaux
3. Alex Lamoreaux
4. Jay McGowan

Great Gray Owl
1. Ian Davies
2. Ian Davies
3. Shawn Billerman
4. Alex Lamoreaux

Belted Kingfisher
1. John D. Reynolds
2. Louis Hoeniger
3. William Higgins
4. Matthew Pendleton

Red-naped Sapsucker
1. Bryan Calk
2. Arlene Ripley
3. Shawn Billerman
4. Jay McGowan

Red-breasted Sapsucker
1. Greg Gillson
2. Ollie Oliver
3. Matt Davis
4. Alex Lamoreaux

Acorn Woodpecker
1. Brian L. Sullivan
2. Charlie Jackson
3. George Gibbs
4. Matt Davis

Downy Woodpecker
1. Ollie Oliver
2. Jack and Shirley Foreman
3. Ollie Oliver
4. Herb Elliott

Hairy Woodpecker
1. Terence Zahner
2. Herb Elliott
3. Ollie Oliver
4. Ollie Oliver

White-headed Woodpecker
1. Ollie Oliver
2. Matt Davis
3. Bryan Calk
4. Shawn Billerman

Pileated Woodpecker
1. David WIlson
2. Shawn Billerman
3. Jay McGowan
4. Shawn Billerman

Northern Flicker
1. Ian Davies
2. Matt Davis
3. Warren Lynn
4. Greg Gillson

American Kestrel
1. Matthew Pendleton
2. Sue Barth
3. Dorian Anderson
4. Ad Konings

Peregrine Falcon
1. Ryan Schain
2. Brian L. Sullivan
3. Jay McGowan
4. Ryan Schain

Western Wood-Pewee
1. Darren Clark
2. Steve Calver
3. Ryan Schain
4. Evan Lipton

Least Flycatcher
1. Jay McGowan
2. Ian Davies
3. Terence Zahner
4. Russ Morgan

Black Phoebe
1. Ian Davies
2. Paul Fenwick
3. Don Danko
4. Ad Konings

Say's Phoebe
1. Arlene Ripley
2. Sean Fitzgerald
3. Arlene Ripley
4. Brian L. Sullivan

Ash-throated Flycatcher
1. Robert Hamilton
2. Alan Versaw
3. Brian L. Sullivan
4. Luke Seitz

Western Kingbird
1. Jerry Ting
2. Ryan Schain
3. Ad Konings
4. Steve Calver

Eastern Kingbird
1. Scott Martin
2. Josh Ketry
3. Jay McGowan
4. Russ Morgan

Warbling Vireo
1. Ad Konings
2. Shawn Billerman
3. Jay McGowan
4. Jay McGowan

Red-eyed Vireo
1. Gordon W. Dimmig
2. Scott Martin
3. Evan Lipton
4. Ryan Schain

Loggerhead Shrike
1. Matthew Pendleton
2. Matt Davis
3. Dorian Anderson
4. Evan Lipton

Northern Shrike
1. Steven G. Mlodinow
2. Jim Hully
3. Nick Saunders
4. Brian L. Sullivan

Canada Jay
1. Evan Lipton
2. Shawn Billerman
3. Melissa James
4. Ollie Oliver

Pinyon Jay
1. Noah Strycker
2. Jeff Bleam
3. Jay McGowan
4. Mike Miller

Steller's Jay
1. Jay McGowan
2. Brian L. Sullivan
3. Ryan Schain
4. Jeff Maw

Blue Jay
1. Scott Martin
2. Patrick Maurice
3. Jay McGowan
4. Dan Vickers

California Scrub-Jay
1. Brian L. Sullivan
2. Greg Gillson
3. Brian L. Sullivan
4. Nancy Christensen

Black-billed Magpie
1. David Disher
2. Alan Versaw
3. Dean LaTray
4. Alan Versaw

Clark's Nutcracker
1. Eric VanderWerf
2. Brian L. Sullivan
3. Eric VanderWerf
4. Ian Davies

American Crow
1. Alan Versaw
2. Steven Kolbe
3. Steven G. Mlodinow
4. Sue Barth

Common Raven
1. Brian L. Sullivan
2. Brian L. Sullivan
3. Greg Gillson
4. Matt Davis

Black-capped Chickadee
1. Scott Martin
2. Greg Gillson
3. Brian L. Sullivan
4. Terence Zahner

Mountain Chickadee
1. Ryan Schain
2. Kent Leland
3. Shawn Billerman
4. Matt Davis

Chestnut-backed Chickadee
1. Alex Lamoreaux
2. Matt Davis
3. Ollie Oliver
4. Brian L. Sullivan

Boreal Chickadee
1. Ryan Schain
2. Bryan Calk
3. Ryan Schain
4. Evan Lipton

Oak Titmouse
1. Matt Davis
2. Paul Fenwick
3. Luke Seitz
4. Kent Leland

Juniper Titmouse
1. Darren Clark
2. Bryan Calk
3. Shawn Billerman
4. Shawn Billerman

Horned Lark
1. Alan Versaw
2. Linda Petersen*
3. Sue Barth
4. Ad Konings

Purple Martin
1. Bryan Calk
2. Mark Ludwick
3. Matthew Pendleton
4. Kent Leland

Tree Swallow
1. Greg Gillson
2. Phil McNeil
3. Matt Davis
4. Noah Strycker

Violet-green Swallow
1. Darren Clark
2. Alex Lamoreaux
3. Greg Gillson
4. Matt Davis

Barn Swallow
1. Alex Lamoreaux
2. Paul Fenwick
3. Brian L. Sullivan
4. Arlene Ripley

Cliff Swallow
1. Dorian Anderson
2. Dan Vickers
3. Dorian Anderson
4. Herb Elliott

Bushtit
1. Ryan Schain
2. Ryan Schain
3. Darren Clark
4. Tim DeJonghe

Wrentit
1. Brian L. Sullivan
2. Paul Fenwick
3. Paul Fenwick
4. Matt Davis

Golden-crowned Kinglet
1. Ryan Schain
2. Luke Seitz
3. Gates Dupont
4. Ian Davies

Ruby-crowned Kinglet
1. Jay McGowan
2. Brian L. Sullivan
3. Matt Davis
4. Luke Seitz

Red-breasted Nuthatch
1. Scott Martin
2. Ryan Schain
3. Christopher Wood
4. Shawn Billerman

White-breasted Nuthatch
1. Evan Lipton
2. Herb Elliott
3. Alex Lamoreaux
4. Herb Elliott

Pygmy Nuthatch
1. Bryan Calk
2. Greg Gillson
3. Janet Theilen
4. Matt Davis

Brown Creeper
1. Scott Martin
2. Scott Martin
3. Scott Martin
4. Adam Jackson

Blue-gray Gnatcatcher
1. Liam Wolff
2. Caleb Strand
3. Keith Leland
4. Jerry Ting

Rock Wren
1. Ryan Schain
2. Bryan Calk
3. Darren Clark
4. Matt Davis

Canyon Wren
1. Arlene Ripley
2. Herb Elliott
3. Kent Leland
4. Nancy Christensen

House Wren
1. Matt Brady
2. Ryan Schain
3. Evan Lipton
4. Ad Konings

Pacific Wren
1. Steve G. Mlodinow
2. Marya Moosman
3. Bryan Calk
4. Matt Davis

Bewick's Wren
1. Darren Clark
2. Bryan Calk
3. Jerry Ting
4. Russ Morgan

American Dipper
1. Dan Vickers
2. Christopher Wood
3. Jay McGowan
4. Jeff Bleam

European Starling
1. Matt Davis
2. Ryan Schain
3. Jay McGowan
4. Linda Petersen*

Gray Catbird
1. Ryan Schain
2. Bryan Calk
3. Jay McGowan
4. Evan Lipton

Western Bluebird
1. Chris S. Wood
2. Arlene Ripley
3. Matt Davis
4. Robert A. Hamilton

Mountain Bluebird
1. Christopher Wood
2. Brian L. Sullivan
3. Shawn Billerman
4. Arlene Ripley

Townsend's Solitaire
1. Nick Saunders
2. Darren Clark
3. Alex Lamoreaux
4. Scott Martin

Varied Thrush
1. Matthew Pendleton
2. Brain L. Sullivan
3. Matt Brady
4. Jeff Bleam

Swainson's Thrush
1. Adam Jackson
2. Brian L. Sullivan
3. Brian L. Sullivan
4. Shawn Billerman

Hermit Thrush
1. Kent Leland
2. Brian L. Sullivan
3. Sue Barth
4. Matt Davis

American Robin
1. Christopher Wood
2. Evan Lipton
3. Jay McGowan
4. David Wilson

Bohemian Waxwing
1. Ian Davies
2. Russ Morgan
3. Matthew Pendleton
4. Evan Lipton

Cedar Waxwing
1. Terence Zahner
2. Jay McGowan
3. Jane Bain
4. Evan Lipton

House Sparrow
1. Evan Lipton
2. Louis Hoeniger
3. Paul Fenwick
4. Ad Konings

Evening Grosbeak
1. Matt Davis
2. Fred Forssell
3. Marya Moosman
4. Alex Lamoreaux

Pine Grosbeak
1. Shawn Billerman
2. Shawn Billerman
3. Evan Lipton
4. Darren Clark

House Finch
1. Scott Martin
2. Jay McGowan
3. Paul Fenwick
4. Ryan Schain

Purple Finch
1. Paul Fenwick
2. Paul Fenwick
3. Paul Fenwick
4. Jeff Bleam

Cassin's Finch
1. Bryan Calk
2. Alan Versaw
3. Jay McGowan
4. Paul Fenwick

Common Redpoll
1. Eric Gofreed
2. Ryan Schain
3. Ryan Schain
4. Andrew Simon

Red Crossbill
1. Luke Seitz
2. Darren Clark
3. Christopher Wood
4. Evan Lipton

Pine Siskin
1. Matthew Pendleton
2. Matt Davis
3. Luke Seitz
4. Jim Merritt

Lesser Goldfinch
1. Matthew Pendleton
2. Matt Davis
3. Paul Fenwick
4. Arlene Ripley

American Goldfinch
1. Don Danko
2. Ian Davies
3. Linda Petersen*
4. Daniel Irons

Grasshopper Sparrow
1. Ian Davies
2. Melissa James
3. Matt Davis
4. Scott Martin

Black-throated Sparrow
1. Luke Seitz
2. Arlene Ripley
3. Arlene Ripley
4. Chris S. Wood

k Sparrow
1. Matt Davis
2. Paul Fenwick
3. Scott Martin
4. Brian L. Sullivan

k Bunting
1. Jay McGowan
2. Marky Mutchler
3. Ad Konings
4. Ad Konings

ipping Sparrow
1. Evan Lipton
2. Daniel Irons
3. Jay McGowan
4. Jay McGowan

ewer's Sparrow
1. Matt Davis
2. Doug Hitchcox
3. Steven G. Mlodinow
4. Ad Konings

x Sparrow
1. Ryan Schain
2. Jay McGowan
3. Ryan Schain
4. Shawn Billerman

nerican Tree Sparrow
1. Scott Martin
2. Gates Dupont
3. Evan Lipton
4. Luke Seitz

ark-eyed Junco
1. Scott Martin
2. Christopher Wood
3. Greg Gillson
4. Greg Gillson

nite-crowned Sparrow
1. Daniel Irons
2. Sue Barth
3. Matt Davis
4. Ollie Oliver

olden-crowned Sparrow
1. Jay McGowan
2. Alan Versaw
3. Brian L. Sullivan
4. Paul Fenwick

White-throated Sparrow
1. Jay McGowan
2. Keenan Yakola
3. Adam Jackson
4. Shawn Billerman

Savannah Sparrow
1. Matt Davis
2. Bryan Calk
3. Arlene Ripley
4. Don Blecha

Song Sparrow
1. Ryan Schain
2. Shawn Billerman
3. Matt Davis
4. Matt Davis

Lincoln's Sparrow
1. Scott Martin
2. Darren Clark
3. Linda Petersen*
4. Sue Barth

Green-tailed Towhee
1. Noah Strycker
2. Don Danko
3. Tom Lally
4. Arlene Ripley

Spotted Towhee
1. Brian L. Sullivan
2. Kent Leland
3. Matt Davis
4. Brian L. Sullivan

Yellow-breasted Chat
1. Bryan Calk
2. Ad Konings
3. Ad Konings
4. Ryan Schain

Yellow-headed Blackbird
1. Matt Davis
2. Alan Versaw
3. Brian L. Sullivan
4. Julie Zempel

Bobolink
1. Ollie Oliver
2. Greg Gillson
3. Shawn Billerman
4. Shawn Billerman

Western Meadowlark
1. Alan Versaw
2. Matt Davis
3. Matt Davis
4. Alex Lamoreaux

Bullock's Oriole
1. Arlene Ripley
2. Matt Davis
3. Arlene Ripley
4. Don Sterba

Red-winged Blackbird
1. Ryan Schain
2. Jonathan Eckerson
3. Dan Vickers
4. Sue Barth

Brown-headed Cowbird
1. Brian L. Sullivan
2. Arlene Ripley
3. Shawn Billerman
4. Linda Petersen*

Brewer's Blackbird
1. Brian L. Sullivan
2. Matt Davis
3. Shawn Billerman
4. Jack Bushong

Common Grackle
1. Christopher Wood
2. Herb Elliott
3. Jay McGowan
4. Evan Lipton

Orange-crowned Warbler
1. Ian Davies
2. Paul Fenwick
3. Matt Davis
4. Herb Elliott

Common Yellowthroat
1. Paul Fenwick
2. Brad Imhoff
3. Darren Clark
4. Shawn Billerman

Yellow Warbler
1. Ryan Schain
2. Shawn Billerman
3. Sue Barth
4. Ryan Schain

Yellow-rumped Warbler
1. Matthew Pendleton
2. Arlene Ripley
3. Tom Lally
4. Ryan Schain

Townsend's Warbler
1. Matt Brady
2. Paul Fenwick
3. Jay McGowan
4. Matthew Pendleton

Wilson's Warbler
1. Ad Konngs
2. Matt Davis
3. Scott Martin
4. Arlene Ripley

Western Tanager
1. Matt Davis
2. Chris S. Wood
3. Arlene Ripley
4. Arlene Ripley

Black-headed Grosbeak
1. Herb Elliott
2. Robert A. Hamilton
3. Jim Merritt
4. Herb Elliott

Lazuli Bunting
1. Darren Clark
2. Ad Konings
3. Arlene Ripley
4. Arlene Ripley

INDEX

ACKNOWLEDGMENTS

These guides were put together with the help of many people. The bird species profiles are derived from the more comprehensive accounts in the *All About Birds Online Bird Guide*, authored by numerous expert contributors throughout the year, with editing and many recent additions made possible by Hugh Powell, Kathi Borgmann, and Ned Brinkley. Maps are based on original *All About Birds* base maps featuring data from NatureServe and updated to reflect known ranges. Early on, Jessie Barry and Ian Davies shared what they would like to see in a new field-guide series. Hugh Powell wrote much of the helpful information on ID at the front of the guides. Tilden Chao provided a selection of photos to begin our search for ID photos. Robyn Bailey, Jenna Curtis, Marilu Lopez Fretts, Holly Grant, Emma Greig, Jay McGowan, Becca Rodomsky-Bish, and Bobby Stickel provided updates on projects and technology. Rachel Lodder's eagle eyes proofread many versions of these books. Caroline Watkins filled spreadsheets and edited copy, assisted with photo permission requests, and hunted down images. Diane Tessaglia-Hymes' design skills brought this project to the finish line with finesse and grace. Miyoko Chu smoothed over the many road bumps along the way, and Brian L. Sockin gave guidance and support. Michael L. P. Retter provided crucial feedback on photographs, range-map adjustments, and copy. Michael's boundless knowledge, enthusiasm, and energy kept the project moving forward.

Last, but certainly not least, I would like to thank every photographer/citizen scientist who contributes photos to the Macaulay Library, the contents of which I scoured for birds of all ages and plumages. For a complete list of image credits, please see pages 285–289. A special thanks to the following photographers who granted use of any of their photographs in this book. I admire their skill and appreciate their generosity: Sue Barth, Shawn Billerman, Jeff Bleam, Matt Brady, Steve Calver, August Davidson-Onsgard, Ian Davies, Matt Davis, Herb Elliott, Paul Fenwick, Fred Forssell, Greg Gillson, Louis Hoeniger, Adam Jackson, Melissa James, Ad Konings, Tom Lally, Alex Lamoreaux, Kent Leland, Evan Lipton, Mark Ludwick, Scott Martin, Patrick Maurice, Jeff Maw, Jay McGowan, Jim Merritt, Marya Moosman, Russ Morgan, Ollie Oliver, Matthew Pendleton, Arlene Ripley, Ryan Schain, Luke Seitz, Andrew Simon, Caleb Strand, Brian L. Sullivan, Usha Tatini, Alan Versaw, Dan Vickers, David Wilson, Liam Wolff, Chris S. Wood, Christopher Wood, Kathryn Young, and Terence Zahner.

Jill Leichter, Editor

Titles in This Series

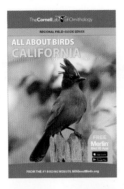
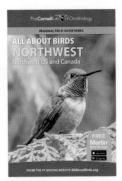

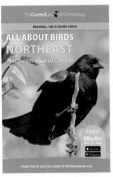

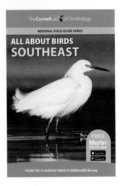

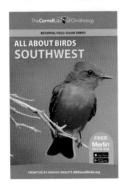

press.princeton.edu